THE GLOBAL CORPORATE BRAND BOOK

The Global Corporate Brand Book

Michael Morley

First published 2009 by
PALGRAVE MACMILLAN

Palgrave Macmillan in the UK is an imprint of Macmillan Publishers Limited, registered in England, company number 785998, of Houndmills, Basingstoke, Hampshire RG21 6XS.

Palgrave Macmillan in the US is a division of St Martin's Press LLC, 175 Fifth Avenue, New York, NY 10010.

Palgrave Macmillan is the global academic imprint of the above companies and has companies and representatives throughout the world.

Palgrave® and Macmillan® are registered trademarks in the United States, the United Kingdom, Europe and other countries.

ISBN-13: 978–1–4039–9663–3

This book is printed on paper suitable for recycling and made from fully managed and sustained forest sources. Logging, pulping and manufacturing processes are expected to conform to the environmental regulations of the country of origin.

A catalogue record for this book is available from the British Library.

A catalog record for this book is available from the Library of Congress.

10 9 8 7 6 5 4 3 2 1
18 17 16 15 14 13 12 11 10 09

Printed and bound in Great Britain by
CPI Antony Rowe, Chippenham and Eastbourne

This book is for Ingrid

This book is for barbarians

Contents

List of figures, tables and exhibits

Figures

Tables

Exhibits

About the author

Michael Morley is President of Morley Corporate Consulting, a firm of management consultants in corporate reputation and branding. He is also Chairman of the Senior Advisory Board of Experts of Echo Research. For nearly 35 years Morley held a variety of senior positions with Edelman and founded the agency's first overseas office, in London in 1967. He went on to establish other Edelman offices in Europe, Canada, Asia Pacific and Latin America. He remains of counsel to the firm.

He is an adjunct professor, teaching in the Master of Science in Public Relations and Corporate Communications program at New York University.

Morley is recognized as an authority on multi-country and global communications and has managed multinational PR programs for companies that include UPS, AMADEUS Global Travel Distribution, NCR, VISA International, British Airways, Ernst & Young, Hoffmann-La Roche, Procter & Gamble, SC Johnson and Hertz.

He is also an expert in nation branding and has worked on behalf of Finland, Spain, Mexico, Korea and India.

He is a Fellow of the Chartered Institute of Public Relations. He served as Chairman of the jury of the IPRA Golden World Awards from 1999 to 2002. In June 2003, Morley was awarded the Alan Campbell-Johnson Medal for distinguished service to International Public Relations. Later the same year he was one of the first six PR leaders named to the ICCO Hall of Fame.

Morley is the author of the book *How to Manage Your Global Reputation*, published by Palgrave Macmillan.

Acknowledgments and author's notes

This book has been a long time in the making and I thank Stephen Rutt, Publishing Director at Palgrave Macmillan, for his patience and guidance. Since the idea was first conceived I was pulled away from working on it by various distractions which seemed more urgent at the time. Over that journey there are many whom I have to thank for their encouragement, advice and practical help.

First among these are Haywood Batchelor, Diana Bhaktul, Kristin Johnson, Stephanie Mattera, Louisa Bargeron, March Cail and Kaeisha O'Neal. They were graduate students in NYU's Master of Science in Public Relations and Corporate Communication course and each voluntarily undertook secondary research for three chapters. I am also grateful to Professor John Doorley, who supervises the NYU program so successfully that it was voted the best PR educational program in the 2009 *PR Week* awards.

There are many others who helped but whose names do not appear elsewhere. They are Annie Phan, Eneida Lamberty, Betty Hunt, George Barbero, and Dick Martin (a real brand expert).

The thoughts expressed are in no small measure the distillation of experiences gained over 50 years of work. For this I have to thank all my employers, partners and colleagues as well as the many clients who placed their trust in me during that time. Special mention must be made of Dan Edelman, Founder and Chairman, and Richard Edelman, CEO of Edelman, and Sandra Macleod, CEO of Echo Research. Nor should I forget clients and competitors, who can often be the best teachers.

When my energy was flagging I was stirred into action by my wife Ingrid and two daughters, Helen Morley and Ann Wool, who pressed me back into harness. Maybe they just wanted the whole thing over and done with. My son Andrew played a similar role while we spent a month in 2008 with him in his adopted country of Australia.

As the book came to its production stages I was given unstinting help by Eleanor Davey-Corrigan of Palgrave Macmillan. Bryony Allen was a careful and caring copy-editor and Linda Norris and her colleagues at Aardvark Editorial brought the book to the point at which it was fit to print.

I caution readers, as I did in my previous book, that when generalizing about, for example, chief executives or chief communications officers, I do not want the flow to get entangled in gender issues or explanations. So when I write "he" it means "she" as well. So take no offence, please. The book is in US rather than British spelling conventions because this is the default system in my laptop computer.

I thank all of those who have provided material, background guidance, checked my text for accuracy, and granted permission to quote them directly or from previously published work. Where appropriate, citations have been made in the text or end notes to each chapter but below is as comprehensive a list of sources and permissions as I can manage.

Introduction: Edelman kindly provided access to the findings of the annual Trust Barometer survey from its inception until the time of writing. Further references to insights from the Edelman Trust Barometer can be found throughout the book. *BusinessWeek* gave me permission to quote from their annual Top Brands Survey 2008. Alan Behr, partner at Alston & Bird kindly provided Exhibit 0.1 (Brand Symbols in common use) as well as the commentary. Ann Wool of Ketchum provided valuable input on Lenovo's sponsorship of the Beijing Olympics.

Chapter 1: *BusinessWeek* gave permission for the reproduction of Table 1.1. Ray Jordan and Marc Monseau provided invaluable help for the Johnson & Johnson case study.

Chapter 2: Amy Kavanaugh and colleagues at Edelman were my source for the section on Starbucks. Ernst Primosch and Kai Schmidburger provided the input to the Henkel case study which used material from (1) an article originally published in the October 2008 edition of *Frontline*, the journal of the International Public Relations Association; and (2) *International Corporate Brand Management – The Henkel Example*, a case study by Bernhard Swoboda, Judith Giersch and Ernst Primosch.

Chapter 3: I am grateful to Jane Hutterly and Kelly Semrau of SC Johnson who provided me unfettered access to company documents and gave me excellent guidance about family companies. Ken Sternad and John Flick provided generous counsel and constructive criticism on my references to UPS, which can be found in this chapter as well as in others. Andrew Bone of De Beers has been unstinting in his efforts to help me give an accurate portrayal of his company and to gain permission for me to reproduce the famous advertisement (Figure 3.1). Dickie Arbiter was a vital and helpful guide, correcting the excesses and inaccuracies in my first draft casting the British Monarchy as The Crown Corporation.

Chapter 4: I have relied on Booz Allen's *CEO Succession 2006* for some important statistics. The section on Herb Kelleher, former CEO of Southwest Airlines, is sourced from "The CEO as brand guardian", July 2007, by Will Rodgers and Christian Sarkar (http://www.zibs.com/ceobrand.shtml).

Chapter 5: John Heilenmann kindly gave permission for me to quote from his article on Steve Jobs in *New York Magazine* (June 18, 2007). Glenn Curtis of Thomson Reuters Financial gave permission for me to quote from *CEO Succession Planning*, July 2007. Joe Griesedieck of Korn/Ferry was a vital resource for the entire chapter and allowed me to reproduce Table 5.1.

Chapter 6: I am indebted to Jane Atkin from whom I learned much while she was at Edelman. Simon Anholt kindly shared his knowledge of nation branding and gave permission for me to reproduce Table 6.1.

Chapter 7: Figure 7.2 is reproduced by permission of Edelman. Ken Sternad and John Flick of UPS kindly checked my account of the section devoted to UPS. John Wiley & Sons granted me permission to quote from James C. Anderson and Gregory S. Carpenter, Chapter 9 in *Kellogg on Branding* edited by Alice M. Tybout and Tim Calkins. The Small Business Administration (www.sba.org) was a helpful resource, as was Mike O'Neill of American Express.

Chapter 8: I am grateful to Rosemarie Yu for her help in all matters legal discussed in this book. Permission to reproduce Table 8.1 was obtained from the publishers of *American Lawyer* and *Legal Week*. My thanks to Yolande Daeninck for checking the accuracy of my section on McKinsey & Co.

Chapter 9: I acknowledge drawing from more than one edition of the Edelman Trust Barometer. Ed Lebar, CEO of Brand Asset Consulting/ Young and Rubicam Brands, and Laura Frank were unstinting in their help and provided guidance, examples and gave permission for the reproduction of Figures 9.1 – 9.4.

Chapter 11: Dr Kent Rhodes (Pepperdine University) kindly allowed me to quote him on corporate culture and mythology. Figure 11.1 and the relevant commentary were first published in an article in the Accenture newsletter *Outlook* (October 2005). I am grateful to Alex Pachetti for his help. Ken Roberts, CEO of brand consulting firm Lippincott, has been most generous in allowing me to draw on his firm's experience and to reproduce Figure 11.2 and the Bentley case study. Pearson Education, Inc. gave permission for the reprinting in Exhibit 11.1 of material first published by Anderson, James C., Narus, James, A., *Business Marketing Management*, 2nd edition, © 2004, pp. 138–9.

Chapter 12: Ken Sternad and John Flick were once again most helpful in my description of the UPS rebranding and Kris Carpenter arranged the permission to reproduce Figure 12.1. My thanks are due to Mary Jo Jacobi for reviewing and improving my description of the evolution of the HSBC brand. Bob Knott of Edelman provided material for my piece on GE's Imagination at Work.

Chapter 13: Palgrave Macmillan granted permission for me to reproduce the graphic in Figure 13.1, which first appeared in my earlier book, *How to Manage Your Global Reputation*. This chapter also contains other material adapted from that book. I am indebted to Randy Nornes, Executive Vice President of AON Corporation, for his guidance and permission to reproduce Figure 13.2.

Chapter 14: I thank Keith Reinhard for granting permission to reproduce the DDB Brand Foundations process described in Table 14.1. But, more than that, for the brand wisdom he has imparted. He and Roger Dow gave permission for the reproduction of Exhibit 14.1. Alan Siegel allowed me to use the Siegel+Gale brand development strategy (Exhibit 14.2) and Figure 14.1.

Chapter 15: I thank Chris Deri and Anne Workman for sharing their insights on stakeholder mapping and permission to reproduce Figure 15.1.

Chapter 16: I am indebted to David Haigh and Camilla Armstrong for allowing the Brand Finance methodology to be described in some detail and for permitting the use of all the figures and tables in this chapter.

Chapter 17: David Rockland kindly permitted the use of Ketchum's Brandbuilder methodology (Exhibit 17.1). John Graham and Rich Eichwald of Fleishman-Hillard provided the AT&T case study.

Chapter 18: I thank Sandra Macleod and Nigel Middlemiss for contributing to this chapter, and for permission to reproduce the table and figures within it.

Every effort has been made to trace all the copyright holders but if any have been inadvertently overlooked the publishers will be pleased to make the necessary arrangements at the first opportunity.

Introduction

Surely there are enough books about branding to make another superfluous. So it would seem, except that a review of the huge range of books available in print shows that they are almost all devoted to brands as products.

In the world of marketing there is a tendency for seeing the world in terms of brands. Popular entertainers are named brands symbolizing their own style of, say, music. Think of all who are known by a single brand name: Tiger, Madonna, Sting, Cher, Beckham and now Obama. Over time, the name of a successful sportsman or entertainer accumulates a value and a loyal following. These same marketers will also see politicians as "brands" representing a defined set of values, aspirations and a promise, along with an emotional connection, that appeal to sections of the public.

BRANDAHOLICS

Perhaps we live in an era in which many of us have become brandaholics. Moreover, the proliferation of annual brand rankings is creating a kind of brandocracy, an elite group in which all ambitious brands are seeking membership.

For those outside the field of marketing this tendency to see the world as a kind of molecular structure of many brands is offensive. Many associate the word "brand" with manufactured and, therefore, inauthentic values. They bridle at the label being applied to anything other than products.

This becomes apparent to anyone engaged in a "branding" project for any organization other than those making and marketing products to consumers. Lawyers, accountants, engineers, healthcare institutions and not-for-profit organizations, even though they have moved from their traditional position as vocational professions into the commercial mainstream, often resent the

1

notion that they are working for an organization that is a "brand". Their sensibilities are less offended by and are more comfortable with terminology such as "corporate reputation" and "corporate identity" or even a "defined culture". Yet, in the public eye, the major professional service firms – lawyers, accountants, management consultants and others, healthcare providers and non-profit and non-governmental organizations – are brands in their own right. In fact, they are among the world's most powerful brands. When measured in terms of public trust, World Wildlife, Amnesty, Greenpeace and Oxfam were listed by Europeans in the top ten of organizations of all kinds in the first of a series of annual surveys initiated by Richard Edelman, President and CEO of Edelman. They were among such icons as Coca-Cola and Microsoft.

Along with the propensity of the public consciously, or unconsciously, to see corporations, institutions, people and movements as brands, we have a world that is increasingly complex, not least where brand identification is concerned.

TRUST AND AFFECTION

When Josiah Wedgwood made and sold his pottery in the mid-eighteenth century he made, basically, one product, under the Wedgwood name. Mont Blanc made pens. Rolex made watches. Gucci made shoes. Coca-Cola made Coca-Cola. Lever Brothers made Sunlight soap. Procter & Gamble (P&G) made Ivory soap. There was a degree of simplicity and clarity that could inspire trust and affection on the part of users in products and producers which were, for all intents and purposes, identified or closely related, one to the other in a direct line.

Now Waterford-Wedgwood makes glass and china, Mont Blanc makes pens and watches, Gucci makes clothes, watches and a host of other products as well as shoes. Coca-Cola makes a variety of beverages, Lever Brothers has grown into Unilever, a giant corporation with food and toiletries added to its washing/cleaning products. P&G has extended its number of categories and markets soaps, detergents, pharmaceuticals, foods and pet foods, beauty products and many other categories. At last count it owned 23 brands, each with global sales of over $US 1 billion. Rolex still makes only watches.

But all of them now have to present their products – and their corporate entities – in about 200 vastly differing markets around the world.

It is the second of these tasks that interests me and should be a topic of special interest to public relations professionals. It prompted me to consider writing this book. There seemed to me to be little literature written about brands that are both corporate *and* global.

At the moment I was turning over the project in my mind, my eye caught a book review in *The Economist* (November 20, 2005) of *Kellogg on Branding*, edited by Alice M.Tybout and Tim Calkins.

In a favorable review of the book, as well as of Kellogg School of Management, by far the brand-leading business school in the marketing discipline, *The Economist* gave the following recommendation: "If you have time to read only one of the many books on branding, make sure it is this one", implying that it covered all you need to know.

IRRESISTIBLE

This was a recommendation too strong to resist, offering the prospect of "one-stop shopping" for my research and within minutes I had placed my order on Amazon.com.

For all its insights and value, the book was a partial disappointment to me because it gave virtually no recognition to the power of public relations in creating and sustaining brand equity. And, perhaps as befits the marketing discipline origins of Kellogg and its selected authors, its focus was primarily on products. I was much wiser for having read the book but given new reason to work on this volume. There was still room for a work that looked at brands that are corporate and global and to examine how public relations can be a potent force in creating and sustaining their success.

But corporate brands come in many different packages. Some are holding companies, simply investment vehicles that own, but do not directly manage, a stable of subsidiary corporations that may or may not have a common thread to link them, beyond being profit machines. Such owners were generally known as conglomerates, a term that has gone out of fashion favor.

Some are multi-brand corporations – P&G is a good example – that own and manage several product brands, or brand ranges in several product categories (for example men's grooming, women's hair care, women's fragrance, and so on). Sometimes major consumer products corporations such as Nestlé, Unilever and P&G market several competing – or complementary – brands in a single category. P&G, for example has Cascade, Dawn, Ivory and Joy, all jostling for shelf space in the dish washing section. These are known as "house of brands" companies, and to varying degrees and in varying ways they now give attention to managing their corporate brands.

FAMILY BRANDS

There are "family" brands in which several generations of, usually, the founding family maintain a brand name that has accumulated a standing over many generations. There are corporate brands that are synonymous with a charismatic leader, when it can be hard to determine which has the greater value, the person or the corporate entity.

Finally, there are corporate brands whose names are the same, for the most part, as the products or services they sell, where the linkage is clear for all to see. It is interesting to note that in the annual *BusinessWeek* issue on the Top 100 Global Brands in 2008, only one product brand – Marlboro at place number 18 – makes it into the top 20. (It is possible to argue that Mercedes-Benz (11) and Gillette (14) are now product brands, owned by Daimler-Benz and P&G respectively, but in most respects these have operated as or are perceived as autonomous corporate entities.) But even 17 out of the top 20 shows the important place held by corporations clearly linked to the brands being sold. All of the top ten share the same brand and product or service name. This is discussed further in Chapter 1.

WHO IS THE CORPORATE BRAND MANAGER?

There is no defined background or career path for those who aspire to the position of global corporate brand manager.

- **Public relations and corporate communications** practitioners often believe they have the right to be the strongest voice in determining the brand. After all, among the responsibilities of the most senior public relations (PR) executive is that of promoting and protecting the reputation of the corporation. This could equally well be described as **corporate brand management**. In the spirit of full disclosure I must declare that it is from this viewpoint that I approach the topic.

But other professions have also laid claim to the mantle of responsibility for determining and managing brands, corporate brands among them. Each approaches the concept of brand from his own viewpoint. While each professional craftsman starts out with skills and training in one specific element of a brand, those who become really successful add mastery of the other components of branding in order to become fully rounded brand consultants or managers.

- **Designers and visualizers** are prominent among brand experts. Starting life creating symbols and logos – corporate and product identities – some add knowledge of the other elements that go into the whole brand and become consultants, often at the head of a specialist branding firm. Even within this community there are degrees of specialization. Some are experts in pictorial design or typography. Others claim a special knowledge of colors, and will persuade you that a particular shade of red for your logo and livery will truly reflect (or reshape) your corporate identity. In special product fields, smell might be the defining characteristic of a brand. The illustrative art path of development is succinctly expressed in the title of a book, *Image by Design*, by Clive Chajet. He was the head of Lippincott and Margulies, a long-established corporate identity specialist which graduated into brand consulting and is now known simply as Lippincott.

- **Lawyers** lay claim to an important place in the brand management hierarchy, approaching the subject from the point of view of, first, selecting a name (and indeed a design) that is distinct from any other existing brand and that will be secure from any costly legal challenge. The brand lawyer will also have to make sure that basic pitfalls are avoided as successful brands are created and move from their home market into the global arena. A backhanded confirmation of the cash value of a brand can be found in a certain breed of entrepreneurs who, like other professional gamblers, register ownership of new and rising brand names in key international markets, make small quantities of product and offer them for sale while waiting patiently for the target brand to expand into international markets. At that point the new company or brand is confronted with a legal challenge from the entrepreneur who owns the rights to the name locally and there is invariably a very costly settlement for a transfer of the brand rights. Fortunes have been made in this way, and not always by the genuine developer and creator of the brand. Once the brand has been established the brand lawyer must turn his attention to protection of the property, which, if it is a Coca-Cola, McDonald's or Marlboro, will be under constant siege with copycat assaults on the valuable name or insignia. Nor do many large markets have the legal framework to make this brand protection task easy.

The table in Exhibit 0.1, kindly prepared by Alan Behr, a partner at Alston & Bird LLP, shows some of the devices and symbols that corporations and other owners of brands or intellectual property use as ways of protecting their assets.

Exhibit 0.1 Brand symbols in common use (Source: Alan Behr, Alston & Bird LLP)

Symbol	Definition	Use
©	The international symbol of copyright ownership	See below
TM	Superscript meaning a trademark	Used primarily for unregistered trademarks, meaning marks for goods and not services
®	International registration symbol for trademarks, service marks, collective marks (marks owned by a collective group or association such as a cooperative or union) and certification marks (marks owned by one party to certify the origin, quality or other characteristics of the product or service of another party)	In the US, only used after registration of a mark by the Patent and Trademark Office. Use of it prior to registration may cause problems in an attempt to register the mark with the US Patent and Trademark Office
SM	Superscript meaning a service mark	Used primarily for unregistered service marks

Copyright notices in the US and elsewhere commonly use the © symbol, add the word copyright and date and have a rights reservation line. The date is important in the US to help assess damages awarded in litigation and also to help calculate the expiration date for certain types of works.

US law requires, in each copyright notice, the use of (1) ©, "Copyright" or "copr.," (2) the year of first publication, and (3) the name of the owner. The standard format:

Copyright © 2008 Alan Behr
All rights reserved.

The © symbol is used regardless of whether copyright is registered. Note that registration of copyright is very important in the US, but many nations have no copyright registration system.

The © symbol is used once on a work, such as on the title page of a book. Trademark and service mark symbols are used next to (but not inside of) the marks to which they relate, in a way that makes it clear to which mark they refer. Most commonly, that use is as a superscript – on the upper right corner of the mark – but there is no hard and fast rule about that. The symbol need not be used every time a mark is used, but it is usually best to use it with a mark in the first or most prominent place that the mark appears on product, packaging, in advertising, or wherever else the mark is applied. The rules for slogan marks are the same as for other marks: it is usually best for the correct superscript or the ® registration symbol to be placed at the end of the first or most prominent use.

- **Name consultants** are individuals or firms, often lawyers, who advise corporations on the most appealing names for their organizations or products. Some organizations register and hold available a bank of available names to save clients the laborious and costly business of selecting a name that is already owned by someone else. Here, too, there are pitfalls for the unwary that can result in the loss of a valuable and sometimes personally invaluable property, as happened in the PR firm where I worked for nearly 40 years. When it was decided to dissolve the operations of a joint venture partnership in one of Asia's key markets, it transpired that the small print of the joint venture agreement conferred ownership of the name Daniel J. Edelman to the local partner in that market. This was not only financially damaging but seemed wrong and unreasonable to Dan Edelman, the founder, who saw it as a personal affront, having his own name taken from him. He was faced with the choice of buying back his own property, as he saw it, or proceeding with a global brand strategy that had another name in a key market. Of course, agreement was reached for the return of the name and a lesson was learned not just in the importance of a name but also in reading the small print and making sure that this prized asset is protected.

- **Advertising agencies** have traditionally been strongly associated with the creation and promotion of brands, especially product brands. Great admen understand instinctively that brands create a bond with their consumers that is not based solely on rational choice. A more powerful emotional connection can be created by inspired advertisements. And because the lion's share of most corporations' marketing budgets has, until recent times, been controlled by the advertising agency, the result has been that senior ad agency executives have traditionally held a position of great influence (often most influence) on brand strategy. Add to this the early internationalization of several large advertising agencies, creating a knowledge bank of different consumer habits and preferences around the world, and they have been in pole position to act as leaders in discussion of branding. Although this position of influence might have arisen through work for products, it was natural that it should be extended into the area of corporate brand strategy. Young & Rubicam Brands, a global advertising agency member of the WPP Group, has developed a proprietary methodology known as Brand Asset Valuator. BAV, as it is commonly known, has been in operation for more than 15 years and has been following brand progress of products and corporations well beyond its own base of clients. Thus Y&R is in possession of historic and trend data about consumer attitudes towards brands and categories and, further, is able to calculate a financial value for a brand. The BAV method and model is discussed more fully in Chapter 9.

- **Marketers**, especially those in consumer products companies, have risen in their careers through roles as product managers, brand managers, brand group managers and category managers and are steeped in experience of the systems of managing brands. Not all will know the secrets of creating the magical brand bond but they will know that it is necessary and will hire experts to find the secret. However, they will know a great deal about the many other elements that are necessary to sustain an enduring brand – financial management, innovation, consumer preference, and so on. They also have the responsibility of supervising the work of the lawyers, admen, PR team and research experts whose combined efforts are needed to achieve success. Marketers are among those who sometimes turn themselves into brand consultants.

- **Sponsorship and event management** specialists have also extended their influence into brand consulting, especially with products and corporations that devote a major proportion of their budgets to these activities. For a Nike, Adidas or Puma, simple visibility for their names and symbols at major sporting events, along with the endorsements of successful athletes wearing or using the products, is central to the creation of the brand. For other corporations with a less obvious connection to sports or even the arts, the ability to reach a mass or discrete audience by sponsorship of a league, team, athlete or event can be a compelling component of a brand promotional program. Coca-Cola, Johnson & Johnson, VISA, GE, Samsung, Panasonic, Kodak, Lenovo, Omega Watches, McDonald's, Manulife and Altos Origin would not each spend close to $80 million simply for the right to be an Olympics TOP sponsor[1] (that is before spending additional tens of millions in advertising, signage and other promotions to capitalize on the sponsorship fee) unless they believe that it confers a huge brand benefit.

BRANDOCRACY

Samsung is an example of a company that has a passionate belief in the power of sponsorship to create a mega brand. Over a short period of 20 years the Korean company has transformed itself from being a relatively unknown maker of OEM components for more famous branded electronics products into one of the world's top 25 brands according to the 2008 *BusinessWeek*/Interbrand rankings.

Samsung had taken the same route as Sony, which had used the Tokyo Olympics in 1964 to vault into the premier league of global brands. Now these two mega brands are being followed on this proven path to success by Chinese PC maker Lenovo, which seized the opportunity afforded by the Beijing Games to establish itself as the newest member of the global brandocracy.

Three years ago, no one knew the Lenovo name. A Chinese company (previously known as Legend) that purchased IBM's PC division, the newly named Lenovo faced the challenge of elevating its position in the global market. The company, already number one in the largest growing consumer market in the world, needed to combat its low awareness among constituencies in other key countries. Lenovo saw its Olympic partnership as a platform to introduce the brand globally and reach millions in countries in which the company looked to gain traction. The *Financial Times* (August 13, 2008) reported that "Lenovo's sponsorship of the Beijing games is the centerpiece of a big and expensive three-year branding push". Ann Wool, Managing Director of Sports and Entertainment at Ketchum, the PR agency that worked with Lenovo on the project, says the computer maker "started a comprehensive program that began long before the start of the Games through a proactive public relations campaign focused on these priority countries outside of China – Japan, India, Australia, France, UK, Germany, Russia, US, Argentina and Hong Kong. The challenge was to ensure the Lenovo brand messaging and core competences would be part of the stories coming out of the Olympic news".

Unlike most sponsors, Lenovo technology and innovation were critical aspects of the smooth running of the games themselves, from the opening to closing ceremonies. Powering the Games, Lenovo had an intrinsic IT link and reason for the partnership. It developed a plan that incorporated the core technology story as well as maximized Olympic athletes, Lenovo's innovative design of the Olympic torch, philanthropic endeavors, interactive online programs and on-site activation in addition to traditional media tactics.

According to several independent surveys and reports, Lenovo either had the most media coverage among Olympic sponsors or was on a par with McDonald's and Coca-Cola. The brand goals the company had set were met or exceeded. Lenovo's brand tracker showed an increase from 21 percent to 29 percent in worldwide consumer awareness and a jump from 44 percent to 62 percent in commercial awareness over the duration of the Olympic campaign.

But Olympic sponsorship is just one element in a company's quest to become a global power brand. A leading article in *The Economist* (September 20, 2008) cites Lenovo and Arcelor Mittal as being on the leading edge of a new phase in the evolution of the multinational corporation. Among the items on Lenovo's long checklist of actions to convert itself into a world brand leader has been Chairman Yang Yuanquing's decision to relocate his family to North Carolina "to deepen his appreciation of American culture, so as to help him integrate his Chinese and American workers".

The creation of "brand events" is related, as we will see later in this book, to the vital importance of "brand experience" in the formation of the brand. This is the realm in which creative minds have grown up in fields such as theater, cinema and music and have been refocused on staging events in which the audience is not just touched by the brand, but is immersed in its aura. Imagination is a firm that started out as the producer of spectacular events on behalf of its clients such as Ford Europe. Gradually, under the leadership of the creative genius Gary Withers and former screenwriter, adman and Unilever marketing director Len Heath, Imagination morphed into a fully fledged brand consulting firm.

- **Market and opinion researchers** are logical candidates to mature into brand consultants. Using the information they glean into consumer (and other stakeholder) preferences, the best of them are able convert this into insights that can help a client understand a brand and then strengthen it. While an important part of the researchers' work involves quantitative elements, they are also in a good position to analyze the chemistry of the brand bond, that attraction that transcends rational choice and is usually the vital differentiating factor. The transition from researcher to brand consultant can perhaps be best illustrated in the related field of electoral politics where the transition from pollster to pundit is not unusual. It is almost the rule in present day politics in the USA, UK and other democratic nations that the researcher/pollster assumes the most influential role in shaping (and sometimes during the course of a long campaign, reshaping) the brand of a candidate. It is now not unusual for a campaign manager to have a market research background. Pollster Mark Penn served for several months as chief strategist for Hillary Clinton's bid to win the Democratic Party's nomination as Presidential candidate while continuing to act – controversially – as CEO of global PR agency Burson-Marsteller.
- **Chartered accountants** (Certified Public Accountants in the US) arrive in brand consulting via the balance sheet where – at least for some

of them – the quest is to measure the intangibles and attribute to them a monetary value. Brand is for many corporations a huge proportion of their total value but this is seldom recognized in their formal annual accounts. In the past, brand value became apparent only when a company or part of a company was sold. If the total purchase price exceeds the net assets it could be assumed that brand value/potential was part of that calculation. This is illustrated by Jaguar cars. When Jaguar was bought by Ford for $2 billion in 1990, the British car maker had negative equity so it was clear that all the additional value resided in the aura – or brand appeal – and loyalty of customers to the Jaguar heritage brand. (Ford, in turn, in 2008 sold the Jaguar and Land Rover companies to Tata of India for $2.3 billion in order to maximize its investments in rebuilding the products and brand of Ford itself.) Now companies are more systematically trying to value their corporate and product brands without any plan to make a sale, and specialist companies such as Brand Finance plc are there to help them do it. The company's CEO, David Haigh, and four of his top executives are all qualified chartered accountants. They believe they have created a best practice model for achieving valuations based on a "relief from royalty" calculation that is more fully described in Chapter 16.

Note

1   TOP stands for "The Olympic Partner Program" and is the only International Olympic Committee sponsorship that offers exclusive worldwide marketing rights to both Summer and Winter Games. In the very act of becoming a TOP Olympics sponsor a corporation sends a clear signal that it has joined the exclusive club of global brands. It is of significance that all the Beijing TOP sponsors are corporate as well as product or service brands.

1

The brand house

Take a close look at the annual "Top Brands" survey conducted by Interbrand for *BusinessWeek*. It is a testament to the power of the corporate-product brand entity, in which the corporate name and the name of its principal products are identical.

Led by Coca-Cola (1), IBM (2) and Microsoft (3) and ending with FedEx (99) and VISA (100), the overwhelming victors are product brands which have given their names to corporations, or vice versa. And all top ten corporations have names that are the same as their principal products or services.

As Table 1.1 shows, nine of the 2008 top ten are the same as in 2007 but Google, with a huge 43 percent rise in brand value came in at number 10, pushing Mercedes-Benz into 11th place.

Table 1.1 Top ten brands, 2008 (Source: Reproduced from the September 29, 2008 issue of *BusinessWeek* by special permission, copyright © by The McGraw-Hill Companies, Inc.)

Rank 2008/2007		2008 Brand value $millions	Country of ownership
1	Coca-Cola	66,667	US
2	IBM	59,031	US
3	Microsoft	59,007	US
4	GE	53,086	US
5	Nokia	35,942	Finland
6	Toyota	34,050	Japan
7	Intel	31,261	US
8	McDonald's	31,049	US
9	Disney	29,251	US
10	Google	25,590	US

While the Interbrand/*BusinessWeek* methodology openly admits to the omission of some important brand heavyweights such as Wal-Mart, for specific technical reasons, it is widely regarded as one of the best surveys of its kind because it attaches a specific monetary value to each brand, stripping out all the various operating costs associated with making and marketing the products.

Brand value is only confirmed or adjusted when a brand is sold, and the valuations done by specialist branding consultants play a key role in the mergers and acquisitions community. The seller wants to obtain the best price when selling the brand asset. The buyer will be looking, as always, for a bargain. This applies when the brand asset is the entire corporation, a name division or a product.

BusinessWeek says it chose Interbrand's methodology because it evaluates brand value in the same way any other corporate asset is valued – on the basis of how much it is likely to earn for the company in the future. Interbrand uses a combination of analysts' projections, company financial documents, and its own qualitative and quantitative analysis to arrive at a net present value of those earnings.

Those corporations with a name that is synonymous with the principal product brand(s) are known as "brand houses", as distinct from corporations that manage a portfolio of different brands and are called "house of brands".

The brand house has a number of inherent advantages when it comes to corporate branding. But these are counterbalanced by some disadvantages. Let's look at the plus and minus ledger:

Advantages

- Allows a clear focus on the "master brand" and a high degree of identification to all the organization's stakeholders: customers, employees, suppliers, communities, stockholders, regulators and activists. No longer are these groups in separate silos. In today's society they regularly interact with each other on an equal basis and often act in dual or multiple roles. Employees, for example, might well be customers, stockholders, activists and community members at the same time.
- Concentration of resources: all PR, advertising, sponsorship or philanthropy is directly linked to a single entity without dilution and builds brand equity in the corporate brand in a way that does not occur when there is no linkage between corporate and product brand. An example

of a radical change implemented to take advantage of this dynamic occurred in June 1994 when the French food giant BSN became Groupe Danone. According to the company, it "decided to drop BSN, which seemed to reflect the company's past rather than looking ahead to the future ... The group thus took advantage of the resonance of its leading brand, which was famous the world over (Dannon in the USA), produced in 30 countries and accounted for about a quarter of its turnover. Danone is the Group's standard bearer and has become the link between the various families of brands: biscuits, mineral waters and baby food were soon being sold under the new name."[1]

■ The power of a strong corporate brand allows for expansion with new products, variations and sub-brands at a lower cost than would be the case for a stand-alone new brand.

■ There is now some evidence that consumers want to know more about the "company behind the brand". They increasingly weigh the way a company behaves toward its stakeholders and its care for the environment when making buying decisions. Equally, product quality, safety and environmental care are among the attributes that shape impressions of the corporation as a whole. These linkages are especially tight and strong in the case of a brand house where the corporate and product name is shared.

■ Brands have a legacy value and this is true of both product and corporate brands, some of which are similar to the aristocracy or dynasties to be found in human society. While some new generations want – at least for a while – to rebel against their parents, there is considerable evidence to show that a majority of children choose and use the same brands as their parents. Thus, a brand with longevity is usually one that understands the essence of its appeal but is able to innovate and adapt itself so as to keep its old and new customers and other stakeholders faithful.

■ A new product or service from an established brand house is assured of distribution and trial if it comes with the message "another innovation from" a corporate name with a high level of recognition and trust.

■ A powerful brand house benefits in recruitment and gets first pick at the best qualified recruits.

■ The brand house benefits from the emotional connection created by the fact that consumers and other audiences *experience* the product or service as individual or business consumers. This is often a more potent influence of brand affection and loyalty than practical performance attributes. It is hard for a hedge fund or holding company to forge a bond of brand affection with any group other than its investors or stockholders and that relationship will surely be weighted heavily in the direction of performance.

- It has not been usual for most corporations to apply brand management techniques to the overall corporate identity and the brand image or equity it has is often the halo effect of its product or service advertising, PR, and promotional and sales activities. This is an "accidental" bonus that does not apply to house of brands companies. Increasingly, however, as the importance of corporate brand equity is recognized and understood, product brand management skills are being deployed at the corporate level.
- A strong corporate brand acts as a "crisis shield" when problems occur – as they inevitably will. A brand with a good reputation will be given the benefit of the doubt and time to put things right, a privilege not usually granted to anonymous or poorly regarded brands.

Disadvantages

- For defensive-minded corporations it is dangerous to have (to use the old cliché) all the eggs in one basket. It can happen that when something goes wrong with one product that is directly linked to the corporate name or in one department, the corporate entity is tarnished and other products become damaged by association. When Coca-Cola corporation was slow and ineffective in managing a product-tainting crisis in Belgium in 1999, a relatively small local problem spread to other countries, damaged relations with government authorities, as well as sales, caused the stock to plunge, caused the CEO to resign and forced a complete revision of marketing strategy. Nike, surely the emblem of a proactive, in your face company took a hit when they were taken to task by NGOs (non-governmental organizations) for unacceptable employment practices in the factories where their products were made. Nike shoes, clothing and sports equipment were all affected, as was the company's reputation. Nike was forced to change policies and pay heavily to recover its brand reputation.[2]
- It can be hard for a corporation to expand its portfolio of offerings when it seems chained forever to its original flagship product. But it might be essential with the investment community, in particular, to recognize that the success of the company is no longer irrevocably linked to the heritage brand, especially when it is perceived to be in decline and has been overtaken by a competitor or revolutionary new technology (as in the case of Kodak, for example).

- The tradition and culture of a "brand house" company can work against the creation of completely new power brands by denying the brand team the independence and marketing oxygen it needs to succeed.
- Finally, there is often less understanding of the importance and science of branding in some brand house organizations than in house of brands corporations. The latter are built on the notion that the brand is king and most company leaders follow a career path through the discipline of brand management. For most corporations it is still a novel idea to apply the techniques of brand management to the corporation itself.

CASE The brand house

Johnson & Johnson has been at one and the same time a power product brand name and one of the world's most admired corporate brands. It is a brand house as well as a house of brands.

Johnson & Johnson consistently ranks very high on all lists of "most admired" companies. It is at the top of *Harris Interactive's* National Corporate Reputation Survey, is regarded as the world's most respected company by *Barron's Magazine*, and was the first corporation awarded the Benjamin Franklin Award for Public Diplomacy by the US State Department for its funding of international education programs, according to a posting in Wikipedia.

I have chosen to place it as a case in the chapter dealing with brand houses because in my view this is its real strength, even though it owns and operates several autonomous corporations, each with its own strong brand identity and its own product or service brands. Yet, the Johnson & Johnson connection signifies more than anonymous ownership; it adds luster to the subsidiary brands and, in my view, imparts more brand benefit than it receives, the tipping point that distinguishes a brand house from a house of brands.

For example, an exclusive preserve of elite, world-class brand house corporations is the group of worldwide TOP sponsors of the Olympics. In the group sponsoring the recent Beijing Olympics, Johnson & Johnson is the only multi-brand corporation that has considered it a good investment to pay the high entry price, joining McDonald's, Coca-Cola, Lenovo, Kodak, Samsung, VISA and other brand house members of this exclusive club.

Also, consider the notorious instance of the Tylenol tamperings in Chicago, where, in 1982, packs of Extra Strength Tylenol were found to have been laced with cyanide. In the public mind Tylenol, a power brand in its own right, is irrevocably linked with Johnson & Johnson with minimal reference to the McNeil Consumer Products Company, the operating subsidiary company that produces and markets Tylenol. Although Johnson & Johnson's decision to recall all packs of Tylenol in distribution in the USA may have had a considerable short-term cost to the company, in the longer term the company has since benefited from the decision taken at that time by then CEO of Johnson & Johnson, James Burke. An event that might have caused damage to the reputation of another corporation enhanced and strengthened the Johnson & Johnson brand.

Those who work for or closely with Johnson & Johnson have little doubt as to why this should be. They see the action taken in the Tylenol case as being the natural and only responsible course for a company focused on its mission and culture, crystallized in a "credo" written in 1943 by Robert Wood Johnson, the son of one of the company's founders (see Exhibit 1.1).

This document is the cement that links all the Johnson & Johnson subsidiaries and all their regional and national operating units around the world, however recently they might have been added to the Johnson & Johnson family of companies. Whereas Johnson & Johnson central management allows its divisions and units a high degree of operational autonomy, they are expected to observe and follow the responsibilities outlined in the credo.

The foresight of the founders and successive leaders of Johnson & Johnson is truly remarkable. If, as I argue elsewhere in this book, stamina is one hallmark of a great corporate brand, then Johnson & Johnson is a fine example. Not only has the company itself endured for over 120 years since its foundation in 1886, the logo style of its name has changed imperceptibly over the years and the credo has continued without alteration of content or style since it was introduced. It would be hard to find any other major global corporation that can match this record. The company has found it unnecessary to react to the many changes of corporate and management fashion that have occurred in the intervening years.

Exhibit 1.1 Johnson & Johnson's Credo

Our Credo

We believe our first responsibility is to the doctors, nurses and patients,
to mothers and fathers and all others who use our products and services.
In meeting their needs everything we do must be of high quality.
We must constantly strive to reduce our costs
in order to maintain reasonable prices.
Customers' orders must be serviced promptly and accurately.
Our suppliers and distributors must have an opportunity
to make a fair profit.

We are responsible to our employees,
the men and women who work with us throughout the world.
Everyone must be considered as an individual.
We must respect their dignity and recognize their merit.
They must have a sense of security in their jobs.
Compensation must be fair and adequate,
and working conditions clean, orderly and safe.
We must be mindful of ways to help our employees fulfill
their family responsibilities.
Employees must feel free to make suggestions and complaints.
There must be equal opportunity for employment, development
and advancement for those qualified.
We must provide competent management,
and their actions must be just and ethical.

We are responsible to the communities in which we live and work
and to the world community as well.
We must be good citizens – support good works and charities
and bear our fair share of taxes.
We must encourage civic improvements and better health and education.
We must maintain in good order
the property we are privileged to use,
protecting the environment and natural resources.

Our final responsibility is to our stockholders.
Business must make a sound profit.
We must experiment with new ideas.
Research must be carried on, innovative progams developed
and mistakes paid for.
New equipment must be purchased, new facilities provided
and new products launched.
Reserves must be created to provide for adverse times.
When we operate according to these principles,
the stockholders should realize a fair return.

Johnson & Johnson

The Johnson & Johnson logo from the 1920s was based on the signature of one of the company's founders.

Exhibit 1.2 Johnson & Johnson's logo

Notes

1 Muzellec, L. and Lambkin, M. (2006) "Corporate rebranding: Destroying, transferring or creating brand equity?", *European Journal of Marketing*, **40**(7/8): 803–24.
2 (1) Michael Morley, *How to Manage Your Global Reputation*, page 104; and (2) Professor Maureen Taylor, "Cultural variance as a challenge to global public relations: A case study of the Coca-Cola scare in Europe", *Public Relations Review*, September 22, 2000.

2
The house of brands

Many of the world's most outstandingly successful brands are owned by corporations that are much lesser known to the general public. And in the past many liked it that way.

Procter & Gamble (P&G) is less recognized than its brands like Ivory soap, Tide detergent, Head and Shoulders, Gillette shaving products, Pantene hair care and a host of its other products.

Unilever is seeking greater awareness as a corporate brand but cannot compare with its mega brands like Dove, Axe, Lipton Tea and Hellmann's Mayonnaise.

Henkel, the German-owned group, has redefined its corporate brand following the sale of its raw chemicals business and is now focused entirely on its consumer products and adhesive technologies which include such names as Persil, Schwarzkopf, Dial, Right Guard, Loctite, Sellotape and Pritt (see case study).

Nestlé, the world's largest food corporation, is linked to its original milk and infant formulas and chocolates with the same name but is less connected with its mineral waters (Poland Spring and Badoit, among others), Nescafé/Taster's Choice, Crosse & Blackwell, Milo and its other brand families.

Nivea outshines Beiersdorf, its German parent corporation, just as Ban deodorant does its Japanese owner, Kao.

Each of these, like many other companies, particularly in the field of fast moving consumer goods (FMCG) owns many other brands that individually might be the equivalent of a medium sized corporation.

Mars, Inc., which in many countries shares the name of its leading brand; the Mars Bar (the USA is an exception), also markets Snickers, M&Ms, Uncle Ben's Rice and other products, and is a world leader in pet foods with the power brands Pedigree Chum and Whiskas. In 2008

Mars took a giant step by acquiring Wrigley's, adding global leadership in chewing gum to its powerful portfolio.

Until recently, many of these multi-brand corporations – to which the term "house of brands" has been applied to differentiate them from the "brand house" – gave little attention to the nurturing of their corporate brand, at least to the general public. In fact, it was felt that corporate anonymity was something of a blessing.

First, it operated on the submarine principle. Most submarines are built with six or more watertight compartments; when one is damaged in an accident or by enemy action the rest of the vessel remains sound and able to operate. House of brands managers feel reassured that if one brand in their portfolio is seriously damaged by, for example, a food product tainting incident, or even a long-term brand decline, this can be balanced by the success of unrelated brands.

Second, one of the axioms of the school of "the product is hero" brand marketing is that no resources should be wasted on any messages or activities that do not strengthen product loyalty and drive sales of the brands. Thus, little money and effort were applied to enhance the corporate brand name. Another tenet of this same school of thought was that the corporate brand name has little to add of value in advertising a product brand; indeed all it did was occupy valuable time or space that could be better used to extol the product's benefits.

This, of course, is a good example of the "chicken and egg" conundrum.

Now more and more, brand houses are getting involved to varying degrees and with different groups of stakeholders in corporate branding.

One company that straddles the description of brand house and house of brands is Kraft Foods, which makes and markets a host of products from Kraft Cheese Slices through to "stand alone" brands like Philadelphia Cheese, Miracle Whip and Vegemite. Kraft now places its logo/name on most of its products and promotes the Kraft brand as implying an extra level of quality and value assurance to the consumer. It is one of the key drivers of sales. But Kraft also has several distinctive or premium brands whose positioning with consumers could be damaged by association with Kraft, which is a power brand in its own right.

At the other end, some companies that have traditionally preferred anonymity at the corporate level and invested all their resources in promoting their individual brands have now, perhaps somewhat reluctantly, recognized the necessity of a good corporate brand reputation, at least with certain audiences.

The first among these audiences are employees, the communities in which they operate and the investment community. Then there are the OFEs (opinion forming elites, which include regulators and lawmakers). Usually there is a ready understanding of the importance of these groups to affect the ability of the corporation to practice its business successfully; but that does not mean that all corporations, therefore, undertake coherent and professionally executed corporate brand management programs.

Let's take a look at each one of these stakeholder groups and see how house of brands corporations have historically taken a different view of each.

First, it must be said that the way each company views corporate branding is driven by culture and tradition. It can be also affected by the way in which the individual sub-brands have been accumulated: by organic growth generated by its own R&D or by acquisition of established brands, brand families or corporations. But it is more likely to be driven by the corporate philosophy. There are companies that may have many brands but manage them directly. Others adopt a "holding company" approach and allow brand units great latitude.

In the case of the former it is more likely that there will be a strong corporate brand presence/recognition among several of the stakeholder groups. Unilever, Kraft and Nestlé are examples. Corporations that are a composite of acquired brands, especially if this occurred recently, and have a decentralized management style, usually allow the sub-brand to dominate in the minds of stakeholders. This is particularly true of conglomerates such as Berkshire Hathaway and Tyco.

INVESTORS

All house of brands companies that are publicly listed recognize the importance of the investor stakeholder group. The stock price is the first thing checked each day by most CEOs, who know that investor confidence is the key enabler of the corporation's continued success (and his own continued employment).

For this reason a significant effort is put into communicating with the investment community. By definition, this requires presentation of the corporation as a complete entity as opposed to merely a collection of units or sub-brands. Several techniques will be used – from profiling the CEO, or leadership team, to speeches outlining vision and strategy – to project the idea of a sound investment. But, few directors of investor relations would think of themselves as managers of a corporate brand.

Based on the notion that investors and analysts are interested only in quantifiable facts, hard numbers, and proven performance, this is where communications are focused. However, a look at how volatile markets can be suggests that so-called experts know little more than we average citizens. So, when the going gets rough and the market heads for a downturn or recession, the money flows out of the unknown corporations and into the safe haven of recognized blue chip corporate brands, where there is a long-standing emotional, as well as rational, connection. In short, trust. Beyond the strength of the corporate brand itself, the market believes that in tough times consumers prefer quality brands over bargain products and even own-label brands. It is instructive to note that one of the world's best known, richest and most successful investors, Warren Buffett, the head of Berkshire Hathaway, says that he only invests in companies whose brands are household names and whose business he can understand. So it is not surprising to find that among the many corporations in which he owns stock, two of the prominent names are Coca-Cola and Procter & Gamble.

EMPLOYEES

All corporations, including house of brands corporations, pay lip service to the importance of employee morale and commitment, and many give a high priority and sizeable budget to their (unfortunately titled, in my view) human resources managers. HR professionals no more think of themselves as employee brand managers than do investor relations managers. Yet, the task in most cases is to create an emotional and rational bond between employee and the overall corporation. This is a fundamental first step in the implementation of an "inside out", or employee-led, corporate brand/reputation strategy (see Chapter 10).

Based on the idea of the employee as advocate and ambassador for the brand – product or corporate – it requires that employees are dedicated to product quality, best practice and good corporate behavior. Further, employees may be called on to speak out on behalf of the corporation in public.

For the house of brands, especially one that has been recently created from an acquisition, rather than by organic growth, winning the commitment of employees to the corporate brand can be especially challenging.

In such cases, the corporate brand loyalty that has been built up in a brand or corporation that has subsequently been acquired by another house of brands needs to be transferred to the new corporate entity, without damaging the commitment to the existing brand. This can be especially difficult when the culture and style of the new owner may be quite different to that which the employee is accustomed, and is exacerbated by the increased remoteness of the master corporation.

To succeed, a conscious and sustained educational and motivational effort is needed.

COMMUNITIES

In today's global economy, local communities are one of the most difficult stakeholder groups to deal with for all corporations, whether they are brand houses or houses of brands. They can often be the crucible in which the behavior of the corporate brand is put to the test on such sensitive issues as outsourcing, offshoring, employment practices and pay, healthcare provision and environmental protection. And, the way the corporation behaves will shape the future of its brand equity in the community and often beyond. CEOs in the US now pause before seeking the financial advantages of relocating the corporate headquarters to a more tax-friendly domicile because they followed with interest the attempt in 2002 of Stanley Works to relocate to Bermuda. A furor followed Stanley's announcement even though the company was at pains to point out that the relocation would strengthen the company financially, make it more competitive and would not involve loss of jobs in its home base of New Britain, Connecticut, where it was founded in 1843. The community public and government outcry forced Stanley to abandon its plans and the storied Stanley brand, a symbol of national pride, sustained at least temporary damage.

In the case of house of brands corporations, there are additional complications that encourage the owners not to pursue a policy of strong corporate branding among business units spread across a number of locations. Many of these are the same reasons as have been described in the case of employees. First, a factory or some other business unit usually has strong brand associations built up over several years under the name, management, policies and culture of a heritage (in most cases, founding) company that has been acquired. Even if a concerted effort is made to rebrand the local unit under the new corporate name, this is often extremely hard to do.

More often than not, the heritage company has historical roots that go very deep and are connected in local lore with a charismatic founder who was a local, or who has a strong local identity based on a personal commitment to the community. This might have taken the form of service in local government and extensive philanthropy. Most important, the company was probably a cornerstone of the local economy, providing jobs and a good living for the residents of the community and livelihoods for independent local trades people. Roads, public buildings, hospitals, schools and universities most likely carried the name of the benefactor, the local corporation.

Apart from being hard and costly to change the name, in today's fast changing marketplace there are arguments against making the effort. The most powerful of these is fungibility – the possibility that many of these heritage units, especially those engaged in manufacturing, may be closed down with the all-important jobs being outsourced or transferred to lower cost units elsewhere or overseas.

Another reason is that the parent organization may want to keep the business unit/local company operating under a separate livery so that it is easier to sell as a self-contained "separate" concern to another corporation. In such cases, corporate management is content that there should be a great distance between the local unit or affiliate and the parent and to convey the impression that the local management has complete authority in decision making.

Mostly, this works well and helps to enhance community support for the enterprise. But when the local unit is shown to be a pawn in the parent's corporate strategy, relations with the community soon turn sour and in turn the corporate brand can suffer, at least in the geographic area of the community affected. For example, when a decision was announced that 12,000 jobs were to be eliminated at an Opel automotive plant in Germany, in 2004, only the very naive could think that the decision was made by the local management. It was, of course, made 4,000 miles away at the General Motors headquarters in Detroit, Michigan, USA; Opel's parent company. For all the storied heritage of the Opel brand, built up over 100 years in Germany, for all the effort to develop good community relations, for all the management messaging about local autonomy, the ultimate decision to fire the workers brought home the truth: that the power lay with a corporation that was anything but local. Germans, especially those in the localities immediately affected, were left yearning for the return of the "good" German-owned Opel and the GM corporate brand was tarnished, at least with one group, for a long time in this market.

DISTRIBUTORS AND RETAILERS

Whereas managers in house of brands corporations are skeptical about the value of adding the name and logo of the parent on a new product as a way to drive consumer confidence and purchase, most do agree that the source of the product does exert influence over the buyers in the chain of distributive trades.

Unless and until Procter & Gamble implements a corporate brand campaign over some years, the P&G logo in small print on product packaging will not be a driver of consumer purchase decision making. On the other hand, for Nestlé and Kraft, the corporate brand will offer a degree of assurance that will help consumers select their various product brands.

But in the case of companies like P&G, Nestlé and Kraft, the corporate brand name *will* have a significant influence in the relationship with the distributive trades, whose importance to the success of the products cannot be overestimated.

When a new product is launched it is much more likely to win the support (stocking, distribution, promotion and display) of the major retailers that will be critical to its success, if it bears the legend "another new product from Procter & Gamble". This kind of strong corporate branding carries several advantages with the distributive trades.

First, retailers such as Wal-Mart, Tesco or Carrefour will know that any new product from companies like P&G, Nestlé and Kraft will have been exhaustively tested with consumers for acceptance and will be the offspring of the highest quality R&D. There will be an assurance of use of ingredients of a good standard. They will know that market research will have established that a demand exists – or can be created – for the new product and that there will be strong and well-directed advertising, PR, and promotional and merchandising support to ensure success. Add to this a strong and long-standing relationship between the individuals at the producing and retailing companies, and a history of successful launches in the past, and it should hardly be surprising that there is little argument about the value of a strong house of brands corporate reputation with the distributive trades.

GOVERNMENT

Government is another stakeholder group with which most houses of brands maintain a direct relationship at the corporate holding company level. Parent company managements are well aware of the potential for government to adopt policies and initiate legislation that can benefit – or severely damage – their ability to conduct their business. This is especially vital for those that are heavily regulated such as telecommunication, broadcasting, pharmaceuticals, energy and transportation, but all corporations are increasingly drawn into the net of environmental regulations, equal opportunity employment, control of ingredients in food products, and so on.

The approach to dealing with governmental matters can have a major impact on the reputation and brand of a corporation and corporate officers have to weigh their approach carefully.

For example, Corporation A might believe that it will be badly affected by the adoption of proposed new laws or regulations that will eliminate a key ingredient from one of its cornerstone products because it is suspected of being a carcinogen. This could lead to a loss of revenue and possible loss of jobs. The corporation, however, does not believe the danger of carcinogenicity in the ingredient has been proven or is real.

If it chooses to fight the proposal in public the company may be in the right; it will no doubt win the approval of all those employees whose jobs are at stake as well as the communities in which they live.

Fear and risk

But at the same time, the corporate brand reputation might be damaged. Politicians and those supporting the new measure are skilled at reaching out to the general public, which will be swayed by two four-letter words: fear and risk. Just the idea of a potential carcinogen in a popular product is likely to strike fear in the consumer, whose reaction will be to avoid taking any risk, especially if there are adequate alternative products available.

The picture of Corporation A seemingly defending its financial interests against sensible precautions on behalf of the safety of users can – however distorted in reality – cause real damage to the corporate brand with an audience much wider than the government stakeholder group itself.

And, if over time it turns out that the ingredient was dangerous, the damage will be all the more serious, sometimes so much so that it can bring down the corporation.

But here is an interesting thing – a corporate brand can have a life after death. Even though a major meltdown can prove a fatal blow to corporate entity, so that it goes into liquidation or is bought at a fire sale price, the value of the corporate brand name might yet retain significant value. This is because stakeholders still have fondness for the brand, which might well not have lived up to its values in the period leading up to its demise. Some stakeholders are discerning enough to know when a brand whose values they endorse has not lived up to its promise; the brand may not be the culprit but rather those who own and manage it. Perhaps, under different management there could be a rededication to the original brand values and the corporation could be revived, or reborn. That's why there is a lively secondary market in "distressed" brands.

Government is included in the handful of stakeholder groups often referred to as opinion forming elites (OFEs) but in this chapter I have chosen to comment on government – meaning elected lawmakers and appointed regulators at both the national and local levels as well as at the supra-national level. These include organizations such as the EU, WTO, NAFTA and ASEAN as well as the UN and its agencies (WHO, UNICEF, and so on) and institutions like the IMF and World Bank. All of these have, to varying degrees, the authority to create laws, make regulations or set standards that can directly affect a corporation's ability to conduct its business and, in extreme cases, to put it out of business altogether. In that sense government is a decision maker, not merely an influencer.

Opinion forming elites (OFEs)

They may not be empowered to make decisions that directly affect a company but they often influence those responsible for making decisions – government, distributive trades, thinktanks, expert commentators, academics and the media, which in spite of the animosity and rivalries that exist between them, inhabit a private world in which they take part in a kabuki dance of mutual self-interest, with the media acting as the focal point. The media need access to news sources such as NGOs (particularly media-savvy activist groups) as well as to expert commentary from such sources as academics and thinktanks. Many publications require a journalist to include at least two independent quotes from third parties in each news story. On the other side, academics, thinktank executives and other experts actually cultivate contacts in the media because they know that frequent appearances can enhance their own reputations, promotion prospects and income. In most cases house of brands corporations do not have the luxury of choosing whether or not to present the face of a unified corporate brand or a series of autonomous brands owned by an anonymous holding corporation. In a way similar to government, OFEs themselves select the entity they are dealing with or commenting on, and in most cases this is the "master" corporation.

All these OFEs are fully aware that on all matters to do with investment, finance and policy, decisions are made at corporate headquarters. And the corporations themselves know that mistakes made by distant, often unimportant units can come back to cause damage to the corporate brand. In the 21st century it is no excuse to claim that the misdeed or mistake was the result of a policy of decentralized decision making.

(This is, indeed, one of the most testing problems facing the management of global corporations today. How do you balance the devolution of power to individual units, which we know produces excellent results, but still ensure that no shortcuts are taken and that corporate standards of ethics, quality control and human relations are not compromised? How do you think and act with respect for the different localities in which you operate and at the same time think and act globally, when often the two cannot easily be reconciled?)

OFEs, because of the closed circle of commentary described earlier, have an inordinate influence on corporate brand perception among consumers. And their views are arguably even more influential in shaping the legislative and regulatory agenda.

Although it is thought by some that "trickle down" communication is less influential than in the past, it still remains important. In recent years, the annual Edelman Trust Barometer has observed that now the most potent influence on people is the view held by other "people like me"; peers, in short. They are more likely to place their trust in the view of someone like themselves than a more distant expert or celebrity.

But it would be a mistake to underestimate the aggregate and mutually reinforcing power of OFEs to affect the brand image of all corporations, including houses of brands.

Activist NGOs are skilled at the techniques of shaping public opinion, often out-thinking their corporate targets. Although their primary target is most likely a corporate "master" brand they will often adopt tactics that focus attention on product brands that are the lifeblood of the organization. Nowhere does this apply more than with houses of brands, and especially those that are anonymous at the corporate level. Thus, a pressure group will select a single prominent product brand, one of the organization's crown jewels and an important contributor to its revenue and profit, to be the emblem of a public relations campaign. In this way they know that damage to the brand with consumers will affect sales in a very real way and have a better chance of forcing the corporation to change behavior.

To target a company with a portfolio of brands in a general way is difficult. When a boycott was called on The Distillers Company Ltd[1] and its brands – which included Dewar's, Johnnie Walker and Haig Scotch Whisky, Gordon's, Booth's and Tanqueray Gin and a host of other labels – it failed miserably. One reason is that consumers were confused and did not have the clarity of a single brand which they could avoid buying.

SUPPLIERS

Suppliers, contractors and subcontractors have been a Cinderella group in many corporations' brand communications strategy. But recent calamities have underscored their importance in the shaping of brand reputation and trust. It has become clear that although there might be little data to suggest that a strong brand approach to suppliers and subcontractors, on the same "inside out" principle as described for employees, will bring significant enhancement to the master corporate brand, there is plenty of evidence that inattention can cause material damage. Just ask Nike,[2] Mattel[3] and Dell[4] which have each suffered brand reputation damage as a result of the practices of their subcontractors.

As the world of production specializes and globalizes and as business efficiency theory encourages the practice of outsourcing and offshoring, house of brands companies and brand houses alike are realizing they must exercise a high degree of control over all aspects of their suppliers' practices and policies. Consumers are not normally concerned with the way in which products are made or marketed but they do get alarmed (and sometimes angry) when they learn that a brand they trust contains a harmful, perhaps fatal, ingredient; or the telephone sales representative they have reached to make a booking on a locally based carrier has very poor English-speaking skills and the conversation is terminated because no mutual understanding can be achieved. Such instances are bad "brand experiences" and bring to the surface other issues of concern. It is quite possible that many consumers might have been unaware that the tainted product brand they have been buying for years is now made in China or that the operator in the travel phone center is based in India. There may be many economic imperatives for reducing the employee payroll, with its high social cost and hourly wage rate, and finding cheaper alternatives with a contractor, perhaps overseas. But if the brand is to remain strong in today's consumer society, a corporation will need to treat its contractor just as it would its own employees.

CONSUMERS

For many people branding is solely confined to the business of marketing consumer products – "brands". Branding is viewed as a composite of the name, package design, advertising, PR, promotion, ingredients and the promise of performance or delivery of a result by the marketer to the customer. While the merits of treating the corporation itself like a brand for many of the stakeholders described in the previous pages seem clear, the debate still continues in many house of brands corporations: Do the benefits of highlighting a brand's parentage outweigh the drawbacks? Many of the items on this balance sheet have been discussed already, and the final decision will be made by each company based on its own corporate philosophy and priorities.

At one end of the spectrum are holding companies that are simply financial institutions, perhaps eager to retain a high degree of anonymity. They buy and sell branded or even unbranded corporations, seeking to enhance or realize their value. Such holding companies have no wish to stress the umbilical cord between parent and subsidiary unit because they might wish to cut it at any time. At the same time, there might be an entirely hands-off approach to management or the subsidiary's management is in control of its own corporate brand destiny, even if it is passed from one owner to another.

At the other end of the spectrum are houses of brands that are built, brick by brick, by people who mostly are marketing and management experts, seeking to create an organization that has stable and growing brands within a clear vision, rather than financiers. (This is not to say that such entrepreneurs and managers are without financial skills.) And, of course, there are a host of corporations that are in between on this spectrum as they struggle to decide in which direction to move.

You might want to liken the different approaches with families. There are biological "parents" and there are foster "parents". The former create their own offspring but might augment the family by adoption. The foster parent provides a temporary home for the children. As the parent corporations weigh the matter, a fairly new consideration has to be put in the balance: this is an increased interest on the part of the consumer (according to some research findings) in "the company behind the product". A growing number of consumers say they want to base their product buying decisions on, for example, the degree of corporate social responsibility shown by the "master" corporation. How do Nestlé, Kraft, P&G and Starbucks treat the coffee farmers in developing countries? How do Nike and Wal-Mart make sure that their suppliers' factories in Asia are safe, there is no child labor and wages and conditions are fair? It is not necessary to be too cynical to suggest that there is still a chasm between good intentions and deed, and it is hard to get evidence that a product has not been bought because its parent company has a poor brand image. Although it is a brand house rather than a house of brands, the approach of Starbucks is instructive.

Starbucks

From its inception in 1971, Starbucks Coffee Company has been committed to ethically sourcing and roasting the highest quality Arabica coffee in the world and early on began a relationship with Conservation International to integrate environmental conservation principles into Starbucks' coffee-buying practices to ensure the sustainable production of high-quality coffee. Today, the company is the premier roaster and retailer of specialty coffee in the world but maintains its commitment to one of the guiding principles of the company's mission – contributing positively to communities and the environment.

Starbucks created its own coffee trading standards called the Coffee and Farmer Equity (C.A.F.E.) Practices. Coffee purchased under the C.A.F.E. Practices guidelines meets criteria around social responsibility in the farming community, economic transparency to help ensure equitable payment to farmers for their crops, and environmental leadership. C.A.F.E standards are broken down into measurable and incentive-based criteria used to evaluate suppliers. Producers with less than 60 percent in each of the social and environmental areas are designated as "verified suppliers." Preferred suppliers achieve scores between 60 percent and 79 percent and "strategic suppliers" achieve scores of 80 percent or higher. The standards were developed in conjunction with the Scientific Certifications Systems (SCS), an independent auditing service with input from coffee suppliers, Fairtrade and the Rainforest Alliance. SCS provides oversight, training, accreditation and auditing of verification organizations. In 2007, Starbucks bought 65 percent of its coffee from C.A.F.E. approved suppliers, and intends to increase that amount to 80 percent by 2013.

In addition to C.A.F.E. Practices-approved coffee, Starbucks purchases coffee through other responsible environmental or economic certification efforts, including conservation (shade grown), certified organic coffees, and Fair Trade Certified coffee. Starbucks is the largest purchaser, roaster, and distributor of Fair Trade Certified coffee in North America, buying 20 million pounds in fiscal 2007. In order to qualify for the fair trade label, Starbucks pays the Fairtrade Minimum Price as set by Fairtrade Labelling Organizations International (FLO) to producer organizations that provide living wages for workers and safe working conditions, prohibit child labor practices, invest in community development, and promote sustainable farming methods. The Fair Trade Certified label ensures that farmers receive equitable prices for their coffee while strengthening their farms for the future.

This is easier for houses of brands that have made the decision to feature the corporate name prominently on all brands. And immediately such a decision is taken – or confirmed – it triggers others, the most important of which are these two: corporate behavior and policies must be above reproach and transparent, and there must be investment in promoting the umbrella brand name if it is to add real value to the product brand.

CASE Henkel

After selling its conventional chemicals operations, in 2001 Henkel redefined its strategy as a consumer brands company in detergents and cleansing agents (Persil, Pril), cosmetics and body care products (Schwarzkopf, Dial, Right Guard) as well as adhesive technologies (Loctite, Sellotape, Pritt). This provided the impetus for a consistent reinforcement of the corporate brand.

As a result, according to Ernst Primosch, Henkel's head of corporate communications, "an unmistakable corporate culture was created, built on a clear vision and binding corporate values, from which a uniform corporate identity was derived, establishing the company as a global corporate brand based on its claim, 'Henkel – A Brand like a Friend'."

Far-reaching implications

"Turning Henkel into a 'branded house of brands' had far-reaching implications for corporate communications activities. Not only did their significance grow with the aim of enhancing the value of the corporate brand in boosting the level of brand awareness and reputation; the structural requirements increased as well. Before the reorientation, Corporate Communications & Corporate Brand Management had been institutionalized in 22 countries. These functions have subsequently been extended to more than 60 countries across the globe.

The core steering elements are the two associated management instruments known as the Balanced Scorecard (BSC) and Strategy Map devised by Kaplan and Norton. Both were specifically tailored to the requirements and needs of the communications department at Henkel", says Primosch.

Internally, Henkel has focused much of its attention on driving its corporate brand strategy through its employee audience using a policy of "codes". These include a Code of Conduct, a Code of Corporate Sustainability, a Code of Teamwork and Leadership and a Code of the Corporate Brand (under development).

The latter will describe how the corporate brand should be understood, communicated and respected. It emphasizes the role of each employee as brand ambassador.

Externally, the situation is more complex and the need is to harmonize the often competing interests of different products, lines of business, geographies and heritage cultures.

Although Henkel is operating within a clearly defined global strategy of aligning product brands with the corporate brand, this moves at a different pace in individual markets reflecting local conditions.

What lies ahead

The next task, according to Primosch, is "to develop benchmarks for the impact on the behavior of business-critical stakeholder groups. In 2006 Henkel implemented a tool for strategic analysis and performance management in rankings, awards, ratings and primary studies".

Henkel's corporate brand is well recognized and regarded in its home market, Germany, where an IPSOS Image and Awareness study in 2003 put Henkel in second place after BMW, and ahead of German icons like Siemens and Continental.

But this recognition was not replicated across the world until the corporate branding initiative began to resonate in other markets and progress has been made. Henkel entered the 2008 Brand Finance 500 in 393rd place for the first time. The assessment gives Henkel a brand equity of $2,148 million, representing 9 percent of the total enterprise value of $24,454 million.

Sources: (1) an article originally published in the October 2008 editions of *Frontline*, the journal of the International Public Relations Association; and (2) "International corporate brand management – the Henkel example", a case study by Bernhard Swoboda, Judith Giersch and Ernst Primosch.

Notes

1 Now part of Diageo.
2 Nike has been strongly criticized for the employment practices of subcontracting factories in Asia. They have taken steps to remedy the situation.
3 Mattel has been pummeled by consumers and lawmakers for allowing the importation of products with harmful ingredients.
4 Dell had to contend with a crisis of flammable batteries sourced from a supplier in Asia.

3
We are family

Family corporations mostly benefit from the same advantages as those whose corporate and principal product names are the same (as described in Chapter 1). They also face the same problems because in many cases, the name of the founding family lives on for decades or longer in the corporate identity. Think of Ford, SC Johnson, Johnson & Johnson, Mars, Inc., Hewlett-Packard, Dell, Sainsbury's and Wal-Mart. But many other huge corporations are family owned without any connection between the corporate name and the family – think of Bacardi, Beiersdorf and Bertelsmann.

Family-owned corporations have specific branding issues of their own. They merit our attention because of their importance to national life.

In almost every society, including Britain and the USA, family businesses are the underpinning of economic life. Bob Hughes, Director of Baylor University's Institute for Family Business, estimates that 75 percent of all businesses in the USA are family owned or controlled.[1] Worldwide this number jumps to 80 percent according to the Cox Family Enterprise Center, which also estimates that family businesses account for 60 percent of total US employment and 78 percent of all new paid jobs (in contrast to voluntary employment). Nor is this large number accounted for by just the massive number of small businesses or "mom and pop shops" as they are affectionately known. In a separate analysis of *BusinessWeek* magazine's list of the top 1,000 companies in the USA, Dan McConaughy, a professor at Rosary College, Chicago, found that one in five had top executives who were direct descendants of their founders. In later studies, he found that companies with strong family ties tend to perform better on average than those with none.

Although statistics are hard to come by, it seems probable that the importance of family companies is even more pronounced outside the USA. In *On Competition* (1992), Harvard's Michael Porter postulates that different capital systems put the USA at a disadvantage to Japan and Germany where "dedicated" as opposed to "fluid" systems allow institutions and families to hold large stakes in companies for longer periods. These "dedicated" investors are focused on management as well as financial performance. India, China, Hong Kong, Malaysia, Philippines and Thailand – every one of these countries has one or more legendary commercial and industrial dynasties.

So, branding is of supreme importance to the family-owned company, especially if it is to give the lie to the contention of the great economist John Maynard Keynes that the founder makes the money, the second generation coasts along and the third goes bankrupt. Fewer than one-third of owners successfully pass family business ownership to the third generation. For this reason it is instructive to give attention to those which have broken this Keynesian law. Clearly, they have organized things better and could act as a model for those family companies aspiring to emulate their success.

Family companies share many stakeholder groups with all other companies. These include:

- the communities in which they are based or maintain a significant presence as an employer
- lawmakers and regulators who are influential in those communities or in the sectors of industry or commerce of importance
- suppliers of raw materials, goods and services essential to the activities of the company
- partners of various kinds in distribution, production or joint ventures
- customers and consumers
- employees and potential employees
- non-family members of management.

In addition, the family company has to ensure it maintains communications with certain specific groups. These are the:

- family executives working in the company
- family shareholders who are not employed by the company
- shareholders and banks and financial institutions whose confidence in the company is essential as a source of capital.

With all stakeholders the company must seek to develop a strong brand positioning. Its communications need to stress the advantages of its status as family owned while countering any possible negative perceptions stemming from the same heritage. For the larger, longer-established family companies, which now have a large group of non-family investors, related shareholders and members of different branches of the founding family at work in the firm, systematic and effective family communications are of the highest importance.

Dissonance and discord in the owning family is immediately sensed as if by radar by non-family members of the company and investors, and this can lead to demotivation which can quickly affect the success of the enterprise.

The family company is also likely to feature more prominently in the social pages and gossip columns than on the business pages of the media. Nor does this only apply to the founder generation. The exploits of the rich descendants of famous, or notorious, entrepreneurs in industry and commerce are often more titillating than the activities of the enterprise that carries the family name. A media scan would probably confirm that the exploits of Paris Hilton garnered much more free media coverage than the hotel chain itself. Does this matter? It often does to employees and shareholders but they probably greatly overestimate the connection made by the general public between an individual heir or heiress and the corporate brand bearing the same name.

Throughout most of my career I have been privileged to have a worm's eye view of the family company at work so my observations are colored by my own experience.

PERSONAL EXPERIENCE

My first encounter with the institution of the family company was my second job – at W.H. Smith & Son, the company that dominated (some say, controlled) the distribution of newspapers and magazines around Britain from the advent of the railway network. Here I learned a great deal about branding but even more about how remarkable men and luck can be more important to the life or death of an enterprise. When W.H. Smith, the legendary founder, died at an advanced age, he had neglected to incorporate the business. By that time Britain had a socialist government that had introduced an inheritance tax, which at the highest level was applied at the surtax level of 99 percent. Thus the working capital of this very large enterprise was dramatically diminished overnight. But, as bad luck would have it, there was to be a second hammer blow. Before the lawyers could incorporate the remnants of the holdings, the eponymous "son" also died, causing a further 99 percent of the remaining 1 percent to be taken by the state. In spite of this the firm survived and continues as a successful publicly held corporation today.

I moved from my role as an editorialist at W.H. Smith to the role of editor at the periodical publishers Maclaren & Son, also a family firm, and from there into the public relations business. Later, in 1967, I joined the firm of Daniel J. Edelman Inc. to start its operations outside the USA. Edelman is now the largest independent public relations agency in the world and the only family and privately held organization of its kind among the 20 leading global public relations firms. It is also a preeminent brand in its field.

I have also had the special experience of working for a number of clients that were family firms.

COMPETITIVE ADVANTAGE

The benefits and challenges of the family-controlled firm are discussed at length – and from the owner's point of view – by Samuel C. Johnson, Chairman of SC Johnson & Son, Inc. from 1967 until 2000, in *The Essence of a Family Enterprise:*

> The preeminent edge for a family firm if it is totally private may well be secrecy from your competition, a cherished privilege among private CEOs. Your competitors don't know what you're doing. They have little idea of how strong you are, where problems might have arisen, or even if you're winning. They can figure your share of a particular market but they don't have the slightest notion of your bottom line.

> A CEO of a public company is beholden to literally thousands of individuals and interests. His time spent actually managing the business, trying to make money, is cut appreciably. The public CEO must take to the road to pump the company's stock, meeting with security analysts, talking to investment bankers, informing *The Wall Street Journal* reporters and newsmen from local papers. He must also spend countless hours with government agencies.

> Logically, one might think public companies would show higher profit margins. But a study of public and private company earnings conducted by the University of Southern California business school – one of the

few ever attempted on this matter, since acquiring data on private firms is difficult – concluded that private companies had earnings margins greatly higher than public corporations. The private outfits also earned higher returns on assets.

In the same book, Johnson concedes that:

Public companies do have some advantages, principally unlimited access to the public equity financial markets and the ability to make acquisitions with stock. Also, in some cases the public market is the only way minority family shareholders can diversify their investments or settle their estates.

PUBLIC SCRUTINY

But public scrutiny and the constant attention of analysts and media are not only a nuisance and disadvantage for the public company. Such scrutiny brings positive corporate branding benefits that are envied by the owner/managers of many private/family companies I know.

The very same scrutiny that can be so irritating is also the means by which publicly held corporations are much more often profiled in the media and are able to position themselves as leaders in their field, often at the expense of privately held competitors. Sometimes this is by design, because such firms prefer to fly under the radar. But more often than not it is simply the result of journalistic imperatives. Business writers have to cater to an audience of investors and potential investors so all their attention is given to companies that are public. Readers and reviewers can make a decision to buy, hold or sell the stocks and shares they write about, otherwise all their articles would be purely academic. There is only marginal interest in the activities of a private corporation and that is if its innovative products or policies might impact the success of its publicly held rivals.

READY ACCESS

For nearly 90 of its first 100 years in business since being founded by Jim Casey in Seattle in 1907, UPS (United Parcel Service) was private and owned by family trusts (Casey had no descendants) and several thousand managers. In spite of the advantages of that status, which helped define the culture and UPS brand for decades, the ability to sell its services was being hindered by the fact that publicly held rival Federal Express (FedEx) was clearly the preeminent brand in the category. This in spite of the fact that UPS's sales volume was over double the size of its rival and many of its services matched or outshone FedEx.

However, the media had ready access to the FedEx CEO and leadership and, moreover, readers/viewers impressed by what they learned about the company could make an investment decision to use the FedEx service. The lack of opportunity for people to invest in UPS was reason enough not to write about the company.

Long before the company made the decision to go public (in 1999) to access the capital needed to finance major global expansion, UPS adopted strategies to counter the problem. Strong media and analyst outreach was undertaken to show that UPS was the most potent player in its market and that any commentary on the package, document delivery and freight market that did not include reference to the company would be a disservice to potential investors.

TRANSPARENT

In any event, as far as disclosures were concerned, UPS's financial position was about as transparent as any publicly held corporation because it operates in a highly regulated industry, had about 30,000 employee shareholders and was unionized with the majority of its 300,000 hourly paid employees in membership of the International Brotherhood of Teamsters. There were no secrets, so the company decided to take the public profile of industry leader and as an innovator investor in global infrastructure and in related services that could be integrated into services needed by 21st century customers.

Not every privately held or family company is in the same position as UPS. As a result, the lack of a regular and repetitive spotlight on their activities in the media means they have less brand recognition than their public competitors. It is the price to be paid for the benefits of secrecy.

LONG-TERM THINKING

Family companies that have survived the generational test have utilized the great gift of being able to think in the long term when the pressures of the market in the USA, Britain and some other countries force the public corporation to think quarter by quarter. Without the three-monthly need to satisfy stockholders who might not have any loyalty to the corporation, the head of the family-owned company can devote himself to building both the tangible and intangible assets, and this means enhancement of brand value. Although the family/privately held corporation forgoes the ready access to large amounts of capital available via the stock market, it can obtain the most advantageous terms for any financing that is needed, creating a virtuous circle in which there is further strength added to the brand.

The family company is often well placed to make significant advances in tough economic times. Although I am not suggesting they fall prey to lack of management disciplines, in slowdown or recessions, they can choose to survive – and gain strength – by accepting temporarily lower margins than would be acceptable to shareholders of publicly held corporations. Quarterly-accountable, publicly held corporations on the other hand may be forced to suspend brand-building activities, and cut advertising and public relations budgets in order to undertake more tactical promotions, as well as keeping dividends acceptable to investors, and all the while are under painful scrutiny by analysts and the financial media. Here is an opportunity for the family-owned enterprise to continue to use advertising and public relations to gain market share and to enhance the corporate brand, putting itself in a stronger competitive position for the day when the market rebounds.

OWNERSHIP – THE POWER TO LEAD

When a family holds a controlling interest in a corporation it can use its power to initiate bold brand-defining moves of the kind that can seldom be attempted by the CEOs of widely held large corporations who have to achieve some degree of consensus in the C-suite and must minimize risk. This is often a personal commitment to something the CEO believes to be important but can be faulted by the cautious or faint-hearted as "bad for business". It is perhaps because the family business patriarch has impregnated the corporate brand with his own identity that he has a keen instinctive sense for what is right and does not need a lengthy detailed analysis of the situation and the options facing him.

Fisk Johnson, current chairman and CEO of SC Johnson, one of America's largest family/privately held corporations tells a story about his grandfather, H.F. Johnson, Jr:[2]

In the early 1960s he got the idea that the company should produce a movie for the 1964 World's Fair in New York. He talked the idea over with his executive committee, and they all resisted. They saw it as a financial risk with an uncertain return. All of them, including my dad,[3] voted "no" to the proposal. But H.F. would not back down. As the story goes, he leaned across the table and told them, "Gentlemen, some decisions are only for the brave", and he went ahead with it. Our film, "To be Alive", went on to win an Academy Award and lots of positive recognition for the company.

It was a defining moment in the development of the SC Johnson corporate brand.

DIFFERENTIATION

It is the ability to take bold and risky decisions that can often differentiate the family-owned corporation from its competitors and give it a profile and character that is more definite, and perhaps appealing, than the risk-averse, publicly held company. Moreover, such decisions can be taken more quickly than at a publicly held corporation where ideas can become ensnared – and possibly emasculated – in a lengthy approval process. And in a world in which the "first" get brand kudos, this can be important. Take SC Johnson (SCJ) again. Sam Johnson (yes, he that was against the idea of the film) had taken over as Chairman in 1967 and in 1975 took a historic decision for the company, one that shocked employees, competitors and the entire chemical industry. Responding to yet unproven research that suggested that chlorofluorocarbons (CFCs) might harm the Earth's ozone layer he banned them from all SCJ aerosol products worldwide. Employees were shocked because the company was the world's largest producer of aerosol products and the ban meant they had to pull out of the business in several countries where CFCs were mandated. Sam Johnson stood firm and publicized his decision, earning a reputation for the company as being in the vanguard of the "green" movement. Others were forced to catch up when the USA and Canada banned the use of CFCs in aerosols – by which time SCJ scientists had developed an equally effective propellant that was also much cheaper to produce.

LONGEVITY AND CONTINUITY

One of the benefits of the family company is that if it survives through three or more generations it has through repetition and the ubiquitous presence of its name, the chance to penetrate more deeply into the consciousness of its stakeholders. Although this is a true benefit in many respects it can also pose its own problems. One of these is that once an image or brand identity has been molded it will set firmly over a period of time and that identity might not accurately describe the company as it is today, let alone the way it wants to be seen in the future, if its plans work out.

If we return to SC Johnson once again, we find a company that has addressed – and is still addressing – this issue. Although the company has been in business for over 120 years, it has been known colloquially as "Johnson's Wax" or "The Johnson Wax Company" rather than by its legal corporate name. In this it was not unusual. Many companies were identified by the heavily advertised brand names of their principal products. In this instance the branding did not matter in the early days because for the first half of the life of the corporation, the products were all wax based. In fact, when Sam Johnson (fourth generation) joined the company after Cornell and later Harvard Business School, he became New Products Director. When he showed the first fruit of his labor, Johnson Aerosol Insecticide, to his father, Sam says: "He looked at me and said, 'it doesn't have "wax" in it'."[4] Now, of course, wax products are a small percentage of the company's range of products but for many, the corporate moniker will always be "Johnson's Wax".

But this has not deterred SC Johnson from making a concerted effort to rebrand the corporation, using the same successful branding techniques that it applies to its category-leading products like Pledge®, Raid®, Off®, Shout®, Toilet Duck®, Glade®, Bravo®, and Edge®.

Over the past century the company has changed from being a "brand house" into a "house of brands" and during the past decade it has been working hard to ensure that perception catches up with reality. Its research determined that there were several advantages in being a family-owned firm and that this should be incorporated in the company's visual corporate ID as well as in product advertising and other forms of communication – SC Johnson, A Family Company. Although the family was central to the way the company conducted its business and put its corporate citizenship policies into practice, this stopped short at the door of the consumer products marketing department. Where product marketing was concerned, the company's goal was to be a fierce competitor and to have a laser-like focus on meeting the needs of consumers. Advertising messages were concerned only with the lifestyle enhancements or performance benefits of the various SCJ products. Any extraneous messages could only reduce advertising effectiveness and there was concern that consumers did not care who owned the company that made the product, so long as it worked as promised. But during a corporate brand management (CBM) process that the company had initiated, interesting data came to light. There was evidence that showed "family ownership" was viewed favorably by consumers who believe that greater care is taken in all aspects of the business at a company where they feel the owner is personally responsible for quality control and other values, especially when the owner's name is on the product. With other research showing consumers to be increasingly interested in the corporation behind the brand, and making product purchase decisions partly based on their views on corporate behavior, the decision was taken to highlight the family heritage of SC Johnson with consumers. This was viewed as giving the products a competitive edge on those produced by rival, large publicly held corporations.

RESILIENCE AND RESOURCEFULNESS

Another company with a 120-year heritage is De Beers, an illustrious name that is synonymous with diamonds, and a colorful history that illustrates the resilience and resourcefulness of proprietors of some family companies. In this case the De Beers family had very little to do with the $6.5 billion corporation. They were Boer farmers who owned land that they sold to adventurer-entrepreneurs and thus gave their name to a mine and subsequently the firm that would soon control the world's supply of the precious stones. Nor were those "adventurepreneurs", Cecil Rhodes and Barney Barnato, the most important families in the corporation's history. In the early days following his arrival in South Africa in 1902, Ernest Oppenheimer worked for his uncle, buying diamonds from De Beers. He then went off and established Anglo American in 1917. Following the success of this, he started buying into De Beers, became a director in 1926 and Chairman in 1929, the story – and brand – of De Beers and the history of diamonds has been shaped by Sir Ernest Oppenheimer and his descendants. His grandson, Nicky Oppenheimer, is the Chairman today. Gareth Penny is the MD, or CEO.

The De Beers story is the stuff of legend, which is ideal for infusing a corporate brand with the elements of adventure, fabulous finds, sudden wealth, intrigue, scarcity and romance. The brilliant slogan of "A Diamond is Forever", created in 1947,[5] made this particular gem the only acceptable certification of the durability of the donor's pledge of love when becoming engaged to be married, discouraged owners from selling their diamonds on the secondary market and underlined the toughness and permanence of the stone itself. Nor, for the longest time, did De Beers seek or need to promote its own name; its sole intent was in expanding the market and maintaining the value of diamonds, sure in the knowledge that 90 out of every hundred diamonds that were sold would have come from their mines or would have passed through the hands of the Central Selling Organization, the London-based market for the world's diamonds over which De Beers exercised tight control.

Figure 3.1 A diamond is forever

The first, huge, test for De Beers came with the Great Depression in the 1930s. The response from De Beers was one that only a tightly controlled family corporation could make. Sir Ernest Oppenheimer's actions would have been inconceivable to a CEO required to satisfy critical shareholders in a widely held corporation. With too many stones chasing too few buyers, De Beers took the dramatic step of closing most of its major mines. Outside producers' operations were kept intact and their stones purchased in order to ensure the industry's survival.

Although there were some attempts to restart production in the late 1930s, these efforts were brought to a halt by the outbreak of World War II and De Beers activities ceased for the next four years. The year 1940 brought another market transformation, the discovery of the vast Mwadui mine by the Canadian geologist, John Williamson. This, followed by huge discoveries in Russia, Botswana, Canada and Australia provided a serious test to the role played by the CSO, but by force of argument, first Ernest and then his son and successor, Harry Oppenheimer, persuaded the Canadians and the Soviets to join the CSO. In this De Beers played the role of custodian. While monopolies, or trusts, are taboo today, they were the "holy grail" sought by all Victorian industrialists: Carnegie, Rockefeller, Frick, Vanderbilt, Gould and Oppenheimer. With all the negative aspects of trusts it is easy to forget that a firm but benevolent monopoly was welcomed by many who benefited. By controlling the spigot of supply, the Oppenheimers ensured diamond cutters, merchants, and the ultimate recipients of the symbol of love that would last forever, had a safe source of income and investment. The importance of family ownership and influence to De Beers came in 2001 when the Oppenheimers reasserted their commitment to De Beers and its future by taking the diamond business private after it had for 113 years been a publicly listed company, a third of which had been owned by Anglo American plc, of which De Beers itself had owned one-third – a cross-holding disliked by analysts and a subsequent impediment on De Beers' share price. Once the deal had been concluded, the Oppenheimers held 40 percent, Anglo 45 percent and the government of Botswana acquired the remaining 15 percent. This was the prelude to the third, and current, phase in the development of the company. De Beers says:

> In the closing years of the last century, the globalising economy rendered De Beers' role of industry "custodian" inappropriate and expensive. In response De Beers set about crafting a new strategy for the 21 st century: a suite of innovative programmes and alliances designed to reinvigorate the industry and to grow demand for diamond jewellery.[6]

In practice this means that De Beers is nurturing its brand as a "trust mark" not only to the diamantaires and retailers but also to the end consumer. Although De Beers is still the single most potent force in diamonds, its market share (around 40 percent) now means it is not sufficient just to promote diamonds; it must promote De Beers diamonds.

The most visible evidence of De Beers as a consumer products company as opposed to a supplier of raw materials is in the luxurious De Beers shopfronts that are appearing in the most exclusive shopping areas of London, New York, Paris and other major cities around the world. These are owned by a joint venture collaboration De Beers has struck with Bernard Arnault's LVMH luxury goods empire.

De Beers is also aggressively undertaking a series of initiatives to forestall and respond to criticism:

- they are the leading voice in the Kimberley Process, the mechanism established to combat the trade in "blood" or "conflict" diamonds
- they undertake a variety of health programs to deal with the AIDS epidemic in Southern Africa (De Beers' local community)
- they spend significant sums on environmental efforts to mitigate the damage caused by mining, for example by creating wildlife refuges out of exhausted mines.

The enormous impact of the Kimberley Process is described by Michael L. Ross[7] in an article published by *Foreign Affairs* (May/June 2008) about the large number of wars in oil producing countries. The results achieved in diamond producing countries might, he suggests, provide hope for a similar situation in oil producing countries. He writes:

> In 2000, six diamond-producing states in Africa were trapped in civil wars; by 2006, none was. Much of this success is the result of sanctions that the UN Security Council started to impose in 1998 against so-called conflict diamonds – diamonds sold by African insurgents or their intermediaries – and the adoption in 2002 of the Kimberley Process, an agreement by an unusual coalition of governments, non-governmental organizations, and major diamond traders to certify the clean origins of the diamonds they trade. After these measures were taken, rebels in Angola, Liberia and Sierra Leone lost a key source of funding, and within a few years they were either defeated in battle or forced to sign peace agreements. In the mid-1990s, conflict diamonds made up as much as 15 percent of the world's diamond trade. By 2006, the proportion has fallen to one percent.

Yet, just as these facts were being recorded, public sentiment about diamonds and De Beers was shaken by a highly publicized and dramatic film, *Blood Diamond*, starring Leonardo DiCaprio – illustrating how hard it is to combat emotive drama, even with strong facts. Brands are in large part built on perceptions, perceptions that can too easily mirror an out of date truth.

It will be interesting to see how the company fares as a partly owned, family entity in the third century of its existence. Will it be like the diamond, forever? In recent years there have been changes. According to Forbes, "under new South African legislation, Oppenheimer was forced to sell 26 percent of De Beers to a black empowerment group, the first major ownership change in a century. Nicky's son Jonathan was replaced as managing director of De Beers' mining division by David Noko, the first black executive to head the company's South African operations" (www. forbes.com/lists/2006/10/2MY9.html).

PUBLICITY SHY

For every publicity hungry CEO there is one or more owner/manager of a private, family-owned company for whom media attention to his business, private life, family, philanthropy, interests and pastimes is anathema. Many simply want a normal life for themselves and their families and to preserve their privacy. Many use their accumulated wealth to protect themselves from the glare of publicity rather than to court it. For many, there is a more compelling reason for this attitude than natural reserve or shyness – it is fear. Many successful and wealthy owners of family companies shun the limelight because they do not want to attract the attention of criminals and terrorists. In the small community of the super rich there is the real and ever-present fear that the family will be a target for every form of invasion of privacy and injury and, in the worst case, kidnappings that end in tragedy. While this is an everyday matter of concern among business leaders in Mexico and other countries of Latin America, where kidnapping and ransoming has become something of a normal business transaction, it is by no means unknown in Europe where it was the kidnapping of Freddy Heineken of the Dutch brewing family that most recently captured the largest headlines.

Thus, the public relations director of a family company is often faced with the task of making the most of the competitive advantages of family ownership and management in his communications with stakeholders while not overstepping the boundaries that mark out the "private space" of the family itself. With good judgment the balance can be found, as indeed it must in a society that is increasingly inquisitive, well educated and concerned that all organizations, public, private or state controlled, large or small, should be accountable. In this respect family control cannot be used as a shield against scrutiny.

THE CROWN CORPORATION

You won't find it on any "World's Best Known" brands list. You will not see it in any ranking by *Fortune* of the most admired private companies. But the British monarchy, in addition to being a societal and governmental institution, is indeed, by almost every measure, a global corporate family brand. In addition to being possibly the oldest mega brand (we will not venture into a comparison with the Vatican or any other religions) it is one of the most widely known around the world. It is the subject of ceaseless media exposure and comment.

It is both a family company and publicly held. It is family because the line of succession is set out with great clarity and on only a few occasions has this line been broken – and then only by someone with at least some claim on the throne. It is the most publicly held corporation in Britain because every citizen owns a share in that some of their taxes[8] are used to offset the costs of the monarch in her role as Head of State. According to the official website, this amounted to a mere 62 pence per head of the population in the year ended March 1, 2008.

Just like any company, the British monarchy – let's call it the Crown Corporation – has tangible assets in real estate, farm stock, a huge collection of art and antiques (technically these are not owned personally by the monarch, but held in trust by her for the nation) and securities; it also has intangible assets that help the Crown Corporation brand. It has all the trappings of normal companies. The corporate identity, or logo, is the national flag and the Royal Standard. It has a slogan or mission statement: "Dieu et mon Droit". It has employees. The Crown Corporation also radiates benefits to other key sectors of the economy. Its palaces and ceremonies are a major attraction to tourists and a boon to Britain's £86 billion tourism industry which also employs two million people. The Royals are also newsmakers, creating jobs for thousands of journalists, paparazzi and publicists, and fodder for a steady stream of books, TV programs and movies.

It licenses its name and insignia (By Royal Appointment) to certain trades people and artisans. It is a major "title" sponsor of organizations such as the Royal Academy, the Royal Free Hospital and the Royal Mail in the form of a Charter, given after years of achievement – for example, the Institute of Public Relations received Royal Charter status on its 60th anniversary – and approved by the Privy Council. Like the owners of most corporations, it engages in patronage. It has a pronounced corporate culture which in this case is called tradition. It has little need to advertise because it generates so much "free" publicity. Here the main problem is to control the messages, insofar as that is possible and to foresee and forestall impending crises; and when they do occur, to contain and repair the damage.

In this the Crown Corporation has been well tried and tested and is an excellent example of the stamina of a power brand. To be sure it has had its ups and downs – as well as an "out" in 1649 when King Charles I was executed and replaced by a commonwealth led by Oliver Cromwell.

The experiment of living without a king floundered after a short time and the monarchy was restored in 1670 in the form of Charles II. The people and the national leaders in parliament decided, based on various practical considerations, compromises between political factions and, importantly, the affection of the people for the institution of the monarchy, rather than any particular incumbent of the throne, that the Crown Corporation was an essential component of the national identity.

In recent times the Crown Corporation has come under strong attack and the institution was shaken from the time of the split between Prince Charles and Princess Diana, her subsequent death and the heir's re-marriage. This turbulence in the Royals' private lives was nothing to do with the behavior of the Crown Corporation as an institution, but can be likened to the impact that a business leader's lurid private life can have on a company's reputation. But the Crown Corporation's resilience was such that it survived and has subsequently recovered something of its reputation.

In this period the experience, skills and reservoir of public goodwill, built up over more than five decades, of the current CEO of the Crown Corporation, Her Majesty Queen Elizabeth II, was a vital element of the successful recovery.

In case you think the comparison of a monarchy with a modern business is fanciful, read this quotation:

Elizabeth both led and managed England as a brilliant executive runs a great corporation, treating it as a dynamic system based perhaps on certain unchanging, transcendent principles, but always responsive to the circumstances of a fluid world. Her saga is also very much a story of today and one that you can use.

Thus writes Alan Axelrod in his book about Elizabeth II's ancestor, titled *Elizabeth I, CEO: Strategic Lessons from the Leader Who Built an Empire.* Axelrod lists 136 tips from her rule for aspiring managers.

Times have changed over five centuries and British monarchs no longer wield executive power over the nation where the Queen acts rather in the role of non-executive Chairman of the Board. But where the Royal household and businesses are concerned she is the hands-on CEO and dedicated guardian of the brand.

The Crown Corporation is a brand with stamina, its national image enduring for centuries rather than decades, ever present in the minds of stakeholders while elected governments of all political shades, and none, come and go.

Notes

1   All statistical information in this paragraph is taken from my article "The family company and its stakeholders", *Journal of Communications Management*, March 1998.
2   *Johnson Journal*, October 2001.
3   Samuel C. Johnson, who was Chairman from 1967 until 2000.
4   *Johnson Wax Magazine*, December 1986.
5   In 1947, Frances Gerety, a young copywriter on the De Beers account at N.W. Ayer in New York, penned the famous slogan "A diamond is forever". This timeless line, first used in 1948, was voted top advertising slogan of the century by the prestigious US magazine *Advertising Age* in a special 150-page issue published in January 1999.
6   www.debeersgroup.com/debeersweb/About+De+Beers/De+Beers+History.
7   Michael L. Ross is Associate Professor of Political Science at the University of California at Los Angeles.
8   In a personal interview, Dickie Arbiter, former Press Secretary to Her Majesty the Queen, said it is "important to emphasize the distinction between the Monarchy as a national institution, the Queen as its titular head, and the Queen – and members of the Royal family – as private individuals. The way in which the Monarchy is publicly funded is quite complex but in essence the sovereign surrenders the revenues of the Crown Estates (which could be likened to the real estate subsidiary of an ordinary corporation) in return for the Civil List, the name used to describe the grant to the reigning monarch, which is voted on by Parliament. This arrangement dates back to 1760 and the reign of George III. Just like commercial enterprises, public and private, the Monarchy has responded to public demands for greater transparency. It now publishes quite detailed accounts on income and expenditures and these are available to everyone on the official website."

4
The brand, cèst moi

As an exercise to wake my audience and to underline the power of personality in corporate leadership, I opened a lecture at an international management conference with ten portrait photos of chief executives on the screen. Delegates were asked to identify them and name the corporations they led. Nearly all answers were correct. When the logos of the corporations were shown on another screen, 100 percent of answers were correct.

It is not surprising. These were individuals often pictured in articles and TV programs and on the front covers of business and management magazines. Their exploits and achievements were well known, often even on an international stage. Young managers sought to emulate them and to distill the essence of their success.

Nor is it surprising that when the delegates at this conference began discussions about the corporations, their opinions were heavily influenced by their view of the CEO. More than ever the reputation, and to some extent the brand, of the corporation is synonymous with the CEO, especially if he or she has joined the ranks of celebrity business leaders, whose every action or word is followed by the media.

What was remarkable was that this conference was not held in the USA, where the CEO personality cult is a well-known phenomenon, but in a remote island in the Baltic Sea. The majority of delegates came from countries outside the United States and Britain, where the historic culture frowns on celebrity and CEOs have traditionally been anonymous. It seems that as businesses, money markets and media globalize, so does the phenomenon of the celebrity CEO: Percy Barnevik of ABB, Olli Mattila of Nokia, Akio Morita of Sony, Ron Sommer of Deutsche Telekom, and Bernard Arnault of LVMH the French luxury goods conglomerate, among others.

There are many reasons for linkage including the most obvious. Any organization is bound to reflect the character of its leader. This is true of a platoon of infantrymen, a football team, a nation or a corporation. Find a strong, wise and inspirational leader and as night follows day you will find a successful unit.

"Take me to your leader," is not just the overworked phrase used in exploration stories, it is also the appeal of reporters and academics wanting to dig deep into a corporation. It surfaces the belief that no other person in the organization has the whole picture or can speak with the same level of authority and that the CEO is the biggest single influence on the actions and performance of the corporation. Similarly the prized speaking platforms sought by aspiring business titans – the Detroit Economic Club, The Executives Club of Chicago and a handful of others – are reserved for only those who hold the CEO title. Thus the mantle of being the face and voice of the corporate brand comes along in the same package as the stock options, corporate jet, expense account and golden parachute negotiated in the "pre-nuptial contract".

CEO AS BRAND MANAGER

There are enormous benefits to be derived from CEOs acting as brand banners so long as dangers are avoided.

One of the dangers is, of course, the fact that every CEO has a finite period in office. So, the corporate image that is too closely twinned with one individual is risky and might be of short duration. According to the management consulting firm Booz Allen Hamilton's study, "CEO Succession 2006", published in the firm's quarterly *Strategy+Business,* Summer 2007 issue, 357 CEOs at 2,500 of the world's largest public companies left their jobs in 2006. And nearly one in three was fired or forced out. In the long-term challenge of creating and building a brand it is worth noting that the average term of a chief executive officer is less than eight years.

One legendary former CEO is Herb Kelleher, co-founder of Southwest Airlines. Southwest is among 100 companies studied by Will Rodgers and Christian Sarkar, writing in the online publication of the Zyman Institute of Brand Science at the Goizueta Business School, Emory University.[1] They point out that Kelleher is the opposite of most CEOs in that he placed the needs of shareholders last, behind employees and customers. Yet the airline has set industry records for maximizing shareholder value.

Here is Herb Kelleher's description of the CEO's role as "brand guardian", as described to Rodgers and Sarkar:

The role of the appropriate CEO is, in my opinion, **most important in both creating and guiding the brand** and, to this end, I met about once per month with our Marketing Department, advertising agency, and Public Relations Department in creative sessions.

The objectives of my participation were manifold:

1. To license participants to be creative, rather than mechanistic and bureaucratic in approach;

2. To license participants to be daring, rather than humdrum in approach;

3. To help ensure that our advertising and PR content were congruent with our strategic and operational intentions, our corporate values and Culture, and our ethical standards;

4. To help ensure that we were paying contextual attention to changes in societal mores, interests, and trends;

5. To help ensure that our advertising and PR resources were being spent and expended in a manner appropriate to our allocation of aircraft seats; impending competitive confrontations; and potential service opportunities;

6. To help ensure that there was continuity and consistency to our advertising and PR over a span of years;

7. To help ensure that our advertising and PR had the potential for a substantive and lasting impact, rather than just an insubstantial, ephemeral presence;

8. To help ensure that the creative process was both unconstrained and a barrel of fun.

Caveat: I wrote "appropriate" CEO above because some CEOs, regardless of their merits in other areas, might deaden, rather than enliven, creative sessions.

There are several factors that contribute towards "the brand, cèst moi" phenomenon. We will examine these along with the outcomes – good, bad and occasionally very ugly.

THE ARCHITECT AND INSPIRATIONAL GENIUS

As mentioned above there are from time to time leaders with an original approach or idea that can change a business paradigm. It involves inspiration, tenacity and the ability to motivate others to participate in the execution of the idea as well as the ability to infect investors and customers with enthusiasm. More often than not such CEOs are the founders of their enterprises and it is natural that there should be no discernable line between CEO and corporation – they are almost identical. Think Steve Jobs at Apple, Richard Branson and Virgin, Fred Smith at FedEx and the late Anita Roddick and The Body Shop. But this is dealt with in Chapter 5, "Transitions – the next generation", in which the major problem of succession of the founding visionary pioneer is discussed.

Here we look mainly at CEOs who occupy a place in a succession of corporate leaders at major global enterprises, in which the corporate brand should be more powerful, better known and understood than any (temporary) leader.

HUMAN INTEREST

Every young journalist trainee learns that the human interest story trumps every other kind of news or feature. Readers are captivated less by events, happenings and statistics than by the stories of people affected by them. Thus, a new medical breakthrough described in terms of statistics of a percentage cured or number of lives saved has less impact than when the benefits are explained as seen through the eyes of a single patient who has been given a new lease of life. People are interested in other people more than abstract ideas or seemingly inanimate organizations. (Have you noticed a new fashion in advertising of describing corporations with the personal pronoun "who" rather than "which", presumably in an attempt to humanize them and make them more friendly and approachable?)

Thus, it is quite natural that the CEO should play the key role of company spokesman, using the interest in him as a person, to define the corporate brand at every strategic opportunity. It is quite proper that this should include both his own personal views on the strategy of the corporation as well as the enduring values that have preceded and will succeed his tenure as CEO.

In fact, it is part of the job description of every CEO that he should be brand reputation manager of his organization not only to external audiences but, equally important, to the internal audience of employees and all ranks of management so that they are constantly reminded of the brand values and promises of their company.

SIMPLIFICATION

In an increasingly complex global economy with large, multifaceted corporations using obscure technologies to stay successful, analyzing and weighing all the factors can be challenging. So many people look for a simpler formula or guide to shape their opinions of a corporation and the most obvious shortcut is to place "trust" in the CEO to deliver a good return on investment or in other respects "to do the right thing". (This is, in effect, what we do with out political leaders in a democracy.)

I am reminded of a near relative who was a regular (but controlled) punter on horse racing. After studying many scientific approaches, past form, past times, past successes at the particular track, handicap, and so on, she decided that she would place her trust in the jockey, rather than the horse. She found that, over the long haul, by placing her wagers on one or two jockeys with a winning record, she achieved a modest return on investment.

By placing trust in certain CEOs we make a simplified corporate brand selection, eliminating the need for assessing massive amounts of data on performance, ROI, transparency, corporate social responsibility, and so on.

According to the financial weekly *Barron's* World's Best CEOs list (August 13, 2007) "the ultimate CEO who matters is Steve Jobs, a co-founder and guiding force at Apple. Jobs' departure probably would result in a greater loss of stock-market value than the loss of any other CEO in the world. Jobs might be worth 20 or so points to Apple shares, roughly $16 billion."

VANITY

Along with the many ways in which the CEO can use his own position to help define and promote the corporate brand, there are less altruistic motives that drive some CEOs to become celebrities, which can put corporate brands in danger. Among people with the talents, drive and ambition to reach the top in business, hubris, vanity and self-aggrandizement will be found in good measure, and corporations jealous of their brand reputation must be on their guard. Just as using the CEO to articulate the brand story is a recommended technique, so the CEO who tries to use the corporate brand – of which he is the temporary steward – to sate his vanity or pursue his own agenda needs to be restrained. There is no surer way of placing the corporate brand in danger.

Another danger to watch out for is the lazy or sycophantic advertising agent or public relations counselor for whom it is a tempting safe bet to make the case to the boss of the client company that "there is no better person to describe the benefits of working with our company/buying our product than you, sir. After all, no one knows it better than you or can speak with such conviction and authority. What's more, our message will have more credibility coming from you rather than a paid actor."

For the sycophantic adviser this approach also helps him cement a relationship based on feeding the CEO's vanity. This must surely account for the large number of business leaders touting their wares on TV ads and for the dangerous overexposure of some CEOs in the "free media" during the good times, only to be left struggling or in hiding when the corporation faces difficulties.

THE HEART AND SOUL

Because the "heart", or emotional connection, is an important element that makes up the appeal of a corporate or product brand, the CEO needs to think beyond the usual numeric performance measures when seeking to establish a strong bond with stakeholders. So in addition to his responsibilities for running the day-to-day business and producing adequate profits while caring for the community, the CEO must also act as the heart and soul of the enterprise. All successful corporate brands achieve a connection with their stakeholders that is beyond the delivery of a high performance product or service. This involves the commitment to a social purpose beyond the commercial calculation, or perhaps central to it. It involves having a point of view, listening to others, humility rather than hubris and the ability to convey both the passion and reason behind the corporation's way of doing business. Success will be evident if stakeholders of the corporation – customers, communities, suppliers, employees, and so on – begin to see themselves as part of a movement, or perhaps a club peopled by others who share a common interest or vision, a bond that transcends a simple commercial transaction.

Apple, Whole Foods, Ryanair and some others included in *Barron's* list of "30 CEO's Who Matter" are companies in which employees and customers take "membership", signifying a relationship that is much deeper than normal.

There are several scenarios to be aware of when embarking on a campaign of "CEO positioning", over and above those mentioned in the preceding paragraphs.

ALIGNMENT

Grasping the true essence of any brand, product or corporation is not easy. To be an effective brand ambassador the CEO needs to understand the underlying and enduring elements of the corporate brand as well as his own character and make sure they are in perfect alignment. This is especially true if the CEO is new, when it is probable he will want to put his own mark on the enterprise. This is perfectly okay, even desirable, if it enhances and strengthens the brand. But this must be approached with care to make sure the new brand positioning and the CEO's views are in harmony and that the likely outcomes are properly researched in advance. No need to paint a picture of the result if the firmly fixed brand identity of the corporation and its CEO's aspirations are out of step.

THE UNSTOPPABLE TRAIN

A fast moving train that goes off the rails is perhaps the most extreme example of non-alignment. But anyone who has spent time close to CEOs will surely have met one who has become so convinced of the correctness and potency of his vision and authority, perhaps based on a previous unblemished record of business success, that he believes it to be more robust and important than the corporate brand itself. Such individuals gather speed in expansion and change either spurred on by a coterie of aides, or with their grudging acquiescence, unable to prevent the disaster they can see coming. Such individuals invariably display dangerous characteristics of egotism and megalomania and are under the illusion that they are indestructible. Sadly it can be both a personal and corporate catastrophe when it becomes all too clear that they have failed and are dismissed.

NEVER FORGET

The institution is always more important than even the most important individual.

Early in my acquaintance with Daniel J. Edelman, my boss and mentor for nearly 40 years, I asked him what had become of the CEO of one of the world's top 20 corporations. He had been prominent in a plethora of articles in the media and in cover stories in the business press, describing his plans for the enterprise. I mentioned I had seen nothing about him in recent weeks. Dan replied, "Interesting you should have noticed. I had the same query so when I met the public relations vice president of the company, an old friend, I asked him why things had gone quiet. He told me the CEO was no longer with the company. I asked 'Why?' He replied: 'Well, he did not live up to the reputation I created for him'." So much for indestructibility.

THE SYCOPHANTS

We have all heard of the "yes men" with whom some weak CEOs surround themselves and who can, in the long term, damage their leader's career and weaken the brand equity of the corporation. Sycophants are worse; they do not wait for questions to become "yes men", they actively encourage their superiors to believe in their own infallibility.

Most of us know the story of King Canute, which is mostly taught incorrectly in schools. He is usually depicted as a stupid old man who imagines he is all powerful and even believes he has the ability to order the sea tides to change from flow to ebb.

In fact, King Canute was one of the wisest and most successful kings of England. Such was his greatness that members of his court began to attribute to him supernatural powers. In order to put them right and to demonstrate he was a mere human he ordered them down to the beach, where he would attempt to turn the tide. He knew full well that he would fail and that would bring his sycophantic admirers to their senses.

Unlike Canute, regrettably, some of our business leaders are insufficiently rooted in reality to resist the charms of their sycophant aides. Poor judgments are made which can damage the corporate brand.

NEPOTISM

The advancement of favorites or relatives is an ever present danger with

CEOs prone to believe "the brand, cèst moi". The pride and vanity of some makes them believe they have the right to offer preferment to members of their own families and friends and that various offices or honors are in their personal "gift", as if they were royalty of an earlier era, or leaders of a totalitarian state. This should be resisted at all costs.

It is interesting that UPS, one of the finest and most enduring of corporate brands, has a strict policy against nepotism which is exercised consistently and energetically even though it sometimes precipitates unforeseen and unfortunate consequences. On a visit to a UPS sorting and phone center in Hartford, CT, my guide to the facility was a female executive. It turned out her family was a "victim" of the policy, which includes a ban on husband and wife working for the company. Like so many couples in the USA, she and her husband met at work, while both were employed at UPS. Once they were married they had to make a decision as to which of them would stay at UPS and they agreed it should be her. He went to work at rival Federal Express where he could use the skill and experience he had acquired at UPS.

In spite of this anomalous outcome UPS knows occasional instances like this are the price to be paid for maintaining a policy of promotion or preferment based on merit alone.

APRÈS MOI, LE DELUGE

As the theme of this chapter was expressed in French by Louis XIV of France, it is appropriate that we consider another French expression, a branding and management consideration frequently associated with dominant celebrity CEOs: succession planning (or lack of it) – *After me, the flood.* Some CEOs become so confident and vain that they imagine they are not only indestructible but are also immortal. They give little thought to the major issue of stable continuity if, for one reason or another, they are either no longer there or unable to perform their functions.

On occasion, there is no succession planning at all. This can be especially dangerous if the departed CEO had single-handedly managed the corporation as a fiefdom, without any structure or deputies, one of whom could step into the leadership role without the enterprise missing a beat.

Equally problematic is the succession plan that does not work. There can be many reasons for this but one that is common among "Sun King" CEOs is that the nominated successor, usually a long-standing member of the management group and the Number 2 to the CEO, has never been trained in making the final strategic decisions. All too often, when the time comes for such successors to take the reins, they are revealed as being strong aides but weak leaders.

The CEO oversight and selection committees of Boards are usually exceptionally skilled at choosing competent leaders based on concrete criteria. But in addition to technical skills and leadership qualities, they might do well to look for who understands corporate brand reputation. According to David Larcker,[2] a professor of accounting at the Stanford University Graduate Business School, a 10 percent positive change in a CEO's reputation increases the company's market value by 24 percent. So it turns out that even intangibles can be measured.

FIRST AMONG EQUALS

Although everyone on the planet responds to leadership, there are many forms of that quality to be found in different parts of the world. People's definition of leadership in any organization is shaped and tempered by the culture, history and customs of the country. This infuses business life and thus has a real impact on corporate brands. In many cultures there is a greater reverence for the corporation than for the individual leader.

When a Japan Airlines jet crashed in 1985 and 520 passengers died, the very first action by the CEO of the corporation was to accept full blame and resign. This is redolent of the philosophy of US President Harry S. Truman's philosophy of "The buck stops here", but is far less visible in the decision making of most western corporations. Of course, everyone knows that the JAL CEO had no *direct* responsibility for the disaster but in Japanese culture his action as the head of the organization was fully expected.

When I was planning the formal introduction of Deutsche Bank to the US business community at a press conference in New York following the acquisition and consolidation of Bankers Trust, I was urging the Chairman and clear "leader" of Deutsche Bank, Dr Rolf Breuer, to make certain statements as CEO. He firmly put me right, pointing out that his correct title is "Vorstands Vorsitzender" of the executive board and that Deutsche Bank, like all German companies, did not have a CEO. He was first among several equal members, so when he spoke, it had to be with words that all his co-board members had agreed. He was eager to avoid personal statements. I countered that the distinction was too subtle for the US American and other international journalists who were to attend. They would in any event describe Dr Breuer as CEO (which turned out to be the case). But I had to recognize that Breuer was sensitive to the German business culture that abhors the cult of personality – but reveres the decision taken after detailed consultation. The establishment quickly cuts down to size anyone who steps out of line.

THE TEAM, NOT ME ALONE

There comes a time in every corporate lifetime when there is the call to build the company brand reputation around a team of executives rather than a single individual. The prompt can be simple good judgment, that it is better to show strength in depth and to have expertise of the highest order in all branches of the corporation's business and an insurance policy for continued success in the future without the risk of too much reliance on a single person. Or it can be a reaction – that sometimes comes too late – when investors and other stakeholders feel that the leader is losing his magic touch and there is neither a suitable replacement nor a successor in sight. The order goes out to all branding and communications professionals: "Promote the full management team, not just the CEO".

There are templates for doing this and properly executed plans can work well – up to a point –but only if the CEO plays a role as "coach", "captain", "strategic coordinator" or another form of effective leader. It is worth mentioning again that in the US and in many other countries there is a compelling urge, not least in the media, to find a single figure that embodies all the qualities, strengths and weaknesses of the corporation.

Notes

1   "The CEO as brand guardian", July 2007, by Will Rodgers and Christian Sarkar (http://www.zibs. com/ceobrand.shtml).
2   Professor Larcker is quoted by Leslie Gaines-Ross in her book *CEO Capital*, published by Wiley in 2003. Dr Gaines-Ross is currently chief reputation strategist at Weber Shandwick.

5
Transitions – the next generation

Virgin after Richard Branson?
Apple without Steve Jobs?
Microsoft without Bill Gates?
Berkshire Hathaway without Warren Buffett?

These are questions that do not just keep investors awake at night. They are also top of mind for employees and competitors. With so much of the equity of their corporations linked to their own persons it is hard to separate the corporate brand into parts. And it is hard to know how the market will react when a planned or sudden transition of leadership occurs. A taste of the consequences can be seen in the case of Steve Jobs following the near collapse of Apple after his ouster in 1996. John Heilenmann writes in *New York Magazine* (June 18, 2007):

> The Steve Jobs story is one of the classic narratives – maybe *the* classic narrative – of American business life. Its structure has been rigorous, traditional, and symmetrical: three acts of ten years each. Act One (1975–1985) is "The Rise," in which Jobs goes into business with his pal, Steve Wozniak; starts Apple in his parents' Silicon Valley garage; essentially invents the personal-computer industry with the Apple II; takes Apple public, making himself a multimillionaire at age 25; and changes the face of technology with the Macintosh. Act Two (1985–1996) is "The Fall": the expulsion from Apple, the wilderness years battling depression and struggling to keep afloat two floundering new businesses NeXT and Pixar. Act Three (1997–2007) is "The Resurrec-

tion": the return to Apple and its restoration, the efflorescence of Pixar and its sale to Disney, the megabillionairehood, the sanctification as god of design and seer of the digital-media future.

In the same article, Heilenmann also states:

Apple's reality is no longer in need of much distortion. On the back of the Mac and the iPod-iTunes tandem, Apple racked up $21.6 billion in sales in the last twelve months, and $2.8 billion in profits. Its stock price has doubled in the past year; AAPL was named to the S&P 100, making it a bona fide blue chip. With what Jobs dubs a "hobby," Apple TV, the company has invaded the sanctum sanctorum of living-room entertainment. Then there's that third, impending business, which revolves around a gorgeous sliver of palmtop gee-whizzery that you may have head about: the iPhone.

Now in its fourth Act, with a hugely successful iPhone launch behind it, Apple is powering its way forward with Jobs at the steering wheel. How the play will end is known – with the leadership moving from Jobs to a successor – but when or to whom, under what circumstances, no one knows. That his departure will have a seismic impact is, however, quite certain. According to the financial weekly *Barron's*, (March 26, 2007) "Jobs' departure would probably result in a greater loss of stock market value than the loss of any other CEO in the world ... perhaps, roughly, $16 billion." It is not too soon to start planning for that eventuality.

PERSONAL EXPERIENCE

My first personal experience of a key transaction was in my first job in public relations at the London firm of Harris & Hunter where I shared an office with Eric Bennett, a seasoned and scholarly ex-journalist and ghostwriter. He was responsible for working on one of the agency's prized clients – Tesco, which now vies with France's Carrefour for the position as the world's number two retailer after Wal-Mart. At that time Tesco's name was inextricably linked with that of its founder, J.E. "Jack" Cohen, who was known throughout the UK for his maxim for retail success: "Pile it high and sell it cheap". Jack was to Britain what Sam Walton became to the USA.

It is a tribute to Tesco's management that it has unshackled its present day success and stellar brand identiy from Jack Cohen as well as from any notion of cheapness. It is known for its quality merchandise and good value and has successfully pushed upmarket and diversified the goods and services offered and expanded its sales channels and geographical footprint.

But it was not so easy in the early days when Jack Cohen decided it was time to pass on the mantle of leadership. His chosen successor was one of two sons-in-law, who were both senior executives and aspired to the top position. The one selected was Hyman Kreitman and a succession strategy and plan was put in place by Jack Cohen himself.

One element of this plan was that Jack, who had become a media darling and had an open phone line to his huge number of journalist acquaintances, would no longer take media calls. After his retirement they would all be routed through to Mr Kreitman – this was his edict, and he put it in writing. We advised the media of the new rules. They grudgingly agreed to abide by them. But as is well known, there can be a big chasm between the plan and its execution, and sometimes the damage can be self-inflicted.

After a few weeks Eric Bennett started getting calls from media chums. They reported that they were following the new rules and interviewing Hyman Kreitman but that after their phone chats they would get a call from Jack to say: "I heard you were just speaking with Hymie, what did he say?" Jack would then proceed to give his views just as he had always done. It is hard for long-term leaders to let go of the reins.

Kreitman's reign was quite short, after which he was succeeded by Jack Cohen's other son-in-law, Leslie Porter.

In due course, Jack's calls to his media contacts slowed to a trickle and relatively soon Porter assigned the direction of Tesco's future to top-flight non-family CEOs who have been responsible for leading its spectacular growth in recent years. The first of these was Ian McLauren who was followed by Terry Leahy in 1997. They have taken Tesco to annual sales of $100 billion and pretax profits of $6 billion.

What's more, they have taken Tesco into 3rd position in brand value in the UK, ahead of Shell and BP, according to Brand Finance plc, a consulting company that measures brands and their value. In a head to head comparison with its rival Carrefour, Tesco is in 34th place worldwide, ahead of Carrefour at 63rd. In their 2007 report on the world's most valuable brands, Brand Finance said:

Carrefour had a clear lead over Tesco in the recent past but Tesco's enterprise value and brand value have since overtaken its rival in branding terms. Carrefour's value is more than $5,000m smaller than Tesco, reflecting the strong underlying strength of the Tesco brand, which enjoys an AA+ rating.

In brand architecture terms, Tesco employs its corporate name in most countries ... Carrefour operates a very mixed multi-brand strategy for different segments of the market.

With succession planning being such an obviously important task of boards of directors and owners of corporations, it is surprising that it does not merit their closer attention.

According to a recent Thomson Financial survey, *CEO Succession Planning*, July 2007, "more than one third of all respondents indicated that their board has not broached the topic in more than one year. In fact, just over 10% said that their boards have 'never' engaged in such planning". Thomson's Glenn Curtis says:

These days boards of directors tend to be so focused on corporate gover-
nance issues and finding ways to enhance shareholder value that they sometimes overlook the issue of CEO succession planning entirely. But this is no excuse. Boards must, at all times, maintain a "short-list" of potential candidates to assume the position should the current chief executive step down or be terminated. In fact, such planning makes good business sense and is necessary if the board is to satisfactorily fulfill its fiduciary responsibility to its shareholders.

The same survey revealed that 80 percent of the respondent compa-
nies claimed that internal candidates were being groomed for possible succession, a process that is too narrow according to Korn/Ferry International's Joe Griesedieck and Bob Sutton.[1] They recommend looking externally as well:

For example, if an external market scan indicates that potential CEO candidates at other organizations possess a higher degree of skills and experience, that insight can and should drive changes to existing executive development programs within the company. Conversely, if the external market scan suggests that a company's internal collection of future CEO candidates far outshines those in other companies, that insight can drive changes to existing retention approaches to prevent internal candidates from being hired away by other companies.

This kind of comparative view enables directors to perform a stronger critical assessment of whether or not their existing CEO candidates – as well as their existing CEO succession planning processes – are sufficient.

In fact, according to a book titled *CEO Succession Planning*, published by India's ICFAI University Press, there are four main kinds of succession, planned or unplanned:

They are – (i) *Crown Heir* wherein the heir apparent is identified and informed by the predecessor CEO, (ii) *Horse Race* which pits several candidates against each other and only the best among them is chosen as the new CEO, (iii) *Coup D'Etat* in which the organization members whose interests differ from the incumbent's make the key decision, and (iv) *Comprehensive Search* where the decision-makers seek a CEO whose background and skills match those required by an intended organizational reorientation.

All four scenarios assume that the transition will be conducted at a measured pace, except perhaps in the case of a "coup d'etat". But quite frequently a crisis of succession is precipitated by the untimely death or incapacity of the incumbent. Contrary to the notion that such occurrences are surprises, it should be a starting assumption that an accident is a likelihood and a contingency plan put in place in good time. Consider the problems recently faced by McDonald's when two CEOs died within months of each other.

Nowhere is this kind of succession planning more important than at corporations where the corporate brand and CEO brand are totally interdependent, as we have seen with Apple and Steve Jobs.

ZEST FOR ADVENTURE

Perhaps even more connected with each other are Brand Virgin and Brand Branson. And with founder and CEO Richard Branson's passion for business risk and partying matched only by his zest for extreme adventure and sports, the employees and shareholders of Virgin companies must be more than mildly concerned about how successful the company will be without him at the helm. The corporate initiatives and models he has created have broken most of the cherished principles of success, and yet by the magic of his personality and presence, they have with some notable exceptions (Virgin Cola) been successful to the point where Virgin is ranked as Europe's number two brand with consumers and Branson is number 222 on the *Forbes* rich list. According to the Virgin.com website, the Group's 200 companies had global revenues of $20 billion in 2006.

And then there is the mysterious disappearance of his friend and rival adventurer/sportsman Steve Fossett on 3 September 2007, on a routine flight in his plane over the Nevada desert. After extensive but unsuccessful searches, he was declared legally dead on 15 February 2008 (his body was finally found in the wreckage of his plane in October 2008). He held over 100 world records in different sports and beat Branson to become the first person to fly around the world in a hot air balloon. This tragedy can only have served to heighten concerns among those with a stake in the future of the Virgin brand, about its continued success if something should happen to Richard Branson.

There is not the slightest doubt that there are many gifted executives leading Virgin's main companies and the 350 other smaller ventures of the Group but most people would be at a loss to name them, so long and deep is the shadow cast by Branson himself in the media. No organization so successful and so large would be able to function without a team of superb managers; and it is safe to say that the Virgin brand aura has been the magnet for many budding Bransons to join the company. It would be foolish to imagine this matter has not crossed Branson's mind. His talent for innovation, combat and marketing probably indicate that he believes the Virgin brand has a dynamic life of its own that will ensure its longevity even if he is not there. But it is equally certain that investors and other stakeholders will be looking for a remarkable figure who will be able to act as the central force at Virgin, generating new ideas and ventures in multiple seemingly unrelated fields, while holding them within the brand family.

CROWN HEIR

As mentioned earlier, Korn/Ferry says that 8 out of 10 companies in their surveys claim to be grooming internal candidates for possible succession. But there are two broadly different ways that this is done. The first involves the "anointment" of a crown prince or princess to the throne well in advance of the departure of the current CEO. This can be the outcome of a "horse race" (the second way of handling a succession from internal candidates), months or years in advance of the coronation or it can be a successor chosen by the CEO and who has served as the corporation's president or COO for a long time, often sharing duties with the top executive.

The advantage of this method is that it is comforting to investors, boards (phew! one less problem to deal with), employees and other stakeholders. It seems to offer the safe haven of managing expectations.

Another advantage is that a CEO promoted from within the company will bring with him a deep knowledge of the corporate culture and the essence of the brand. This can sometimes take a long time for a CEO hired from the outside to learn. Corporate brand is to a large degree shaped by the corporate culture. And culture clash has been known to undermine some CEOs' ability to be effective and they soon depart of their own volition or under pressure.

But there have been enough recent high profile examples of this method to suggest it is not guaranteed. And in cases where the retiring CEO picks his own successor single-handedly, great care should be taken to ensure that his last executive decision, after a string of successes, does not turn out to be a failure, as in the case of the legendary Robert Goizueta, CEO of Coca-Cola. His nominee was Douglas Ivester. Ivester's tenure from Goizueta's death in 1997 until his departure in 2000 is regarded as a failure in its own right, not just when measured against his illustrious predecessor and mentor. Shareholders who had become addicted to a buoyant stock price and excellent returns under Goizueta – even during the "new Coke" miss-step – now had to be content with a lagging investment.

But, as is so often the case, it needed a defining moment to precipitate Ivester's premature retirement in 2000. This came in the form of what has become known as the "Belgian tainting crisis" in 1999.

In this case Coke, under the leadership of Douglas Ivester, allowed a small local incident to escalate into an international crisis which led not only to Ivester's downfall but to a drop in the price of the stock and a loss of reputation, all of which has taken a long time to repair.

The case, as analyzed by Professor Maureen Taylor of Rutgers University, is included in the chapter on Crisis Communication in my earlier book, *How To Manage Your Global Reputation*. (In this book I proposed a new "law" of crisis management: "The negative reputation impact of a crisis is directly proportionate to the length of time it takes for the CEO to take control and reach the scene.")

In this instance Coke sought to manage the crisis "long distance" from Atlanta and it took one week for the company and its CEO to issue an apology.

Since then Coca-Cola has had two CEOs, both long-serving executives with the company, first Douglas Daft, an Australian, followed by Neville Isdell who came out of retirement from his native Ireland to take over the top job. Now his own successor as CEO has been anointed and appointed – Muhtar Kent, a 30-year veteran of the company. Isdell will stay on in the role of Chairman, at least until April 2009. The split of the chairman and CEO roles will be a first at Coca-Cola even though it is the general rule among public companies in the UK. The board will determine in April 2009 whether to keep that arrangement or return to having the roles held by one person.

It must be irritating to Coca-Cola to have the spotlight so often put on their failures but that is the unfortunate lot of the leader and shining example in any sphere. Every small event at Coke will be examined and parsed if only because it is the king of corporate and product global brands in almost every independent league table, including the Brand Finance 500, where it has a brand value of $43,146 million, well ahead of Microsoft and HSBC. The conclusion must be that Coke has a brand resilience that may be unequalled. Brand Finance comments in its annual brand rankings for 2006, published in May 2007:

Created in 1888, the brand is the second most understood English word globally and is consumed in over 200 countries.

It has survived health scares, the commercial failure of "New Coke" and becoming a focus for anti-capitalist and anti-American sentiment in various parts of the world. The brand has also extended to cover various flavours and variations, including Diet Coke, Cherry Coke, Vanilla Coke and, most recently, Coke Zero.

Despite these issues, Coca-Cola's value is nearly double that of its rival Pepsi, whose brand is calculated at $23,948m.

The world's number three brand was Citi in 2007 but in the 2008 league table it was overtaken by another bank, HSBC. While the full fallout from the mortgage crisis is still unknown, Citi has suffered both huge losses on its balance sheet and the loss of its CEO, Charles Prince III, who was another example of the "crown heir" (in this case we will avoid the obvious pun) style of succession.

The architect of Citigroup as it exists today was Sanford I. Weill who created the institution through a blizzard of ever-larger acquisitions culminating in the merger of his Travelers Group with John Reed's Citicorp, whose flagship franchise was Citibank. Weill and Reed shared the role of

Co-CEO for a while but as many on Wall Street foresaw, it was not long before Sandy Weill was in sole charge. As Leslie Gaines-Ross observes in her book *CEO Capital*: "Experience shows that job sharing between equals works only as a convenient way to complete a deal quickly, but it hasn't succeeded long term as a means of running a company." She says this is particularly true of US companies.

The year 2002 saw a number of scandals hit Citi after the stock market plunged. This was the cue for Sandy Weill to relinquish his CEO role to his Number 2 and anointed successor Charles (Chuck) Prince, while he continued as Chairman for another four years.

Fast forward to 2007 when, after years of a sluggish stock price, Citi had to disclose that it was a victim of the sub-prime mortgage meltdown and announced the first of a series of losses and write-downs totaling $20 billion by April 2008. Chuck Prince was an early casualty and was pushed out to unfurl his golden parachute.

But this time there was no planned, smooth handover to a crown prince or princess and the reins were taken temporarily by Citi board member and one-time Treasury Secretary Robert Rubin, until it was announced early in 2008 that the new CEO would be Vikram Pandit, a recently recruited addition to the Citi management team from Morgan Stanley.

Meanwhile a few hundred yards away J.P. Morgan Chase, a combination of two of the world's most illustrious banking brand names, now led by Jamie Dimon, was less exposed to mortgage risk and became the selected vehicle of the Federal Reserve to rescue the investment bank Bear Stearns from bankruptcy – at a bargain basement price.

Who knows what was going through the mind of Citi investors and Sandy Weill himself at this turn of events in which the *New York Times* in March 2008 called Dimon "the world's most important banker". After all, it might have been heir apparent Dimon in the Citi CEO's office had he not been fired by Sandy Weill in 1998 after spending the previous 16 years as Weill's protégé, Number 2 and partner in arranging the series of mergers that created Citigroup. He had to jump-start his career once again which he did by joining BankOne as CEO in 2000. Dimon became President of JP Morgan Chase when it acquired BankOne in 2004, and took over the CEO's office following the retirement of William B. Harrison.

THE HORSE RACE

The horse race describes the method of CEO selection from within that is employed by many extremely large and successful companies, among them Procter & Gamble and General Electric. It is the procedure that in the current generation of CEOs has produced A.G. Lafley at P&G and Jeffrey Immelt at GE.

Such companies as these pride themselves on the care with which they recruit, train and mentor each successive level of leadership. The process begins at the initial selection process for entry to the organization. From that moment it is a *series* of horse races rather than a single event because in large companies candidates for the CEO's chair will have been through several functional posts in a number of different countries; and they will have been tested for "CEOship" by holding the top position in a large autonomous unit. The heads of these divisions usually constitute the field of runners in the final race for the triple crown title of Chairman, CEO and President. According to Jeffrey Sonnenfeld and Andrew Ward, firms such as P&G and GE, as well as Johnson & Johnson, IBM, and the *Washington Post* are classified as "academies" that not only develop their own cadres of management but "have served as training grounds for many great leaders. In fact, at one point in their careers, GE's Jeff Immelt, Microsoft's Steve Ballmer, eBay's Meg Whitman and AOL's Steve Case all worked for Procter & Gamble".[2]

It is almost a rule that candidates who fail to take the crown leave the firm and often turn up as CEOs of other firms.

But this can also happen earlier if it seems that there is going to be too long a wait for the incumbent to vacate his seat.

When John Chambers of Cisco, one of Silicon Valley's longest-serving and best known CEOs, confirmed his intention, in 2007, to continue for another three to five years, it was too much for two of the people tipped as a possible successor. First Mike Volpe left to become CEO of another company and Charlie Giancarlo, Chambers' Number 2, resigned to join an investment firm.

But Warren Buffett, 78, has confirmed that although he still feels he has some way to go, he is aware of the importance of succession at his Berkshire Hathaway.

In his annual newsletter for 2008, awaited as eagerly in financial circles as children anticipate a new J.K. Rowling Harry Potter story, Buffett drops some of his trademark hints. He said he has three internal candidates to succeed him as chief executive, and four candidates to run Berkshire's $107 billion stock-and-bond portfolio as chief investment officer. He has also hinted that youth may be a priority for his board. "Anybody who takes my (CEO) job would do better if they have a long run ... say 15 years."

In all the methods of grooming and selecting the chief executive of a large corporation, I suggest that one measure of all candidates should be an assessment of their understanding of the critical importance of branding to the future success of the enterprise, at both corporate and marketing levels.

According to Joe Griesedieck,[3] Vice Chairman and Head of the CEO Practice at Korn/Ferry, specific knowledge of branding is seldom, if ever, on the checklist of candidates for the CEO position. At the same time he stresses that a critical element of the CEO's role is as the brand guardian, even if the day-to-day task falls within the remit of the Chief Marketing Officer or Chief Communications Officer. However, he points out that if the CEO candidate fulfills all the requirements being sought, the corporate brand should be in safe hands.

Table 5.1 Attributes for a successful CEO (Source: Korn/Ferry)

- Integrity ... strong sense of ethics ... courage to do what's right.
- Insight ... self-awareness and insight into others.
- Decisive ... takes responsibility for making decisions.
- Appreciation for the value of people ... human capital.
- Communicator ... engenders trust through open and frequent communications.
- Strategic ... understands the core competences of the enterprise and builds upon them.
- Willingness to take risks.
- Encourages innovation and change ... drives it.
- Builds strong teams and encourages teamwork across and throughout the organization ... is able to recruit and retain good talent.
- Global perspective ... is interested and pays attention to what is happening in the world ... and the opportunities and risks that global events and developments represent for the company.
- Ability to work effectively with the board ... to keep the board informed ... and to have the confidence to share and debate issues openly with outside directors.

The fact that brand value is intangible may make judgments of caliber unnerving to members of a selection committee who are more at ease with the P&L and balance sheet, and questioning candidates on how they would deploy or reallocate the tangible assets of the company. This difficulty of understanding and approach is all the more pronounced among certain companies. Engineering, professional services and component manufacturers are just a few examples of firms that do not have a heritage in marketing branded products. Most management talent moves up the ladder in R&D, production and other functions and this can sometimes lead to a dismissive attitude towards the "soft" management skills involved in reputation and branding.

In companies that market consumer products with substantial research, advertising and PR budgets, the situation is potentially easier. First, all concerned "get" the fact that brand equity may be intangible but it can be measured. Second, most candidates will have years of experience in the techniques of creating strong product brands. Third, it is a short step for such candidates to apply those same skills to the corporate brand if selected to become CEO.

Companies without a strong history/tradition of branding should recognize that they will be losers in the globalizing and commoditizing economy of the 21st century. They would do well to co-opt an expert onto their selection committee who will help choose – and then help train – the candidate who understands the need for differentiation as an essential first step to creating a competitive and enduring brand. Moreover, the selection committee and candidate should be respectful of the corporate culture and heritage of the corporation that has been fundamental to the formation of the brand. Not to do so can be extremely painful, as Home Depot found when they selected Robert Nardelli as CEO in 2001.

Confidence high

The prospects were bright and confidence was high. After all, Nardelli was one of three "finalists" to replace legendary CEO Jack Welch who was retiring from GE, a job that finally went to Jeff Immelt. The other contender was Jim McNerney who left to join 3M but soon after was recruited to become CEO at Boeing.

Nardelli had had a stellar career at GE, which he joined in 1971. He worked in various divisions and left GE for three years, returning in 1991. In 1995 he was appointed CEO of GE's Power Systems Division, a huge enterprise in its own right. According to Welch, Nardelli was a notable success at GE Power Systems, which was losing money and had trouble with unions before Nardelli took over and invested in products, cut costs and improved labor relations. Nardelli created joint ventures around Europe and efficient, environmentally sensitive power products at a time when the market demanded them, making power one of GE's most important businesses.

Welch is not the only Nardelli fan who thinks he is the right choice for Chrysler, where he took over as CEO in August 2007.

Board members Ken Langone and Roger Penske also believe that his achievements at Home Depot, where he helped increase revenue, profits and the number of stores, were under-recognized.

But the lagging stock price and his rich pay package, along with his unwillingness to listen to shareholders alienated investors. And at the other end of the spectrum he had not managed to win over the Home Depot employees, the vital interface with the customers, in spite of his well-known work ethic and efforts at making a connection. He cut back workers' hours thus alienating long-serving and experienced sales persons.

Another Nardelli supporter is Noel Tickey, a professor at the University of Michigan who ran the CEO Leadership Development program from 1985 to 1987, and has written a profile of Nardelli.

Tickey told the Associated Press[4] on Nardelli's appointment at Chrysler: "What he brought to Home Depot actually was a lot of GE. He's hard-headed – he'd still be (at Home Depot) if he hadn't stuck his head in the sand"; and on his $210 million severance package: "That's one of his tragic flaws, but it wasn't tragic enough to stop him from re-emerging."

The tipping point was reached at the much-publicized 2006 annual shareholders' meeting at which Nardelli installed large digital timers that cut off speakers after one minute. Jena McGregor of *BusinessWeek*[5] described the event as "a 37 minute session that was attended by none of the company's directors and where shareholders were not allowed to ask Nardelli questions, [that] was one of the low points in the history of corporate governance."

While Nardelli's tenure at and departure from Home Depot have been much analyzed as an example of the new-found power of shareholder activists, an egregious reward package and a failure to achieve a lift in the stock price, there has been less attention given to culture clash and an underestimation of the power of the Home Depot brand.

Highly defined brands

Both GE and Home Depot are highly defined brands but are different in many obvious and less obvious characteristics.

Proponents of "living the brand", also known as inside-out branding, in which the values of the company are communicated through the actions of management and employees in a thousand different ways every day might consider this episode as a proof case.

Nardelli may have brought "a lot of GE" to Home Depot but perhaps sufficient care was not taken to understand the differences in Home Depot's "magic formula" to ensure the transplant was not rejected. Korn/ Ferry's Joe Griesedieck thinks that all the achievements of Nardelli at Home Depot were undermined by his inability to understand the company's culture: "This particular blind spot ultimately resulted in deteriorating relations with the Board and associates on the front lines and allowed Lowe's, Home Depot's main rival to gain share."[6]

Home Depot was an organization that had in a relatively short history established a pronounced corporate culture that came directly from the personalities of its founders, Bernard Marcus and Arthur Bland, and their ideas and policies played right through the organization to the customers. They recruited and trained former plumbers, electricians and other craftsmen and this won the Home Depot brand a reputation for knowledge, helpfulness and expertise.

Tesco, Citi and Home Depot are just a few of the corporations that have faced change of leadership with varying degrees of success. Apple and Virgin are two whose approach to succession is eagerly watched by investors and analysts. In these cases and all others it seems clear that a sound understanding of the brand should be one key factor in the selection of a new CEO.

Notes

1 "Completing the CEO succession planning picture", July 7, 2007, by Joe Griesedieck and Bob Sutton (can be found at www.kornferry.com in publications archive).
2 *Firing Back*, Sonnenfeld and Ward, Harvard Business School Press.
3 Personal communication.
4 6 August 2007.
5 11 June 2007.
6 Personal communication.

6
Location branding

Many countries, regions and cities have been branding themselves with varying degrees of success. From "Cool Britannia" (UK) to "Asia's World City" (Hong Kong), and the "coming out" of modern China at the Beijing Olympics, the development and promotion of location brands is now a well-established phenomenon, with widespread efforts having been made by national and local governments alike in an attempt to establish an image for their country, region or city that confers status and drives competitive advantage on the new world stage.

My own first experience in this field began with Finland in 1968 and continued over the next 20 years.

It is hard now to recall the problems that country faced in its relations with the western world in which, in fact, it was firmly rooted. It was trying hard to shake off the association of Finland with the 3 S's – Sauna, Sisu (a Finnish word meaning grit or stubbornness) and Sex – as well as the term "finlandization" foisted on it on by the German politician Franz Josef Strauss. This was an adjective he coined to describe countries so in awe of a huge and powerful neighbor they lose all will of their own and obey the wishes of the hegemon. The suggestion that their country was a pawn of the Soviet Union was an offence to the proud Finns.

Strauss was a clever politician and understood Germany. But he did not understand Finland and Sisu. That small Nordic country of 5☐ million people is now ranked as the most literate, wired, and economically successful country in the world, well ahead of its giant neighbor to the East. Even in those early days, Finland recognized the power of coordinated communications in creating a national brand.

The quantum of effort, however, has not always been matched by success – with many location branding programs failing to deliver sustainable commercial or reputational advantage.

In considering the requirements for a national branding initiative, I'll start by listing some critical factors for success. These are based on widely understood industry "best practices" and on the combined experience of expert colleagues.

BRANDS MUST BE TRUE TO THEMSELVES

While brands can, and should, represent aspirations (in order to act as agents for change), they should never risk disappointment or dissatisfaction upon delivery.

Creating a brand promise which then fails to deliver, can generate a more negative perception than if the promise had never been made in the first place. Brands should be an amplification of what is already there – not a fabrication.

Take the example of "Cool Britannia". A few years ago, a British Council survey revealed that people outside the UK perceive the British to be competent in one area – the past; and so a "thinktank" was created with the aim of giving Britain an image overhaul.

"Cool Britannia" was the description given to this effort to characterize the new national identity so as to attract foreign investments with its implied promise to people and businesses located there that they too could be cool just by association. The problem was that half of the British population are not "into" cutting-edge fashion, design, music and the arts. Additionally, many industries actually thrive on traditional values such as honor and reliability. The brand Cool Britannia was not inclusive enough and amplified only part of Britain. And as a result, the effort is widely seen to have failed. If an image chosen to represent a country does not represent its people, how can they believe it themselves? How then can it be believed elsewhere?

Nation branding expert Simon Anholt believes that the real problem was that Cool Britannia, which was never the *official* slogan, became the issue, rather than the reality. He told me "Our main mistake was talking to the media about it, and forgetting that what we were trying to do was promote Britain, not promote the campaign to promote Britain."

This imperative was underlined emphatically in a recent general election in India, the world's largest democracy. The brand slogan coined for the incumbent party – India Shining – appealed greatly to the 100 million Indians who had joined the middle class, as well as to approving developed nations in the West. But the idea was rejected by the one billion voters who have not shared in the country's new-found prosperity and still live just above or below the poverty line.

BRANDS MUST CAPTURE THE SPIRIT OF THE PEOPLE AND THEIR SHARED PURPOSE

In this respect, the core of a location's brand must reflect the spirit of the people – not least because this is directly and deeply connected to the spirit of the place.

Remember a brand is not built on reasoned argument or entirely rational judgment. It is in equal measure the result of the emotional bond that is created between you and the product, organization, country – whatever the brand may be.

For example, the spirit of Hong Kong is directly related to the spirit of its people – witness their unstoppable energy and "can do" attitude to life ("hoh yi"). The spirit of Ireland is defined, in large part, by the people's genuine warm welcome, their wry and witty "craic" (humor) and their sense of optimism. In Wales, "hwyl", the spiritual yearning of the country – its resilience (from a history of heavy industry and limited income) and the strength of feeling in communities – resonates widely through its poetry and music, as well as the experience of everyday life.

USE THE BRAND AS A CHANGE AGENT AND EVOLVE IT OVER TIME

While it is important to ensure that the location is actually able to substantiate what its brand is saying about it, the branding effort does not have to be restricted to what is already there.

The brand can aspire to the potential of a location's competitive advantage. In other words, a proposition can be crafted that is capable of immediate expression, representation and launch, but that can grow over time as various initiatives get it closer to delivering on the true relevant differentiation.

In this respect, the location's brand can also be used post-development to discern what other activities, industries or projects should be jump-started because they complement or reinforce the brand.

ENSURE BRAND POSITIONING CAN BE BROADLY APPLIED

While it may be useful at times to highlight one particular facet of a brand (in order to shift attitudes), that facet should nonetheless be presented in its broader context. The widely acclaimed success of Spain's rebranding program attests to this.

Twenty-five years ago, Spain was suffering from the effects of having been under the long-term grip of the Franco regime. As such it was isolated, poverty stricken and not really part of modern Europe.

Today it has transformed itself into a modern European democracy with much improved economic prosperity. It is the destination choice for holidays, second homes, retirement and party-goers. How did this happen?

Spain's success is largely down to an active, orchestrated and multifaceted modernization program using Joan Miró's sun to symbolize a much more fundamental step change in economic and social development.

It started on the day of the restoration of the monarchy with the accession of King Juan Carlos, when the Spanish Ministry of Information approached Edelman to assist with an international communications program as Spain started on the path toward democracy with a view towards entry to the EU, a mission long since accomplished.

Ostensibly led by a national and regional advertising campaign, the program was, in reality, strengthened by the privatization and rapid global expansion of Spanish multinationals such as Telefonica into Latin America, the rebuilding of cities like Bilbao with the Guggenheim Museum, the films of Almodóvar and the international prominence of such actresses as Oscar-winner Penelope Cruz and the impact of hosting the Barcelona Olympic Games.

And on the Olympics as a kind of defining event for any brand, it will be interesting to see if the surprisingly successful Athens Games can be consolidated into a longer term advantage for Greece or if the effect was simply fleeting and eclipsed by the impact of the subsequent spectacular 2008 Olympics in Beijing.

ENSURE UNITY OF VISION AND COMMON OBJECTIVES

In creating a successful location brand, it is also critical to ensure that there is a common goal among participants and a sharp sense of purpose to achieve results. Absence of unity can cripple a branding initiative, with the lack of an agreed core purpose making it difficult – if not impossible – to create broad-based adoption of the brand.

In the Spanish example above, filmmaker Pedro Almodóvar, clothes designer Adolfo Dominguez and architect Santiago Calatrava pooled their artistic talents and worked together as a team to assist the government express a Spain that was fresh, free and more competitive.

Likewise, when Singapore set out to become the "Switzerland of the Pacific Rim", this aspirational positioning was made credible by the Confucianist mindset of the dominant Chinese business community – an exceptionally powerful unifying force.

As a small country, Singapore also ensured that the three most potent communication "voices" (Singapore Airlines, Tourist Board, Ministry of Trade & Economic Development) worked closely together and consolidated their budgets.

Research also shows that all types of "buyers" want evidence that there is a mind behind the brand and its offer – a collective and conscious force that can be relied upon to keep the promise made by the brand. Prospective tourists need this to ensure their visits will be well managed. Inward investors want reassurance about legislation and infrastructure. Buyers of products or services seek reassurance of quality control. A location's brand is thus considerably more than icons and imagery. It is evidence of a collective will to offer and deliver a competitively attractive proposition.

BENCHMARKING THE BRAND

Countries intent on branding – or rebranding – themselves know they need to benchmark themselves against other countries, including those they wish to emulate, or overtake. Many have joined the Anholt-GFK Roper Nation Brands Index, a joint venture between place and nation branding pioneer Simon Anholt and the international GFK Roper research firm. This Index measures six dimensions that combine to form each country's brand image.

By breaking down the composite image into its component parts Anholt provides a country with a formula for managing each element that contributes to its brand reputation as well as an objective measure of progress and success. The six components are:

- **Exports** – Determines the public's image of products and services from each country and the extent to which consumers proactively seek or avoid products from each country of origin.

- **Governance** – Measures public opinion regarding the level of national government competency and fairness and describes individuals' beliefs about each country's government, as well as its perceived commitment to global issues such as democracy, justice, poverty and the environment.
- **Culture and heritage** – Reveals global perceptions of each nation's heritage and appreciation for its contemporary culture, including film, music, art, sport and literature.
- **People** – Measures the population's reputation for competence, education, openness and friendliness and other qualities, as well as perceived levels of potential hostility and discrimination.
- **Tourism** – Captures the level of interest in visiting a country and the draw of natural and man-made tourist attractions.
- **Investment and immigration** – Determines the power to attract people to live, work or study in each country and reveals how people perceive a country's economic and social situation.

According to Simon Anholt's website (www.earthspeak.com):

The best example of a national rebranding from our own times is undoubtedly that of modern Japan. The effect of Japan's economic miracle on the image of the country itself was quite as dramatic as its effect on the country's output. Only 40, or even 30 years ago, "Made in Japan" was a decidedly negative concept, as most western consumers had based their perception of "brand Japan" on their experience of shoddy, second rate products flooding the market. The products were cheap, certainly, but they were basically worthless. In many respects, the perception of Japan was much as China's has been in more recent years.

Yet Japan has now become synonymous with advanced technology, manufacturing quality, competitive pricing, and even of style and status. Japan, indeed, passes the best branding test of all: whether consumers are prepared to pay more money for functionally identical products, simply because of where they come from. It's fair to say that in the 1950s and 1960s, most Europeans and Americans would only buy Japanese products because they were significantly *cheaper* than a western alternative. Now, in certain valuable market segments – such as consumer electronics, musical instruments and motor vehicles – western consumers will consistently pay more for products manufactured by previously unknown brands, purely on the basis that they are perceived to be Japanese. Little wonder that Dixons, a UK retailer of consumer electronics, gave its new house brand a mock-Japanese name, Matsui, in order to borrow a little of the "public domain" equity of brand Japan.

Japan Inc.'s remarkable success provided the model for other nations to join the big league of brands: South Korea with Samsung, Hyundai, LG and Kia, all of which have achieved mega brand status individually and have helped lift the country's own reputation at the same time.

Now China, with the declared intention of creating 100 global brands within a few years, is following fast on the path from "cheap" to superior quality. Computer maker Lenovo has learned from Sony, Panasonic and Samsung and has used the Beijing Olympics to make its mark on the world stage.

PRIORITIES

All of which makes me ponder the question: Which is more important to promote first? The country of origin or the corporate or product brand?

One view was urged on me by an important mentor. He declared: "You must promote the country first, the corporation second and the product brand last!"

His point of view was that you are unlikely to trust a corporation or value its products unless you know about the country of origin and hold it in high regard. I now question the sequence of this rule because you do not change people's views about a country by communicating its merits. It can only be done by changing reality, and one of the ways is through innovation, production and marketing of quality products that can command premium prices – brands. For as long as the national/country brand is weak, there is no reason for an aspiring brand to highlight its national origin. Sony, Panasonic, Honda, Toyota and Samsung did not wave the national flag (except in their home markets which they sought to protect as long as they could). Rather, they went flat out to achieve technological leadership, efficient production and unbeatable quality. At this stage product brands play a vital role in improving the country brand image to a "tipping point" at which it achieves a positive rating. Only at that point can the brand be paid back with the reinforcement of a label such as "Made in Germany" or "Made in Japan". It seems clear that there is no ideal sequence to be followed and the greatest success can be achieved in the shortest term by synchronized efforts by the national governments and institutions, corporations and their product divisions working in concert.

Government and institutions have the task of creating the framework in which companies and their brands can compete and succeed in the global marketplace, building on national resources and the gifts of the population. This will include working for a stable society that will help attract long-term foreign direct investment. It must pursue active public diplomacy which includes using all modern means of communication. It also needs to attract high profile sporting and arts events and business conventions.

Products and services are where opinions are formed about brands, corporations and, ultimately, about the country of origin. It should be noted that not all of the strongest "nation" or "country" brands have been successful in creating a stable of corporate or product global brands. For instance, for all its success as an economy and as a country brand, Singapore has not given the world any major brand other than Singapore International Airlines. In contrast, the success of Samsung has helped Brand Korea, Nokia has been key in helping Brand Finland and Lenovo and Haier are doing the same for China as are Tata, Wipro and Infosys for India.

In the most recent Nations Brand Index, which surveyed 50 countries, the top and bottom then were as displayed in Table 6.1.

The linkage between nation/place branding and corporate and product branding will become increasingly confused in the years ahead. The effect of globalization will mean that it is no longer possible to think of one country being the domicile of a corporation, the place where it is owned and its products are designed, developed and manufactured. My "Japanese" Canon camera was, on close inspection, made in Taiwan, my "American" Jeep was produced by a German-owned company, my "Korean" Samsung mobile phone/MP3 was made in China and my Honda Accord was made in America.

Simon Anholt is not concerned. He told me, "it doesn't matter how complex these things become – consumers will always simplify them in their own minds because that's what the branding instinct is all about. Everybody knows that Rolls-Royce is no longer really a British brand, but everyone continues to perceive it as one. Brands often have a 'nationality' which overrides questions of country of design, country of ultimate ownership, country of manufacture and so on."

Table 6.1 Anholt Nations Brands Index Q4 2007 Results
(Source: © 2005–2008 Simon Anholt)

All questions overall ranking	Score	Rank
Germany	127.8	1
UK	127.1	2
Canada	126.8	3
France	126.5	4
Australia	124.5	5
Italy	124.2	6
Switzerland	124.1	7
Japan	123.9	8
Sweden	123.5	9
United States	122.0	10
Netherlands	119.7	11
Norway	119.6	12
Denmark	118.9	13
Spain	118.8	14
Scotland	118.3	15
New Zealand	118.1	16
Finland	117.3	17
Ireland	116.2	18
Belgium	115.2	19
Wales	114.5	20
Portugal	111.4	21
Brazil	107.7	22
Russia	105.7	23
China	105.2	24
Singapore	104.5	25
India	103.3	26
Mexico	103.2	27
Poland	102.5	28
Egypt	102.1	29
South Korea	101.6	30
South Africa	98.3	31
Malaysia	98.0	32
Turkey	96.9	33
Estonia	96.0	34
Lithuania	95.7	35
Latvia	95.5	36

THE MEXICO MODEL

Let's look at one country as an illustrator of branding enhancement – Mexico. Mexico already has a strong brand identity. But is it the brand that incorporates the values seen by the country's most farsighted leaders?

Interestingly, Edelman has been privileged to work on tourism and inward investment with various administrations in Mexico over the years, so I have a firsthand understanding of the amazing qualities of this country, including the "spirit" of its people, its rich pre and post Columbian cultural heritage, its spectacular geography and its huge economic potential.

When preparing to promote Mexico tourism in the US and Canada in 1998, we conducted some research among consumers with interesting but unsettling results: most of the people surveyed had a positive image of Mexico and the actual intent to travel there, yet when asked where they would like to travel to, they invariably mentioned other countries – Britain, France and Spain, as well as some Caribbean destinations – as their top choice. This has changed dramatically in the past five years, in tourism and other aspects. Millions of people visit the country every year, generating revenues that compete favorably with income from oil and, more recently, from the remittances Mexican immigrants send from abroad.

Between 1998 and 2003 Mexico received almost one quarter of all inward investment in Latin America, not only from the US, Canada and Europe, but also from Asian countries, especially Japan and Korea. Tequila and Mexican beer and food have become staples in most developed countries, and many Mexican companies have expanded internationally, some of them beyond their natural markets in Latin America, the South-Western US and Spain.

How has this impacted perceptions about Mexico? It appears that the accumulation of positive impressions about Mexico has yet to crystallize in a coherent brand perception of the country as a source for quality products and culture, as a premium place to invest and do business, and as a tourism destination.

A possible explanation is that, while many brands and institutions have increased their presence abroad, they have done so separately, with successful yet diverging strategies. The tourism industry has already taken steps to correct this situation, coordinating the efforts on national promotion and the promotion of individual destinations under a single brand umbrella. While it can still be improved, this initiative, which involves the private sector and all three levels of government – national, state and local – can serve as a focal point to add communications of other sectors in a coordinated effort.

The recent "Beyond Your Expectations" theme of the tourism campaign is true not only to the foreigners' experience of the country, but to how many Mexicans perceive themselves. As such, it captures the spirit of the country and still forms a platform for change, with so many Mexicans wishing to take the country beyond their own expectations. And it is certainly applicable to exports and inward investment, for the world to perceive the country as the ninth largest economy, the home of powerful companies, the supplier of quality goods and manufactures to the largest number of commercial partners any country has in the world.

Coordinating the efforts of the public and private sectors, of institutions, companies and commercial brands, and of the increasing number of individuals that represent Mexico abroad in culture, science and sports, is not easy. But it is desirable, possible and – most importantly – it could be the most rewarding next step.

7

The boring business of B2B

For many people in marketing communications, being assigned to work in a business to business company (or for agency people, a B2B client) is the equivalent of banishment to Siberia.

Goodbye to branding excitement, creativity, fame, recognition, riches, generous budgets and fun.

Hello to anonymity, a club whose members talk about nerdish principles, pricing, process, best price, volume and loyalty, discounts, and where brands are blackballed.

Nothing is further from reality in the 21st century. In fact, the importance and huge size of the B2B market mean that it is fertile territory for those who understand branding and reputation and have strong communication skills which can be transferred from the area of consumer products marketing. Businesses selling to each other have a huge appetite for the kind of creativity that they see being routinely applied in the consumer sector.

The value of branding (and in the brand hierarchy, the corporate brand itself) is recognized as a matter of course in the many corporations that sell to consumers (B2C), to businesses or professional users (B2B), and the government (B2G). (For many corporations the government is the biggest single customer for their products or services.)

For example, SC Johnson & Son has a large unit that sells industrial quantities of its cleaning products to professionals for use in schools, hospitals, offices, and so on. Kimberly-Clark sells its Kleenex brand and other products for use in hospitals, doctors' offices, and factory and office restrooms. While consumers may know General Electric (GE) for its light bulbs, cookers and home electrical equipment, the majority of the company's sales are from its power, engine, medical equipment and other divisions to industrial companies, utilities and governments.

More than in most other lines of business, in B2B the creation of a strong corporate brand flows in a straight line to benefit the marketing of products and services. Corporate brand benefits trickle down.

Of course, the dynamics of B2B vary with the industry but, more importantly, with the size of the target business. This might be minute when compared with the selling organization.

For instance, American Express, UPS and AT&T, each among the world's largest corporations, have identified small and medium sized businesses (SMBs) as key customer groups and develop special marketing programs geared directly to this group of entrepreneurs which, when taken together, account for a very large and, usually, growing segment of most markets around the world.

At the same time, Fuji Film has identified the discrete and growing market of "home office" proprietors as a major potential source of revenue for its products. The growth of high speed internet connections has empowered millions of people to establish enterprises in their homes and thus they have need to access a wide range of business products for the first time. In many cases these are consumer products which have been enhanced and adapted for use in business. For example, American Express, Visa, and MasterCard all offer a range of special "business" finance cards with features designed to meet the needs of a range of business people from the sole proprietor to the multi-brand, multinational corporation.

The "pathway to purchase" as I call the process by which B2B corporations win and retain both very small and very large customers is basically the same. The main difference is that with a sole proprietor of a small or medium sized business, the selection and decision-making process is concentrated in a single person. In a big corporation major purchase decisions are undertaken in a series of steps. Each of these could involve a number of different people who might have predetermined attitudes to the brand. This can be seen in Figure 7.1.

In the case of a small company, all steps are concentrated in a single person who stands on the bridge between acting like a private consumer on one side and a business manager on the other.

Companies that succeed with this small-business-owner audience invariably do so by ensuring their brand has appeal to both sides – commercial and personal.

All B2B corporations that have successfully established themselves as brands have done so with very clear goals in mind. They understand:

■ First, that brands can earn loyalty. This can help win a price premium, ensure "automatic" renewal of contract or repeat purchase and save money by reducing the need for constant reselling.

- Second, it differentiates a corporation and product when prices are equal or the field is commoditized.
- Third, it allows a relationship to be established in which you can transform your corporation's status from vendor to partner of your client or customer. This really is the holy grail of all business marketing strategy.

Let us examine in some more detail the elements hidden in each of the stages along the pathway to purchase.

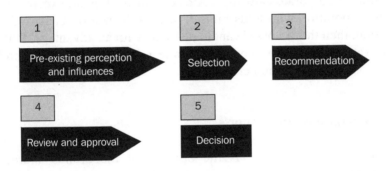

Figure 7.1 Pathway to purchase

STAGE 1: PRE-EXISTING PERCEPTION AND INFLUENCES

Every potential customer or client has been subjected to influences or messages that have shaped his perception of a product or corporation. This might be inaccurate or vague or perhaps based on input from only one source. It might be negative, neutral or positive. It might be strong and front of mind or barely perceptible because there has been no reason until now to know or care about the corporation.

Here are some of the main influences that will have shaped the latent perception of your target customer – or other stakeholder – as you start out on the pathway that you hope will have a favorable outcome.

The relationship experience

A major influence to the latent perception of your corporate brand is any previous experience gained via a relationship the customer may have had with your organization. This need not be as contradictory as it seems. Although on this particular pathway the target is a potential *new* customer, he might have had a previous experience with another company, or with another division of your corporation. It could be that the target has an existing relationship with the brand as a private consumer. A private individual with a checking and savings account at Citibank and an American Express (Amex) charge card, will have pre-formed impressions of the master brand of each organization. If that individual decides to start or buy a firm and has a strong affinity with those two companies, he will probably open a business account at Citi and order a corporate card from Amex. And if he is an executive at a larger corporation who finds himself with influence on bank and card selection, then the "known" candidates start with an advantage. Perhaps there was once a direct vendor–customer relationship that was broken off for one reason or another.

Word of mouth or peer reports

Another potent influence is the opinion of the brands shared by colleagues, family and friends. The Trust Barometer survey conducted annually in several countries by Edelman, the world's largest inde-pendent PR firm, has found that the opinions of "people like you and me" are now the most powerful shapers of our perceptions and are more trusted than media, government, academics and other expert third parties (Figure 7.2).

Media echo

Both trade and general media will have had an important influence on the latent perception of the target. If the corporate brand has a high level and frequency of media coverage, this will be reflected in the target's latent perception even if he has not so far been directly involved in a relationship with the company. Awareness might be accompanied by a favorable/neutral or unfavorable rating depending on the tone of the media coverage.

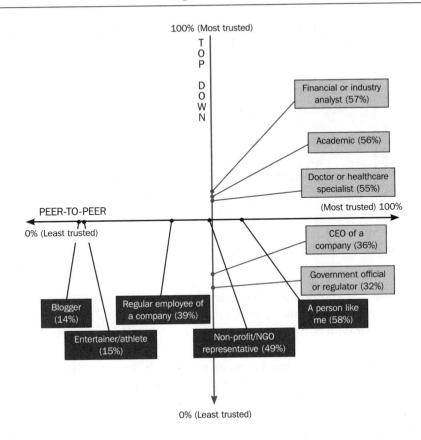

Figure 7.2 The trust barometer (Source: Edelman Trust Barometer Survey 2008)

Third parties and opinion forming elites (OFEs)

Every specialist field has its body of leading experts who are the well-spring of opinion which then cascades or trickles down, especially in businesses engaged in complex technology. Their views will have shaped the latent perception of the target most often through the media but sometimes directly via papers given at conferences, lectures, and so on.

Advertising

Paid media will augment the "free" media coverage mentioned earlier and will especially impact awareness if ad spending is high and targets are regularly "touched" by them, even if in a fleeting way. It is a mistake to underestimate the power of simple repetition in creating awareness of a brand.

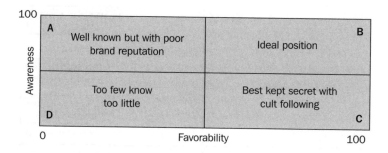

Figure 7.3 Corporate brand position

Figure 7.3 shows three possible starting points of B2B companies seeking to establish a strong brand reputation that will help all operations, in particular with customers/clients:

- Company A is in the most difficult position. It is extremely well known but held in poor esteem by most people. To reach the ideal position B, it has the uphill task of changing the existing or latent perceptions held by the majority of its targets.
- Company B may seem to be sitting pretty and indeed it is in an ideal position of being widely known and universally loved. But as all brand leading icons know, it is a daily task to retain that hard-won position against energetic and innovative competitors and by those who take pleasure and pride in finding and publicizing any problem or weakness in the iconic corporation's conduct of its business. The protection of the corporate brand equity should be a task of a dedicated officer at the highest level of company management.
- Company C is in an enviable position. It is loved by those who know it, but that is a very small group. Its challenge is to extend its circle of admirers without compromising the service and quality elements that have contributed to its – limited – success to date.
- Company D is possibly in a more typical position. It is not very well known and its targets have no particular opinions about or feelings towards the company. Here the task is twofold: to reach a larger audience with the company story while educating it about the quality and benefits of its offerings.

GLOBAL CHARTING

Alas, one table or chart will seldom, if ever, suffice for the large, multinational corporation, or one aspiring to go global.

When Oz Nelson took the reins as chairman of United Parcel Service (UPS) in 1988, the company was still, 80 years after its foundation, essentially a US domestic package delivery service, with its own operations in neighboring Canada and Germany. In October 1988, Nelson, who had been investigating and then planning UPS's transition into a global player, announced the company's plans to acquire 20 local delivery companies in Asia and Europe as a first step on the road to becoming the world's leading company in its field.

A chart in 1988 would have shown quite different pictures in the USA and the "new" markets UPS intended to enter.

In the USA research consistently showed that there was 99 percent awareness of UPS. Favorability was strong but in need of work. Americans had a lagging knowledge of UPS's increasingly fast service, its investment in technology and its expanding fleet of jet aircraft. In the "new" markets UPS was completely unknown and in the position of Company D on the chart. With this knowledge, UPS implemented a dual market and communications strategy to make its target stakeholders both inside and outside the USA better informed about UPS and more favorably disposed to the brand.

In the USA the company would capitalize on its universal recognition but undertake communications to educate business customers about its $5 billion investment in technology and aircraft, its ever-faster delivery service and its wider service offerings to cover more of the needs of its customers.

In the new markets different strategies were needed to introduce UPS to wary potential first time users, a hard task in markets where there were existing local or international service providers.

One hurdle UPS had to leap was the belief on the part of customers in Europe that a newcomer would have insufficient understanding and ability to respond to the special local conditions of the market – a concern that existing local suppliers were eager to stimulate.

UPS decided to adopt a strategy to accelerate the achievement of a "local" image by arranging a major defining activity. They launched the UPS Europe Business Monitor, which surveyed the opinions of a wide selection of CEOs and chief financial officers (CFOs) of corporations in each of the major markets, seeking their views on prospects for business in the year ahead and on issues that would affect them, positively or negatively. The responses received not only gave UPS executives a privi-leged window into the concerns of companies they hoped would become customers, it also gave them the opportunity to communicate how much they knew about local conditions and to show they could be a strong ally for local companies in a fast-globalizing world.

This single initiative had other practical benefits. The results of the survey were unveiled at a video conference, chaired by a former French prime minister, that was beamed to customers and media gathered in key cities. Sales representatives were armed with UPS Europe Business Monitor presentations for use at a series of events in key European cities, which were heavily attended by prospective customers who would not have accepted the idea of a simple sales presentation from UPS. In fact, when it came time to recommit to the next phase of surveys, it was the UPS business develop-ment people who were the strongest advocates for continuing.

The Business Barometer project is now in its 15th year. From Europe it has expanded and there are now UPS Business Barometers in Asia, Latin America, Canada and the USA and it is an integral component of the UPS corporate brand.

STAGE 2: SELECTION

Recognition

Brand awareness and a reasonable favorability rating are an essential start-ing point if you wish to be considered as a vendor/partner by the prospec-tive customer/client. The most galling thing that you will hear when you find out that your company was not even invited to bid on a contract or engagement is the response: "Oh! I didn't know you did that." It is bad business for your company not to be known at all but it is almost as bad for there to be big gaps in customers' awareness of the full range of your offerings. These are no doubt constantly changing and improving. Aware-ness is the ticket price of entry to the game or contest.

Once your company is "on the list" and under consideration, the favor-ability rating of your brand comes into play and will have an important bearing on the outcome. The favorability score will set the scene for an often complex selection process driven by the brand association (Table 7.1). Anderson and Carpenter[1] write:

As a result of a successful positioning, placing a brand within an exist-ing hierarchy, and implementation, brands become endowed with value.

Brands are intellectual assets – the thoughts, feelings, and images that a brand evokes in customers' minds. Brand value, or *brand equity*, is derived from the impact that those thoughts, feelings, and associations have on customers' behavior and, ultimately, their purchases. Brand associations can be divided into three categories: Superordinate, Focal and Subordinate.

Table 7.1 Brand association hierarchy

Superordinate	The emotional connection, which is critical in brand choice. Links the brands through history of use, to lifestyle, aspiration to join a select group, or "club". The most powerful of the brand associations because it can encompass or trump the next two.
Focal	These associations define the brand and describe the most obvious brand attributes, for example "ease of use", "low maintenance", "good service", "best value for money".
Subordinate	When combined, a host of smaller and less significant brand associations that are often cosmetic (color, shape, sound) can all add to the brand aura but can easily be imitated.

When an actual contract or engagement is being bid for, the brand associations described will be harmonized with a number of proximate considerations to affect the recommendation and decision. Often a checklist of required attributes will be prepared and scored by the person(s) responsible for making the selection. Typical of these will be:

- *Value proposition:* This is the price to be paid compared with the service or product.
- *Support and training:* What is being offered to ensure that the customer's employees are able to make best and full use of the product; and how much is this worth?
- *Updating:* Will there be regular updates/upgrades?
- *Service:* Will there be guarantees of swift service and minimal down time?
- *Delivery:* Is on time delivery guaranteed?
- *Finance:* Can the supplier arrange good financing terms, if needed?
- *Meets specifications:* A basic requirement is that the product/services offered should exactly meet the specifications set out by the customer.

All these sound prosaic but are closely related to the focal and subordinate associations. If lacking in any serious degree, the candidate company and its product will be ruled out of further consideration. If satisfactory, the superordinate associations will come into play and could well decide the outcome.

STAGE 3: RECOMMENDATION

In the case of sole proprietor or owner-managed smaller companies, the process leapfrogs Stages 3 and 4 and the selection stage is followed immediately by a decision; there is no need for further review and deliberation.

The third step in the path to purchase, when being conducted by a major, multi-layered organization, is that a recommendation is made by the person (or selection committee) assigned the task of identifying the company that best meets their needs and this is put forward to an executive committee or, sometimes in the case of major expenditures, the board of directors, for review and approval.

In most cases the recommendation, whether written or given verbally, will concentrate on the practical benefits and value proposition of selecting the recommended candidates. In fact it is not unusual for the selector studiously to avoid the less quantifiable brand associations because he will want to demonstrate that he has not been swayed by any irrelevant considerations.

Some recommendations might strongly advocate a single candidate. Others will produce a shortlist with a first, second and third choice.

STAGE 4: REVIEW AND APPROVAL

While the selection process will have been conducted in a large company by an expert individual or team with skills in such matters as technical performance or purchasing terms, the recommendation will probably be considered by an executive or sub-committee without that depth of knowledge. As a result the comfort and security of a well-known brand with a good reputation can influence the final decision, especially on big ticket items.

If the recommendation has a shortlist and the winner is a lesser known brand to the non-expert members of the selection committee, the final decision may be switched to the number two or three contender, if the brand is strong and offers a high degree of comfort, even though a price premium might be involved.

Never underestimate the motivation of avoiding blame in decision making. "Well, I opted for the most reliable brand" is something most of us would like to be able to say, when it seems in the longer run not to have been the best decision.

STAGE 5: DECISION

The final destination in the pathway to purchase is the decision that is taken. Your offering is selected or rejected. But this is not always as cut and dried as it may seem – especially on big ticket items involving perhaps a number of products, subcontractors and continuing provision of service, or even insourcing or outsourcing. Nothing is finally settled until contract signing. The buyer may want to haggle on price ("We want to go with you but one of your rivals is offering a much more attractive price. We'd like you to meet it"!), or ask for warranties on certain key delivery dates, penalties for failure to meet deadlines or specifications, and so on. This is where negotiating skills are paramount but it is also true that a power brand will have a better chance of standing firm than a Brand X.

OTHER BRAND BENEFITS

The foregoing focused on the mechanisms from marketing through sales and the added power of a strong brand in this process, which I have described as the pathway to purchase.

But the principles apply also to the establishment of relationships with other audiences which have the power to help or hinder the progress of the branded corporation.

An example might be government (perhaps both lawmakers and regulators) whose decisions could have a material impact on the company's ability to operate and succeed. It might be a slightly different pathway but the main stages will be similar and the standing of the brand will be helpful in reaching the desired destination.

SMALL AND MEDIUM SIZED BUSINESSES (SMBs)

In most countries around the world the economic importance of small business is now recognized and supported by government agencies or initiatives to encourage the growth of this sector.

This is true even in the USA, which many associate primarily with mega multinational corporations. The USA established its Small Business Administration (SBA) in 1953 and its efforts have gathered pace ever since.

The SBA[2] says that in 2007 alone it "backed more than $12.3 billion in loans to small businesses. More than $1 billion was made available for disaster loans and more than $40 billion in federal contracts were secured by small businesses with SBA's help."

The SBA goes on to say that "small business is where the innovations take place. Swifter, more flexible and often more daring than big businesses, small firms produce the items that line the shelves of America's museums, shops and homes. They keep intact the heritage of ingenuity and enterprise and they help keep the 'American Dream' within the reach of millions of Americans."

There is also a belief among politicians and economists in many countries that small businesses are the most important source of new jobs and employment. And, of course, when "fertilized" in this way many small businesses grow to become much larger enterprises.

In the case of a sole proprietor, all steps in the pathway to purchase are taken by a single person who starts with latent perceptions of the company and brand, who will make a selection, perhaps taking advice from external or peer sources, and will make the purchase decision.

Marketers of business-to-business services and products have caught on to the fact that this is not only a large market for their products but one that has particular needs. They have not only sought out ways in which they can help the small business owner run his business more efficiently but have developed and introduced products and services specifically tailored for this market. They aim to become the small business owner's partner, providing an array of back-office services and advice.

American Express (Amex), itself a global power brand that is near the top of every brand and "most admired" league tables, was one of the earliest companies to see the opportunity in the SMB market and devise a strategy to become an essential strategic partner for small business owners. Starting with a strong brand presence in travel and entertainment and with a deeply ingrained customer service culture, when the company made a concerted effort to enter the small business market in the late 1980s, the latent perception of people running small businesses was very favorable to American Express. For small businesses, often competing against larger competitors with deeper pockets and more resources, American Express was assured of a welcome, especially as it had researched the concerns and needs of its potential customers in advance.

Suddenly the Davids of the business world had an ally in their rivalry with the Goliaths.

What is more, American Express had accurately assessed the schizophrenia of its small business customer base. Business owners were also personal customers, many of whom were existing Amex card holders. For many there was a blurred line separating business and personal finance.

With the launch of American Express OPEN in 2002, the company enhanced the products and services it offered business owners and fulfilled the need of small business owners to manage their business and private accounts efficiently. And the system was kept simple and easily accessible. Customer feedback was encouraged so that there has been a stream of constant enhancements and new services on offer.

Loyalty to the card is encouraged by the Membership Rewards program where a percentage of expenditures earn points which can be exchanged for travel or other goods. An attraction for small business owners who have two Amex cards, one for business and the other for personal expenses, is that the rewards from each can be combined to purchase rewards.

Amex has also negotiated discounts with suppliers providing services that are much used by SMBs – FedEx, Hertz car rental and Flowers.com are examples.

Although American Express had historically been a charge card with no spending limit (the account balance must be paid in full every month), in 1987 it recognized the needs of business and personal customers to have a more flexible means of managing cash flow and making investments in equipment and other improvements. So, a credit card was introduced which also protected the Amex franchise from inroads being made by VISA and MasterCard. A facility was also introduced allowing charge card holders to extend monthly payments over a period.

Equally important in conquering this market is that Amex has worked hard to take the agony out of managing and monitoring spending for the small business manager. This is based on a simple but fast way of paying bills and the option of downloading statement data straight into Quick-Books and other accounting systems.

American Express has used its power to become a – maybe even *the* – leading brand in the small business arena by surrounding its customers with an array of services and options. It is seen by many of its users as an essential partner rather than an interchangeable vendor.

Notes

1   *Kellogg on Branding: The Marketing Faculty of The Kellogg School of Management* (9780471690160/0471690163), pp. 181–218 edited by Alice M. Tybout and Tim Calkins. Copyright © 2005 Alice M. Tybout and Tim Calkins. Reproduced with permission of John Wiley & Sons, Inc.
2   See www.sba.org.

8

Professional service firms

Professional service firms have emerged from their cosy, clubbable and protected past into the bright sunlight of 21st century global free trade. The most successful practitioners have understood the importance of branding to their continuing success. Most practice principally in the arena of business to business: accountants and auditors, management consultants and lawyers all now rely on business clients for the lion's share of their revenues, as also do advertising and PR agencies, architects and even branding consultants. Others, medical practices among them, are still primarily engaged in relationships with individual consumers.

First let's look at the characteristics of any pursuit that lays claim to the description "profession" and which have traditionally described individuals and groups of practitioners. Professions are:

- *Vocational:* most people entering the traditional or learned professions do so as a calling.
- *Self-governing:* the professions of medicine, law, the church, teaching and the military are marked out from other pursuits in that they have traditionally been allowed to set standards of practice and behavior and to police and judge those who are admitted to membership. They are also responsible for training and examination, the accumulation of a body of knowledge and much else besides. Although ultimately subject to the law of the land, these professions are allowed in most cases to judge their own. To be disbarred, cashiered, defrocked, or suspended from medical practice, means not only disgrace but possible penury.
- *Competent, expert and qualified:* a professional is expected to be competent and expert in his craft and to have achieved a professional qualification. In this sense the word is used equally to describe a good plumber or doctor. In addition to an educational qualification, there is

also a period of articles/indenture/apprenticeship (on-the-job training) required before qualification.

- *For reward or payment:* in this sense a professional is contrasted with an amateur as a matter of factual distinction. Nowadays, however, the contrast is often used pejoratively with the suggestion that amateur signifies a lack of competence. In this sense, for example "she approached the matter in a very professional way", the word might be a synonym for "businesslike" and "thoughtful."
- *Principled:* this is another synonym (perhaps incorrectly used) by some wanting to emphasize the ethical component of professionalism (such as in the phrase: "First, do no harm").

The quest for commercial success in the law firms, accounting practices, hospitals and medical practices of the USA, UK and many other countries has made them indistinguishable from profit-driven industrial corporations. In most cases, the restrictions that marked out the professional partnership from the commercial enterprise have been removed. These involved a ban on advertising, PR and marketing; poaching clients was frowned upon.

Most professions are in the throes of a titanic struggle to hold on to key traditional elements of professionalism as they adjust to the changes taking place. Not always with success.

The established professions have been on the retreat, losing respect and trust as well as some of their traditional rights to be self-regulating. The Enron, Andersen, WorldCom, ABB, Vivendi and other corporate scandals have spurred lawmakers in the USA and other countries to pass new laws and regulations because they do not believe in the willingness or ability of the professional accounting firms to put their own houses in order.

CHANGING WINDS

The professions have been shaken out of their comfort zones in recent years by changing winds. Those that could foresee the direction of those winds have filled their sails and been successful. Those that did not or sought to defy the weather have had a difficult voyage and many have ended shipwrecked.

Among these winds was globalization, which posed great difficulties for most professions because they are intrinsically local. Law and medicine, for example, require practitioners to be licensed locally when they move from one country to another – their qualifications are not always portable.

And as industry and commerce have globalized at a rapid pace, professional service firms have had to extend their international footprints in order to keep their relationships. The most farsighted, of course, planned their international expansion in step with their clients, or even ahead of them to gain a competitive advantage.

The globalizing economy called for capital investment on a scale that was not available to most professional service firms. In the first place the traditional structure was that of a partnership in which each partner had to raise sufficient capital to cover his share of expansion and not all partners in professional firms agreed with the concept or need for global expansion. Many were frightened by the risk involved.

Along with globalization, the professions (especially the ancient ones) were under closer scrutiny. An increasingly well-educated and activist public meant that the behind-closed-doors self-regulation procedures of the past were called into question. In societies that were becoming increasingly litigious (America, the UK and Australia deserve special mention) insurance premiums to cover against malpractice claims of various kinds have grown so big so fast that some doctors, for example, have given up practice.

As a result, most partnerships have been converted into hybrid partnership/limited liability company structures that offer individuals some protection of their personal assets in the event of the failure of their firms.

For the rest of this chapter we will narrow the focus of professional service firms to auditing, management consulting and law firms so that we can examine in some greater detail the six building blocks that form a brand identity in this sector.

- **Personal relationships**: As important as it is for any brand to build personal relationships with its stakeholders, it is the foundation on which professional service brands are built. Recommendations and endorsements by trusted advisers and peers fuel the growth of the business and relationships that are correctly nurtured are at the heart of client retention. It is usually much more expensive to replace a lost client than to keep it.
- **Background:** It is a characteristic of most successful professional service firms that they are homogeneous. Not only has it been historically customary for a son or daughter to follow a parent into a family firm but this has continued even with the many amalgamations that have absorbed small local or regional firms into the large global giants. It is also common for firms to recruit talent from a limited number of universities and through a network that is a reflection of the firm's leadership. This goes a long way to defining the character of the firm's brand.

- **Expertise:** Today's professional service firms are multidisciplinary organizations of some complexity. All strive to be the "victor ludorum" and some even to be considered best in each specialty but that is seldom the case. Each firm is invariably partially trapped in its history. In the case of accounting firms, this might mean one is known as the best in class for audit, another for tax. The matrix becomes even more complex when overlaid on a map of the world; in spite of all valiant attempts to replicate strengths globally it is extremely difficult to do this with organizations that are constantly growing through acquisitions. Thus it is not unusual for the profile of a firm's office in, say, Boston to be different to the branch in Bangkok or Budapest, at least for a period of adjustment.
- **Consensus culture:** Although professional service firms have their fair share of larger than life figures who carry huge amounts of revenue based on their talents, successes and personalities, the great global firms have had to work within a consensus culture that would irritate most CEOs of industrial organizations. Every significant proposal for, say, the opening of an overseas office or a merger has to be carefully weighed because the executives are also the owners of the firm. Each decision might mean that several thousand partners have a vote on whether to forgo income in the short term in order to realize the fulfillment of a strategy and a payout in the long term. This calls for deliberate and careful planning and strong diplomatic skills on the part of the leadership. But once a decision is made it often results in a staff that is more committed to building and living the brand (even if brand terminology was not used in making the case for the investment) and provides the firm with a team of brand ambassadors.
- **Success:** Success in the management of its own affairs, the prominence of its leadership within the profession and success on behalf of its clients is a vital brand attribute.
- **Reflected reputation**: Just as clients want to be with the winners, they are also eager to come under the reputational umbrella of a highly regarded professional service firm. The most reputable clients seek to ensure that they do not associate with professional advisers that might cause them damage. Other companies trying thoroughly to improve all aspects of their business operations rightly believe that they will not only get practical help but will also gain reflected reputational advantage by engaging the finest firms. Of course, a fine reputation and strong brand can be the targets for companies that have no intention of changing their questionable practices but are merely seeking to hide behind an impeccable front and are willing to pay a high price for that service. This is where the tensions can be seen between the standards of the old

professional codes (to be rejected by one was to be rejected by all) and the new commercialism in which annual revenue targets must be met. There is great pressure to ensure that juicy fees do not end up at a rival. A strong sense of brand value helps in such situations as does a memory that can recall the demise of the great global accounting firm of Andersen. Groucho Marx summed it up with his quip that he would not want to join any club that would have him as a member.

Each of the groups of professional service firms is confronted by a particular set of circumstances that affect global branding considerations for individual firms and the sector as a whole. Nowhere is this more evident than in the accounting sector.

ACCOUNTING

Accounting firms were early entrants into global branding and it is not hard to see why. As industrial and commercial enterprises started to internationalize their operations they needed help to understand the financial regulations and customs of the new markets they were entering and they expected this help to come from their trusted internal and external advisers. Now, while it might be good business practice to adapt some company policies and procedures to accommodate local customs, the most tangible outcome of the auditors' work is the annual report and accounts. This, by definition, is a single, unchanged document whether it is being read in San Francisco, Stockholm or Shanghai. The early pioneer firms were happy to oblige but first they themselves had to find expert resources in all the key markets around the world which had the skills to act as local partners. In a gross oversimplification, this was done by creating a unified globally licensed brand name. Local firms of sufficient quality and resources were recruited to join a federation of firms which had the rights to use the name and to provide seamless service to each other's clients. It is a remarkable model that has worked brilliantly for decades and led to the creation of four great firms (known by some wags as "the final four") as well as a number of second tier firms that also offer worldwide service. The big four brands are PricewaterhouseCoopers, Ernst & Young, Deloitte and KPMG.

Accounting firms are the only professional service organizations that made it into the Brand Finance 500 rankings for 2007. The clear leader of the "big four" is PWC (PricewaterhouseCoopers) which comes in at 98. The details are as follows in US$M:

Enterprise Value $71,366   Position 98
Brand Value $7,850   Brand Score/Rating 90/AAA+

For most people, most of the time, the assumption is made that each of
these firms has a structure and operates much like a multinational industrial
company. That is far from the reality. In fact, in their case "brand" might be
a more exact term than "firm" because each comprises a number of independent firms that have agreed to maintain certain standards, use uniform
methodologies, share clients and pool knowledge for mutual benefit under
a distinctive name and design. Each remains a separate legal entity, has its
own management in each country, with its own partner income and profit
pool. It has to operate within the laws of the local jurisdiction, and its clients'
financial transactions and reports are governed by local national regulators.

While the umbrella brand can be managed for the most part, it is now
increasingly coming under strain. The accounting firms have so far benefited from the bifurcated structure – global brand on the one hand and a
collection of private local partnerships on the other. In litigation, the big
four stress their local autonomous structures to militate against massive
liabilities and damages being imposed on the global enterprise. But where
the proactive marketing of their resources to clients is concerned, they
adopt the posture of unified brands. It will be interesting to see if this
ambiguous position can be maintained in the future.

The federated structure remains in place in spite of the fact that for
many years the leaderships of the firms that now make up the "big four"
have been trying to move from the federated model to that of something
approximating a single corporation. But certain barriers have stood in their
way, which have so far proved insurmountable.

LAW FIRMS

Law firms face many of the same considerations as accounting firms, only
for them the tension between operating locally and globally is even greater.
Except in certain areas where international or regional legal conventions
apply – maritime law and the laws agreed between members of the European
Community are examples – local laws trump international. In deference to
the globalizing economy and in response to clients with global interests,
some major national law firms in Europe and the USA have sought to build
confederations along the lines of the accounting firms, assembling a group
of sizeable firms in each of the main world markets under a single banner.

But the best description for all but one of the world's major law firms would be "multi local". They might be power brands in their own countries but the value of the franchise diminishes beyond the national border.

The exception, Clifford Chance, has made a bold effort to become a global firm or brand. A legal powerhouse in its own home market of the UK with thriving practices in Europe, the Middle East and Asia, it knew that it could not complete the jigsaw or claim to be global without stronger representation in the all-important market of the USA. In 2000 it took the bold and risky step of concluding a merger of its small American practice with the well-established New York and Washington DC firm of Rogers and Wells which would operate under the Clifford Chance name. This catapulted Clifford Chance into position as the world's largest law firm, and ensured that its progress would be examined under a magnifying glass.

In the drive to conclude the merger deal Clifford Chance probably underestimated the degree of culture clash that would emerge as it set about bringing cohesion between the American firm and its British head-quartered parent. First, Clifford Chance had to deal with powerful person-alities with name brand equity to rival the company they worked for. Second it was also looking to harmonize the reward structure between the USA, UK and other offices. This presented a culture –and cash – challenge because the American reward system favored star power and was based on the principle of "you eat what you kill". The British model, which had taken the company to its pinnacle of success, rewarded its lawyers on the "lock step" principle and leaned towards a sharing of rewards. Thus it is not surprising that the merger was followed by a number of defections of well-known lawyers based in the USA who foresaw a diminished personal income. But damaging as these were, Clifford Chance was not deflected from its goal of creating a single global firm and in this quest its strongest single allies were its clients, who needed a global law firm with multi–local capability to serve their needs. What's more, the hard won reputation secured new engagements from corporations seeking the kind of global representation not readily available from law firms that, perhaps, were too focused on their own desires rather than those of their clients.

In recent rankings Clifford Chance retained its position as the world's largest law firm, measured by revenue. In legal trade publication *The Lawyer*'s (sister publication to *The American Lawyer*) 2007 Global 100 index of international law firms, Clifford Chance occupied top spot with $2.2 billion in revenue (Table 8.1). Second place Linklaters came in some way below with roughly $2 billion. Although the gap between the two has shrunk slightly in recent years, Clifford Chance has clearly consolidated its first transatlantic mover advantage and preserved its position as the leading international law firm. Completing the top ten firms in the index are Skadden Arps Slate Meagher & Flom, Freshfields Bruckhaus Deringer, Latham & Watkins, Baker & Mckenzie, Allen & Overy, Jones Day, Sidley Austin and White & Case.

Table 8.1 Top ten law firms by revenue, 2007 (Source: *The American Lawyer/Legal Week*)

Rank	Firm	Revenue ($bn)
1	Clifford Chance	$2.20
2	Linklaters	$2.07
3	Skadden Arps Slate Meagher & Flom	$1.85
4	Baker & McKenzie	$1.83
5	Freshfields Bruckhaus Deringer	$1.82
6	Allen & Overy	$1.64
7	Latham & Watkins	$1.62
8	Jones Day	$1.31
9	Sidley Austin	$1.25
10	White & Case	$1.19

MANAGEMENT CONSULTING

In no other field of professional service does a single brand occupy the unique position of McKinsey & Company in management consulting, where it is the clear leader. Such is its renown that in every other field of professional service, firms seek to emulate its achievement. It is not unusual to read in the Objectives section of the strategy documents of other professional service companies a simple statement that runs as follows:

To become the McKinsey of … (fill in name of the profession)

In this statement of brand power much is implied without the need for further clarification: that a perfect virtuous circle has been established in which the brand attracts the best recruits, trains and rewards them well; they do excellent work for clients who recommend the firm to others, further strengthening the brand. If, as in the case of McKinsey, the firm is credited with having created and shaped a sector of expertise and has established itself as a market leader, the cycle becomes one of continuous reinforcement.

McKinsey is also an "academy" whose alumni populate the C-suites of many of the world's larges corporations, thus forming another charmed circle. Today, McKinsey claims that 70 percent of *Fortune*'s Most Admired companies are among its clients.

Having reached its position of preeminence, the firm's challenge is to hold its position as the substantive current thought leader in its field. McKinsey does this through two main instruments. The first is its magazine the *McKinsey Quarterly* which has a reputation to equal that of the *Harvard Business Review*. The second is the McKinsey Global Institute, a research establishment that studies global issues and business trends, issuing reports that are valuable to the firm's clients and other stakeholders and a major resource for its consultants.

The McKinsey "brand" is shaped by the culture of the company, which in turn has been created out of the deeply held values of the firm, which have endured through eight decades and ten managing partners, including Ian Davis, the current incumbent. These values are enshrined in the McKinsey credo (Exhibit 8.1) that the firm will succeed if its clients are successful.

Exhibit 8.1 The McKinsey credo (Source: *mckinsey.com/about us/what we believe*)

McKinsey partners and employees must:

- **Put the client's interests ahead of our own.**
  This means we deliver more value than expected. It doesn't mean doing whatever the client asks.

- **Behave as professionals.**
  Uphold absolute integrity. Show respect to local custom and culture, as long as we don't compromise our integrity.

- **Keep our client information confidential.**
  We don't reveal sensitive information. We don't promote our own good work. We focus on making our clients successful.

- **Tell the truth as we see it.**
  We stay independent and able to disagree, regardless of the popularity of our views or their effect on our fees. We have the courage to invent and champion unconventional solutions to problems. We do this to help build internal support, get to real issues, and reach practical recommendations.

- **Deliver the best of our firm to every client as cost effectively as we can.**
  We expect that our people spend clients' and our firm's resources as if their own resources were at stake.

We believe in the power of one firm. We maintain consistently high standards for service and people so that we can always bring the best team of minds from around the world – with the broadest range of industry and functional experience – to bear on every engagement.

No one could accuse McKinsey consultants of humility but nor are they given to overt self-promotion. In this regard the firm is redolent of the more reserved view of publicity that prevailed among professional firms in earlier generations.

Management consulting boasts many outstanding firms with global reputations – Booz Allen Hamilton, Boston Consulting Group and others – but the fact that McKinsey has been able to keep clear water between itself and its rivals is testimony to the fact that brand behavior is more important than brand publicity.

9
Not-for-profits

The world was initially skeptical when the first Edelman Trust Barometer in 2001 reported that the corporations that were at the top of most previously published brand rankings were outperformed by some of the best-known non-governmental organizations (NGOs). In Europe, Oxfam, Amnesty International, Greenpeace and World Wildlife Fund were in the top ten list of most trusted names, along with Microsoft and Coca-Cola.

How could this be?

The answer is simple. First, the criterion for measurement in most published lists, for example the Interbrand/*BusinessWeek* rankings, would automatically exclude NGOs from consideration. They do not meet the financial criteria. Second, other than those directly connected to these organizations, no one thought it of importance. NGOs were considered either a nuisance that got in the way of conducting business or organizations with worthy goals deserving support but, please, without too much commitment of time or thought.

The broad classification of not-for-profit (NFP) covers a wide array of organizations: narrowly focused (MS, cancer research, war injured, mosquito nets against malaria), very local (United Way/Community Chests, local hospital or children's home) or regional and global (Amnesty International, International Red Cross and Red Crescent, Doctors Without Borders/Médecins Sans Frontières, Greenpeace). Some are simply charities with strict articles of association forbidding any deviation from a strictly non-partisan agenda (WWF, Red Cross, Save the Children). Others have a goal of social change (Greenpeace, PETA). At the extreme there are those activist organizations that seek to influence the political agenda.

Although published brand rankings may have excluded NGOs, they have long been recognized and thoroughly studied as brands by Young & Rubicam Brands (Y&R). This global marketing communications company has over the past 15 years developed and refined a methodology and reservoir of brand knowledge in a division called BrandAsset® Consulting™ run by Ed Lebar, which maintains and updates a global database of brands and their performance year by year. Their database contains a number of leading names from the not-for-profit universe.

However, not until Edelman's study of opinion leaders in several countries, were NGOs thought of as "brands" – brands that were very often in competition with corporations for the support of stakeholders, including customers.

Now that it had become measurably apparent that many NGOs were more trusted than some of the most powerful corporate brands, the thinking began to change in the C-suites of companies around the world. Strategies began to change. Instead of adopting an arrogant stance and ignoring a combative NGO some corporations initiated dialog. Where the game plan had been to question, criticize and destroy the reputation of an NGO, it was replaced by a policy of engagement. Adversaries became, in some instances, partners.

Some examples of this change are described in Chapter 15, on corporate social responsibility, but in this section we will examine how NGOs have become global mega brands (and many others have achieved the position of leading brands in their own countries).

For a closer look at popular attitudes we will return to Y&R's Brand Asset Valuator which for 15 years has been following more than 35,000 brands in 48 countries with 500,000 respondents. Among these are not-for-profit brands.

The BAV model is based on the concept that every brand has four pillars – Energized Differentiation, Relevance, Esteem and Knowledge.

Figures 9.1 and 9.2 show how the pillar patterns can drive brand acceptance and purchase which BAV then divides into leading factors that impact the future (Energized Differentiation and Relevance) and lagging factors that drive current performance (Esteem and Knowledge). The natural conclusion is that working on Energized Differentiation and Relevance will be the most effective way of strengthening the brand and this combination is described as "brand energy". Esteem and Knowledge combine to define "brand stature".

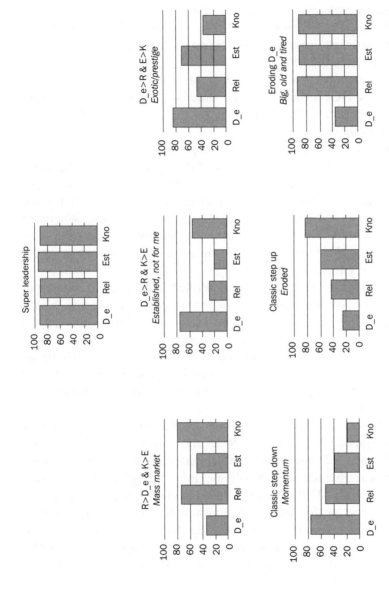

Figure 9.1 Stages of brand development (Source: Courtesy of BrandAsset® Consulting™/Young & Rubicam Brands)

Brand Strength

The brand has captured attention and interest and can build relevance and penetration. This often reflects a new, noteworthy, niche or luxury brand. This condition also suggests the brand has more creativity than functionality.

D^E >R — REL

Examples:
iPhone
Mini
Innocent
Rolls-Royce
Guitar Hero

High levels reinforce the brand is relevant and energized. It is a leader, commanding high margins as well as volume.

D^E R — REL

Examples:
Disney
Google
Nike
Sony
Microsoft

The brand's uniqueness has faded and price or convenience becomes a dominant reason to buy. The brand faces commoditization. This opposite condition indicates the brand is overloaded with rational meaning and low on creativity.

D^E <R — REL

Examples:
Wal-Mart
Exxon
Hanes
Tylenol
U.S. Postal Service

Brand Stature

The brand is liked but not well-known. Consumers are curious and there's a desire to find out more. The difference in the two pillars measures the real love for the brand.

E >K — EST KNO

Examples:
Trader Joes
Coach
Cole Haan
Uni-ball
GlaxoSmithKline

The brand is both well-known and well-regarded. Brand has successfully established itself in the hearts and minds of consumers.

E K — EST KNO

Examples:
Home Depot
VISA
Coca-Cola
McDonald's
Ford

The brand is better known than liked. It has become too familiar and consumers are likely looking for better options. The quantitative difference in these two pillars measures the distaste for the brand.

E <K — EST KNO

Examples:
Spam
Slim Fast
Marlboro
Playboy
Lucky Charms

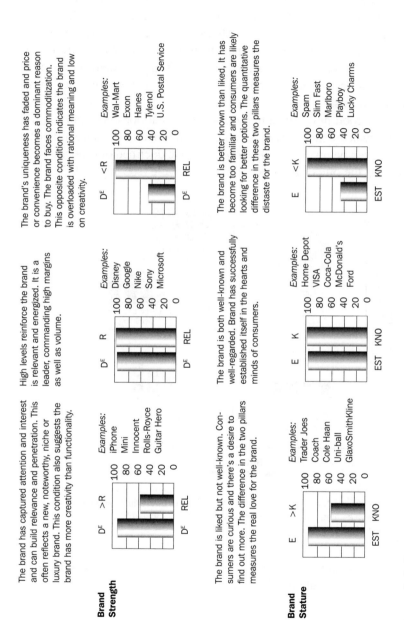

Figure 9.2 The relationship between each pillar tells a different story in the brand's development (Source: Courtesy of BrandAsset® Consulting™/Young & Rubicam Brands)

Every product and corporate brand has a life cycle and the BAV Model for Brand Diagnosis provides a dramatic visual depiction of the current state of health of a brand based on the assessment of the four pillars. The goal, of course, as with most quadrants of this kind, is to drive towards a position in the top right hand corner. In this case however, calibration must be delicate because it is a short distance from the ideal position on the way to, or at the pinnacle, and being on the way down or a declining brand in BAV terms.

But there is good news for a brand life cycle that does not apply to the humans who manage them. Brands can be maintained in a leadership position and can even be resuscitated when they have declined or eroded; there is no changing the outcome of the human life cycle (see Figure 9.3).

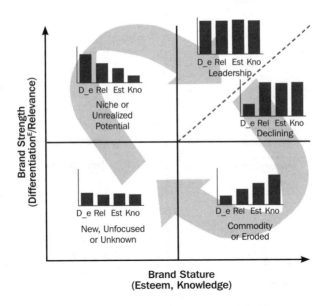

The life of a brand can often be plotted on the PowerGrid as Strength increases first, followed by Stature and eventually losing Strength and becoming Eroded

Figure 9.3 PowerGrid of brand life cycle (Source: Courtesy of BrandAsset® Consulting™/Young & Rubicam Brands)

In the case of charity organizations Brand Stature (the combination of Esteem and Knowledge) is of special importance. It has a major influence on people's preference, likelihood of donating to and loyalty to a particular organization. This should not be a particularly surprising finding except that BAV has data that shows in quite precise terms just how strong such bonds can be. After all, many of us may have experienced the benefit of the work of a charity on our own behalf, or on behalf of a relative or friend; or an NGO that is engaged in a pursuit with which we are in complete sympathy.

However, this is all the more reason for charities and NGOs to work hard on their Brand Energy if they are to push themselves up into the desired position or to arrest a decline.

BAV has detected some marked differences in the way men and women view charities. Figure 9.4 shows the results of a study conducted in the USA in 2005. Although many organizations are viewed in the same way by both groups, there are a few pronounced differences which will have been noted by the boards and executives of the charities concerned and should have led to a new branding or communications strategy.

While Doctors Without Borders, Habitat for Humanity and Ronald McDonald House can take momentary satisfaction from their strong showing among both men and women, UNICEF and the Salvation Army have a great deal of remedial work to do with men and women respectively if they are to gain their support and donations.

There are many factors that contribute to the brand of a not-for-profit that are not usually relevant in the case of businesses. While I was generally aware of this special situation, it was burned into my consciousness on a memorable occasion.

I was traveling from London to New York on a routine trip and had settled myself in, congratulating myself that I was the only occupant of a row of three seats in economy class. After we were prepared for the flight and ordered to fasten our seatbelts, a last minute passenger was allowed on board and led to my row of seats. He was no longer young but lean and fit and he vaulted over me to take the window seat. Any initial annoyance at the loss of my space and comfort evaporated as my travel companion and I got into conversation. He was James P. Grant, who for 22 years ran UNICEF. Using his passionate commitment to public service, his organizational skills, his unerring media-savvyness and his ability to charm global celebrities to donate their names, time and money to the cause, he had turned it from a small UN agency into perhaps the most important force for improvement in the condition of children around the world.

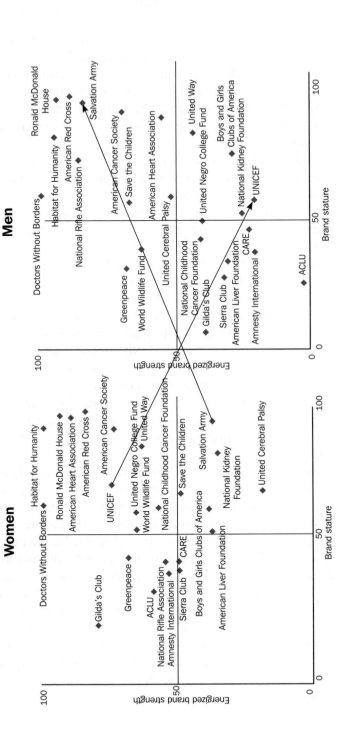

Figure 9.4 Gender support for charities (Source: Courtesy of BrandAsset® Consulting™/Young & Rubicam Brands)

Why, I asked, was he so late on the plane and sitting near me at the back in economy class?

He explained that he had just rushed from a globally televised celebration of UNICEF's 50th Anniversary, because he had a commitment next day in New York. And, yes, although British Airways, like most other major airlines, knew who he was and eagerly pressed him to accept complimentary upgrades to business and first class he would – and could – never accept. He explained that for most journeys it made no difference to him where he sat. Even if the extra comfort might be welcome on long hauls it would be improper to spend public funds in that way. And, he added, imagine the gleeful media outcry if he were ever seen in business class, with headlines hinting that this was where donors' funds ended up, damaging trust in the UNICEF brand.

Then for the next two hours he shared with me the hard-to-solve problem which was at the top of his mind at that moment and with which he had been wrestling with only partial success. This was to change the tradition of large families, especially in farming societies in the developing world. He explained to me that because infant mortality has always been exceptionally high, families believed that by having many children they were creating better chances for one, two or three to survive and continue the family and farm. But now he was intent on finding ways to educate families in these societies that they could have just as many surviving healthy children with fewer births. The tragedy of the awful loss of life was no longer necessary.

This encounter with one of great global philanthropic executives of recent generations might help to illuminate what might be called the *six sins or virtues* that contribute to a strong or weak not-for-profit organization.

The acid test for success among NFPs and NGOs is the volume of donations. While most of us feel compelled to make donations based on compassion for the victims of illness or circumstance, or commitment to a particular cause, another half of our nature will find reasons why we should not and that allow us to keep our purses closed.

POLITICAL

People will support NGOs that come very close to being political organizations if they are in tune with their own political leanings. An example might be the National Rifle Association (NRA) in the USA which aggressively promotes and defends the right of individuals in America to own firearms; of Friends of the Earth in the UK which has an activist environmental agenda. These are obviously political and individuals might choose to support them with donations or not. But many NGOs operate in a grey area in which rumor and innuendo help to shape perception. At the extreme, conspiracy theorists ascribe hidden political motivations to some of the most apolitical organizations, ensuring that their officials are consumed by perception correction and damage control activity.

SYMPATHY WITH GOALS

This is strongly related to the preceding paragraph but relates to activities of NGOs that might not be connected to the political debate. The prospective donor will ask himself whether the NGO is pursuing goals in line with his own or whether there is a hidden agenda that is offensive to him. For example, many people choose on religious grounds not to support certain charities, however worthy, if they are advocating contraception, abortion or, in the case of sexually transmitted diseases, promote any preventive measures other than abstinence.

SCAMMING AND SKIMMING

Donors are increasingly wary of NGOs that appear appealing but might actually be, at one extreme, engaged in a criminal confidence trick, a scam, or, at the other, merely operating unprofessionally or incompetently, or skimming. It is because of the existence of the scams that other useful and innocent charities suffer since donors are scared into exercising extreme caution. Certainly criminal NGOs get exposed and shut down in due time but those who manage them are smart enough to make sure that at least some money gets to – well-publicized – examples of people in need to keep funds flowing as long as they are allowed to operate. The charge of skimming – although it is seldom expressed in that way – is much more common and scandals from time to time tarnish the luster of even the most reputable brands. A key statistic for potential donors is the percentage of funds the organization uses to cover its overhead running costs against that which goes to the purpose for which the organization exists. In the USA the Office of Personnel Management's rule is that charities should spend no more than 25 percent of their revenue on fund raising and other overhead expenses. When this gets out of balance it means that reputational damage is sure to follow. Excessive spending by the leadership of charitable organizations on such items as first class travel, luxury hotels, banquets, companions, pet projects, jobs for relatives and chums, and boondoggles of various kinds are especially sought after by the tabloids. The organizations will invariably seek in vain for more "balanced" commentary if they are within the technical operating costs guidelines. It takes several years for a not-for-profit to recover from a crisis of this kind.

DONATION DIVERSION

Donors are increasingly insistent that their contributions go to support specific activities and are not diverted to other priorities. The United Way movement in the US has seen a significant shift towards donor-directed giving in recent years. United Way was started as a way to enable people to give part of their salaries or wages to a central charity that would seek to make the fairest possible allocation to a wide variety of local charities that had been professionally screened. But recent research revealed that donors wanted to make their own choice and thus all United Way annual appeals now allow for individuals to state their preferences and direct all or part of their donation to a specific organization.

When donors' expectations are ignored or overturned they get angry. The American Red Cross learned this in the aftermath of the catastrophic events of September 11, 2001. In the days following 9/11 the outpouring of sympathy was matched by the outpouring of money to the Red Cross for use in connection with this tragedy. In fact, the sum of money received was so great that it was more than could be used for that purpose and the surplus was placed in the general fund. The fact that the money would undoubtedly find its way to excellent use did not assuage those who felt that they had donated for a specific purpose, not to the general fund. There was an outcry, the Red Cross suffered much unwanted publicity and loss of reputation and changes were made among the top-level volunteer board members and in the executive office.

DONATION LEAKAGE

One of the most trying problems facing aid organizations, in particular, is that of ensuring that donations reach the point of need intact. The fact that this is extremely difficult does nothing to comfort donors. Sad to say, they are often right when they choose not to give and say "my contribution will never get to the people who really need it". There is a rigid cycle to media coverage of any natural tragedy. Phase one is devoted to the disaster, the plight of the victims and the need for aid. In many cases people are encouraged to send donations to specified organizations and often huge sums are raised (as following 9/11 and the Asian Tsunami). In phase two, coverage will seize on any "miraculous" rescue but will also begin to examine any inadequacies in disaster response. In many countries this ends up with stories about funds being siphoned off by corrupt government officials or trucks with desperately needed supplies of food and medicines being commandeered by criminal gangs and sold for profit. The third, sad, stage is that the topic moves out of the news altogether as attention is turned to another event. In these cases the NGOs can only try to communicate their achievements and stay untarnished by the donation leakage.

TRANSPARENCY

Transparency and effective communication are vital to every not-for-profit organization, not least to make sure that donors' expectations are being met and that their contributions are being handled with care, efficiency and probity. The American Red Cross might have avoided the post 9/11 crisis if, as soon as it had seen that it had more money donated than it could usefully spend directly on victims of that disaster, it had informed donors and involved them in the decision as to how the excess should be used. Instead, the Board unilaterally made the decision to transfer the money to the general fund and the public only found out later.

Total transparency creates a sense of confidence whereas opacity breeds suspicion that militates against generous giving. This is true both in times of calm and times of crisis. In normal times NFPs need to communicate consistently. Not only should they have a proactive strategy of explaining the needs they serve and their value to society, but they should also be meticulous in explaining exactly how the money they receive is spent and the measures they take to keep overheads at a minimum. The obvious place is in the annual report, but there are many opportunities over the other 364 days of the year to repeat the message.

In emergencies the need is all the greater for the reasons mentioned above. Invariably those NFPs that are primarily concerned with delivering aid in times of crisis launch special appeals and receive an influx of additional donations. To ensure the integrity of the brand is enhanced and not damaged, organizations need to implement even more intensive communications programs – not always easy at a time when the organizational resources are strained. The messages need to be both emotional – showing how individuals in need were saved or helped, how ingenious solutions were promoted – as well as pragmatic, making clear that funds were being used wisely and that the majority of donations were reaching those in need. Both of these communications tracks need to be followed. To focus on one track only is insufficient.

Following the tsunami on December 28, 2004, which claimed more than 300,000 lives from Indonesia to India and Somalia, I was asked by The Global Alliance of Communications Organizations to undertake a study of how communications performed in helping combat suffering and how it could play a more effective role in the future. In the course of my investigations I met with various experts around the world, all of whom underlined the critical role played by communications before, during and after cataclysmic events. Their opinions were summed up by retired vice admiral Marsha Evans who at that time was Chief Executive of the American Red Cross. She told me: "There are two challenges in each disaster. First, the relief work itself, but a close second is communication and fund raising. Reporting to donors and keeping them up to date is a vital function."

10
Living the brand

Experts are agreed that the experience of a brand is a vital pillar underpinning its foundation. The total brand experience embraces logo, recommendation, promise, public relations, advertising and ready availability as well as brand encounters. But no component is as important as the bond created between the stakeholder and the corporation's employees – the people who embody the brand's values and are responsible for delivering on the promises made.

It is important to underline that in this context the description "employee" embraces every person empowered to represent the company or who works in the supply chain. It includes the CEO and his colleagues in the C-suite, top and middle management, hourly paid workers, part-time workers and contract workers. In this era of outsourcing and offshoring it also includes those who work on contract in telemarketing organizations and in the factories of subcontractors. It encompasses commission agents and PR agency staffers who are engaged to act as company spokespersons. External audiences have neither patience nor inclination to make distinctions between the differing contractual statuses of these groups. They are all representatives of the brand, which grows stronger when their efforts are successful. But when things go wrong, even in a distant part of the world and in a supplier organization that is not owned by the corporation, and standards – ethical, humanitarian or quality – are compromised, the brand can be put in peril.

In researching this chapter I was pleasantly surprised to discover that the topic of "living the brand", also known as "inside-out branding" or the "brand-driven organization", is well recognized in business today, and for those who are interested there is a sizeable body of literature devoted to it, ranging from the academic/theoretical to practical counsel based on best practice case studies. It has been recognized by experts in management, marketing communications and human relations, all of whom from their various standpoints believe in brand management as a critical business function.

My own observation and thinking for this chapter has been importantly augmented by the writings of Scott Davis, Donald T. Tosti and Rodger D. Stotz, Manto Gotsi and Alan Wilson, Nicholas Ind and Libby Sartain.[1]

INSIDE-OUT BRANDING

For those engaged in customer and client contact businesses, it is not necessary to define and defend the proposition that inside-out branding is important. Hoteliers, restaurateurs, air and cruise ship lines and most bricks and mortar retailers know that their success is built in quite large measure on the interaction experience between guests, travelers and shoppers and the front-line personnel who are there to serve them. All offer training, uniforms and the other items on the usual "identity" checklist and are thus able to reach an acceptable standard. The best organizations understand, however, that training has to go much further and that employees need to be instructed and motivated to leverage simple good service into a positive brand experience.

Jan Carlsson, the man who transformed Scandinavian Airline System (SAS) in the 1980s from a European carrier into a much-studied brand, did it by empowering his employees in a way that shocked his peers in the industry. Knowing that brand equity can be slowly eroded while passengers with complaints waited a long time for a resolution, he gave each cabin attendant the power to make an immediate settlement at the site and time of any problem. The attendant could – and often did – write out a voucher in-flight for free travel to a disaffected passenger. Thus a negative brand experience was immediately changed into a positive one. And not just for the passenger concerned, but by all the others who witnessed the episode. Experience showed that the empowerment worked; it was not abused either by the attendants or by the travelers. Money was saved on settlements and legal bills and customers were retained and became SAS ambassadors.

Meanwhile, Richard Branson had a stream of customer-focused ideas to enhance the already well-defined brand experience of his Virgin Atlantic airline. Transatlantic passengers in the Upper (Business) Class cabin were offered free neck/head massages or manicures, ensuring they disembarked in a glow of satisfaction. And on the flight to Hong Kong passengers could be measured for a tailor-made suit; the sizes were sent ahead by radio so that the tailor could do a first fitting on the day of the passenger's arrival. So instead of time hanging heavy on passengers, Branson put idle in-flight hours to practical purpose by creating a unique and memorable brand experience.

But in the case of travel, hospitality and many other businesses, the cabin crew or hotel desk clerks and their equivalent are no longer the only gatekeepers of the relationship between brand and customer. That vital responsibility is increasingly entrusted to either an impersonal virtual relationship through a website or a telephone sales clerk who is probably located in a global phone sales center. Many of these are now in India; others are in Europe (many in Ireland). In America, Utah has established itself as a center because of its high proportion of members of the Church of Jesus Christ of Latter-day Saints (Mormons). Many of them have become bi- or multilingual after spending their obligatory two years of missionary work abroad.

Frequent business travelers are increasingly mastering the business of arranging travel and other reservations online. Not only are they becoming more adept but the sites themselves are becoming increasingly user-friendly because the airlines, hotels, and so on, know the make-or-break importance of this first brand encounter.

But it is not always possible to conclude a booking online even for the most tech-savvy person and they end up in dialogue with a booking agent, often in Mumbai or Hyderabad, whose English might be excellent but unusually accented and hard for some Americans and British people to understand. (In the spirit of full disclosure, I have to confess that I have had more than one quite bizarre conversation in which we were at cross-purposes for much of the time. And this in spite of the fact that having been born in India and lived there many years, my ear is attuned to the manner of local speech.)

Experiences such as this for organizations that pay an exceptional degree of attention to their brand management, such as British Airways, mean that telemarketing must be a matter of some concern. Given the degree of management of the brand at all other points (online, at check in, baggage handling, pre-flight, boarding, waiting lounges, in-flight comfort, service and entertainment, and so on), the chance of a mishap at the very first experience of the brand could be fatal for the first-time customer and disconcerting even for a loyal regular patron.

The potential for mishap is one reason why travelers (and buyers of other products) are directed to a website where they can explore purchase options and conclude the transaction. A second reason is the immense saving when compared with the cost of labor and phone use, which enables the site owners to offer financial discounts to people making purchases online. Thus the site itself becomes a pivotal element in the brand experience, so there is new science developing which seeks to make web booking not only functional but a pleasurable experience that adds to the ethos of the brand.

FIRST CONTACT

As important as is the first contact, very often by telephone, between customer and corporation, brands are built, to use a metaphor, brick by brick over an extended period of time. Once a connection has been established it needs to be nurtured as the initial brand experience matures into a composite of a series of brand experiences, some good and most likely a few bad. While Jan Carlsson used his leadership position at SAS to empower cabin staff to solve problems without recourse to head office, Geoffrey Salmon, at a very successful food processing company in Britain, Telfer's Meat Pies, exercised his leadership in another more direct way – one that had a powerful effect on customers and employees alike. In common with most other food companies Telfer's had a customer service unit (aka complaints department) which handled calls from customers. Mr Salmon (his family owned J. Lyons & Co. which had bought Telfer's) made it his practice once each week – always at different times – to have all customer calls directed to his private phone. It was his way of keeping his finger directly on the pulse of consumer concerns and complaints, and brought to life the turgid tables of customer satisfaction studies. When the customers found they were speaking directly to the boss they were instantly converted into brand advocates; and a motivating message was sent to all Telfer employees about the importance of quality, meeting the brand promise and in maintaining strong relationships with stakeholders.

Another company with many customer-facing employees is UPS which in 2008 was listed as the US company with the second-most employees after first-placed Wal-Mart. Given the special nature of UPS's business, one-third of their 360,000 employees in the USA visit their corporate customers to deliver or pick up packages every day of the working week. Thus UPS has a personal ambassador in direct touch with its customers with an extraordinarily high degree of regularity and this sets up a relationship between the UPS driver and individuals at customer companies that is personal. UPS manages to combine high efficiency (the times between stops, spent with customers and so on is constantly measured with precision and improvements are constantly introduced) with friendly and helpful customer service. UPS is unique in that the entire senior management of the company started or had a spell as a driver, so knows the importance of this interface and that all employees need to live the brand. That is probably why UPS is the only representative of its business sector in Brand Finance's World's 500 Most Valuable Brands 2008, in 38th position, up from 42nd in 2007.

The corporations that sustain a successful brand by living it – in short, by their behavior – have certain defining characteristics which, for the sake of memorability, I classify as the six "V"s. Each "V" in turn – Vision, Values, Vitality, Veracity, Victory and Volunteerism – has a number of independent components.

Many companies nowadays have statements of vision, mission and values and many have been through an VMV process in which these were defined and expressed and communicated to the corporation's internal audience. How much the process affects the strength of the brand through employee behavior depends, however, on the level of commitment on the part of all levels of management in sustained education, communication and motivational activities.

Let's examine the six Vs and their components one by one.

VISION

- **Clarity**: The vision must be easily understood by all employees and expressed in simple language.
- **Inspirational**: It should have the power to inspire employees and make them allies in its attainment.
- **Aspirational**: The bar should be set high (but not so high as to be clearly out of reach). The wording should express how the corporation wants to be rather than how it is now, thus motivating employees to strive for the goal.
- **Broad**: The vision should be expressed in terms that are broad enough to have longevity, taking into account the dynamics of society and economics. But at the same time not so broad as to be generically useable by any other corporation in any other field (for example, "Our vision is to help create a world in which poverty is a distant memory", will not do).

■ **Employees**: The critical importance of employees as engines in the attainment of the vision should be recognized and stated. They should be regularly reminded of their role.

VALUES

■ **Principles**: The values are the principles of behavior of the corporation and, like the vision, must be expressed with clarity. These values should drive corporate decision making and actions by individual employees of the corporation. Commitment to values drives corporate culture, and corporate culture is an important contributor to the brand.

■ **Permanent**: Core values should be permanent and should not change. They should be the same this year and next; they should be identical at units of the same corporation in Indiana and India, in Britain and Bangladesh.

■ **Respectful**: A hallmark of the finest corporations is the value of respecting local customs and traditions. They achieve this by adaptation of procedures where appropriate but never compromise principles. This can sometimes mean hard choices – for example deciding not to work in a market if the only way would be to breach a principle.

VITALITY

■ **Vigor**: It is insufficient to declare "mission accomplished" when Vision and Values have been established. To have meaning and an effect on the brand the declarations have to be translated into action by the employees. Ways have to be found to enlist them in this ongoing quest through effective communications, events and incentives.

■ **Refresh**: It is hard to ensure continued commitment to "living the brand" and there are several ways in which it can be derailed. Common among them are: the arrogance that comes with success when employees feel that no more needs to be done; the despair that comes with lack of apparent results; the inertia that comes when repetition leads to boredom with the process.

■ **Reinterpret**: Brand Sclerosis is my name for a disease fatal to brands whose arteries have become clogged. Brands need to be periodically reinterpreted or reinvented to show their relevance to the present – and the future – world and society. Also, corporations themselves are in a constant state of change. Some use a core business strength to build a much larger portfolio of offerings organically or through acquisition. Others decide to do the opposite and shed non-core businesses. Some change their business entirely. But the brand image does not move in step and always lags behind the reality. So corporations must choose either a gradual brand evolution or a less frequent revolution. Each small or major rebranding event is an opportunity to remind employees of the evolving brand attributes and encourage them to live them day by day.

VERACITY

- **Truth**: Tell the truth. This is a good rule in normal times and builds confidence in the brand. It is especially important when dealing with issues or in times of crisis when the attempt to conceal or bend the truth is a temptation. Work on the basis that the truth is known by a number of people internally and will eventually come out; then there will be secondary damage to reputation.
- **Honesty**: It is better to be honest than merely truthful. Truth can mean bare facts sufficient to satisfy the legal definition, whereas honesty involves a full explanation. It might, for instance, explain the various options considered by the corporation and the possible consequences. Honesty means the provision of enough contested information for an informed judgment to be made by employees and in turn by external audiences.
- **Distortion**: Truth does not always travel well, so global employees must think carefully about how messages will be received in different countries and different cultures. Statements can get refracted or distorted as they pass through international borders. Two kinds of mistakes are possible. The first is to ignore differences of perspectives and beliefs and to push ahead with conviction that right is on your side, so no explanations or translations are needed. The other is to try and curry favor by modifying the truth for different audiences.

VICTORY

- **Survive and succeed**: These are the two commercial requirements of every corporation. Without commercial success all the other "V"s become moot or can be compromised as managements become increasingly desperate. But remember, in great companies the "V"s are the foundation on which success is achieved. They are not a reward or luxury for companies that have made money through unscrupulous practices.

- **The edge**: Brand leading corporations have an edge over competitors, the result of innovative products and policies.
- **Winning team**: Employees are inspired by being members of a winning team.

VOLUNTEERISM

- **Citizenship**: Volunteerism and corporate philanthropy have long been distinctive features of commercial life in the USA and have played an important role in animating "living the brand". As commerce becomes increasingly global, corporations rooted in other countries are increasingly integrating these two elements into their wider commitment to corporate social responsibility.
- **Support the firm**: A corporation can dramatically amplify the awareness of its efforts to be socially responsible and charitable by informing employees of initiatives that are being undertaken and philanthropic donations. Employees can in turn relay this information to others and might also donate their own time and money to augment the firm's contribution.
- **Support the employee**: Employees each have their own causes which they support with time and money. Enlightened firms can encourage "living the brand" by supporting their employees through matching funds or other schemes.

Joint selection

It is appropriate that corporations should have their pet causes that they support. These are usually organizations or initiatives to which the leadership of the corporation is personally committed. The leadership in turn seeks to enlist the support of as many of its employees as it can to increase contributions.

It is also appropriate, as mentioned above, for corporations to support the pet projects of employees.

Some corporations – Marks & Spencer, the large UK retailer, is a trailblazer – have found effective ways of synergizing their societal and philanthropic efforts through a "democratic" process of joint selection. The basic formula is that the corporation adopts a "Charity (or cause) of The Year" and solicits suggestions from all employees as to which that charity should be. Depending on the size of the company there may be one or more charities of the year. From all the names submitted a committee selects a shortlist – this may be five, ten or twenty candidates. Each submits a manifesto describing its work and value with reasons why it should be chosen. This shortlist is then circulated to all employees, who vote for their preferred charity and, based on this, the winners are selected.

The advantages of this approach are many and can be an important enabler of "living the brand". By limiting the number of charities, those selected receive more significant and measurable help. The electoral process allows all contenders to profile their work, even though they may not be winners. Because of the "fair" and inclusive selection process management and employees will give an increased level of financial support and personal time commitment. An annual process of this kind keeps the importance of social and philanthropic activity regularly renewed as the focus for support changes year by year.

Note

1   Scott Davis is managing partner of the Chicago office of Prophet, a management consultancy specializing in the integration of brand, business and marketing strategies. He is author of *Brand Asset Management: Driving Profitable Growth Through Your Brands* (Jossey-Bass, 2000), and co-author of *Building the Brand-Driven Business: Operationalize Your Brand to Drive Profitable Growth* (Jossey-Bass, 2002). He received a BS from the University of Illinois and an MBA from the Kellogg School of Management.

Donald T. Tosti is principal of Vanguard Consulting. He may be reached at change111@aol.com.

Rodger D. Stotz is vice president and managing consultant at Maritz Performance Improvement Co. He may be reached at Rodger.Stotz@maritz.com.

Manto Gotsi and Alan Wilson, University of Strathclyde, Glasgow, UK; "Corporate reputation management: 'living the brand'", *Management Decision*, London: 2001, **39**(2): 99–104.

Nicholas Ind, brand consultant and author of *Living the Brand*, published in association with *Marketing,* and other books.

Libby Sartain, Senior Vice President Human Resources and Chief HR Yahoo, Yahoo, Inc., 701 First Ave., Sunnyvale, CA 94089, (408) 349-6063, libby@yahoo-inc.com.

11
Mergers and acquisitions

Mergers and acquisitions (M&A) is the furnace in which most of today's great corporate and product brands have been forged. Some have been strengthened but more have been diminished. Some revered names have been eliminated altogether.

Something must be seriously wrong in the world of M&A because all the information we have at our disposal should either put a stop to the (statistically lemming-like) rush to combine corporations or radically alter the way in which the deals are done. Yet the pace and value of M&A activity increases every year.

It seems few CEOs, strategists and M&A evangelists (and there are many of these, making their fortunes as corporate matchmakers or enablers) have troubled to review the data on M&A. There are many sources but all suggest that more than half of all mergers are failures and according to Forbes' *Investopedia* (June 9, 2008) "historical trends show that roughly two thirds of big mergers will disappoint on their own terms, which means they will lose value on the stock market".

Why then does the pressure to merge and acquire continue to gain pace? Have our business leaders chosen to ignore the amber lights? Do they not read the cautionary case studies in economic journals and which are taught in MBA classes? Or do they have so much hubris that they feel they will be immune to the problems that are so well documented?

First, it is important to understand that corporate leaders are alpha males (and, yes, alpha females) who are driven to win and exercise power. They have read the books that tell them they must eat or be eaten; that they must not only be superior to competitors but eliminate them if possible; that to be bigger is to open up opportunities denied them at their present size; that they must show regular progress up the *Fortune* 500 rankings or the ranking of the largest firms in their own sectors; the need to be in the news; the desire to score over peers and rivals; the anxiety over being left behind when competitor corporations combine (which usually starts a rush of other mergers in the industry).

If all these often-undeclared drivers were not enough, then come the rationalizations. These can be real enough and have been the rationale for many successful mergers when executed well. These include the following:

- that more flags must be placed on the map if they are to be truly global
- the potential of rewarding synergies
- to buy market share
- that a new skill or business must be added if customers are to be offered the full range of services/products for their needs
- to block a move by a competitor
- to move the corporation into a more promising and profitable area of operation (a greener field).

And for a failing enterprise there is the compelling reason that the merged entity will bring salvation (when so often it can lead to the demise of both parties). Sometimes the failed enterprise might see itself as predator but more often than not as willing prey, hoping to negotiate a nice price.

And all these forces are given encouragement by a powerful group of cheerleaders, the many branches of the M&A industry itself.

Important among these are the investment banks, law firms, M&A consultants, chartered accountants, corporate image and branding experts, communications consultants (internal, PR and advertising). All have a vested interest in promoting deal activity because that is how they earn their livings.

And it is a big business. In 2007 the top five law firms in the USA acted as counsel to principals in no fewer than 386 deals with a value of $1,538,411 million.

WHY SO MANY MERGERS FAIL AND OTHERS SUCCEED

A merger will fail if it is undertaken for the wrong reasons, if it is ill-conceived, does not serve a genuine business purpose or is poorly executed. If I am correct in my analysis of the more primeval forces that drive many leaders to seek out acquisition targets then it is not surprising that a large percentage are doomed from the start.

Mergers undertaken for the wrong, or fuzzy, reasons usually founder along the way for a combination of reasons. The dating corporations can consider themselves lucky if the "divorce" occurs before the potential partners get to the altar because this will save them the greater agony of trying to make an unlikely marriage succeed. The alternative is a very costly break up and separation; and few will have prepared a prenuptial agreement to assist that process.

The well-thought-through merger will arrive at the holy grail of the M&A cult, which is to capture the full potential value of combining the corporations – so often expressed as the equation 1+1=3.

Many of the causes of failed mergers are to do with financial miscalculations, overoptimistic forecasts, market assessments and a host of other factors that are more properly dealt with in other books. My purpose here is to review those factors that are connected with protecting and enhancing brand value.

CULTURE AND EMPLOYEES

In Chapter 10 we described the critical importance of employees in "living the brand" and the influence of corporate culture in framing employee attitudes and behavior. At no time is this more vital than during the complete merger cycle – before, during and after the combination occurs. According to Dr Kent Rhodes of the Graziadio School of Business and Management at Pepperdine University:[1]

> Cultural cohesion is most often the critical asset in the eventual success or failure of the overall deal … most mergers and acquisitions rarely deliver the highly anticipated synergies between companies. Throughout a merger or acquisition, people in an acquired company often complain that they don't know what is happening, express fear about losing their jobs, and feel demoralized as to the future of their contributions. Failed mergers that otherwise have a sound strategic and financial fit are typically the result of the irretrievable loss of intangible, messy-to-measure and difficult-to-implement human factors on which the company's tangible assets ultimately rest.

Dr Rhodes is not alone. Among many who agree are Ravi Chanmugam, Walter E. Shill and David Mann, M&A experts working for Accenture. Writing in the firm's newsletter, *Outlook*, they report that:[2]

Accenture asked the Economist Intelligence Unit to survey senior executives and managers on the topic of post-merger integration. "Cultural differences and cultural resistance" were cited most often by respondents as the thing that surprised them most during the post-merger integration process. This confirms our own experience, which suggests that even some management teams that identify cultural fault lines early on in the M&A process fail to incorporate their insights into the design of their merger integration.

The most successful acquirers of the future will see culture as a tool in three ways. First, they will look at cultural differences during the target identification and bidding phases, assess the potential impact of those differences, and incorporate their analysis into the valuation and bid. Second, they will try to avoid the pitfalls common during pre- and post-merger planning, and actively incorporate the elements of each company's culture that best support the desired combination. Finally, they will proactively use culture to create value through the use of high-visibility retention, promotion, termination and structural organizational design decisions.

Culture and the ability to adapt to change are critical to success:

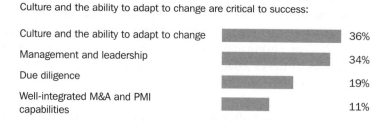

Culture and the ability to adapt to change	36%
Management and leadership	34%
Due diligence	19%
Well-integrated M&A and PMI capabilities	11%

Figure 11.1 Critical elements of successful M&A (Source: Economist Intelligence Unit Survey/Accenture Analysis)

Within this three-step process Dr Rhodes urges that attention be paid to the power of mythology:

Mythology is the group of stories, ideas or beliefs that become a part of an organization. While these stories are not necessarily based on facts, they usually reflect historical accounts of greatness or tragedy and will likely show up in the organization either as a respected legend or common gossip. Mythology in a company can serve either to create a culture of inspiration or a culture of mistrust. During the process of mergers and acquisitions (M&A) integration, managers should identify organizational myths. If those myths serve inspirational purposes or appropriately link current work to the company's history, creating ways to acknowledge such stories could improve the odds of talent buy in.

THE RUNAWAY TRAIN

Anyone who has been a member of a merger team on either side or working in the "clean room" (see The "intelligent clean room", below) as an adviser cannot fail to have been struck on many occasions by the overriding drive to close the deal. This motivation can be so powerful that it can blind the protagonists to serious problems whose resolution are (sometimes fatally) postponed to a later date. Or major mistakes relating to the capture of long-term value can be made.

More often than not the signals are very clear that a deal needs to be aborted or at least renegotiated but it is very hard to stop a chief executive and his cohorts once, as they say, the train has left the station. Once a public announcement of an intended merger has been made it is as if there would be an unbearable loss of personal reputation of the CEO if it were halted or to be derailed. And, of course, there would be a serious loss of fees to the third-party cheerleaders. It takes an exceptionally strong leader to change course.

In my own experience I have to doff my hat to Phil Laskawy, Chairman and CEO of Ernst & Young, who in 1997 aborted an announced merger with KPMG after a careful review of the terms and future prognosis of the combined entity. He concluded that it would not be in the best interests of his firm to cement the deal.

BRANDING IN THE MERGER PROCESS

"In the heat of everyone's desire to close a deal, too many mergers and acquisitions are wrapping up with little formal review of the long-term impact of the companies' brands", cautions Ken Roberts, CEO of the brand strategy consulting firm Lippincott.

Too little attention, or failure to understand how each brand works, can result in overpayment for assets not used, value-destroying constraints on future business strategy, or barriers to post-merger integration. It is essential to place a timely focus on how brands shift demand in order to validate and shape the deal, and to guide customers and employees smoothly through the transition.

Brands do have an asset value, but that value is more volatile than it is for most other assets. A brand's value is not fixed in isolation: it is as much a consequence of the M&A deal and subsequent strategy as it is an input to them.[3]

THE "INTELLIGENT CLEAN ROOM"

Successful execution of the lifecycle approach to merger integration (see story below) boils down to tactical excellence. One of the most effective M&A tactics is what Accenture calls the "Intelligent Clean Room".

Earlier clean rooms were narrowly defined due diligence mechanisms with which third-party experts could examine sensitive information on prospective M&A partners in a physically separate and legally isolated space. Accenture has updated the concept through the application of a value-capture perspective.

Rather than waiting until the deal formally closes, the Intelligent Clean Room allows detailed, side-by-side company analysis and integration planning before approvals are finalized. The analysis is done by third parties, not company employees, so the prospective merger partners can continue to act as competitors as required by US Department of Justice rules.

Working within DOJ limitations, the source and priority of many high-value synergy initiatives can be determined. Intelligent Clean Room processes can include the building of detailed financial models for assessing cost synergies on a business-unit basis or even a line-item basis, creating tools for tracking synergies, assisting the legal teams with regulatory findings, setting up post-merger governance models, and administering the overall project calendar.

For the Cingular Wireless and AT&T Wireless union, Accenture was engaged to design and conduct Intelligent Clean Room pre-merger planning. The stated objective was to capture maximum value in the critical first two years of post-merger operations. To this end, more than 40 professionals, with specialized skills – including sales and marketing, customer care, network experience, supply chain management, HR and IT, along with brand consultants, Lippincott – set up work at an Intelligent Clean Room in Atlanta. During the eight months from announcement to close, key aspects of the combined companies' business were examined, analyzed, modeled against value-capture objectives and assigned priorities. The process covered areas ranging from retail distribution to billing processes to advertising effectiveness.

The Intelligent Clean Room for Cingular and AT&T Wireless was significant for its use of explicitly defined "leading indicators" – anticipatory metrics such as dramatically increased call center volume or product returns. One working (and ultimately correct) premise, for example, was that traditional post-merger integration timelines to integrate systems and fix problems would be too long if customer defections ran high. The Cingular–AT&T Wireless team made preemptive use of daily and weekly interim data to identify and address problems before they became serious issues.

Exhibit 11.1 What about the name? (Source: Anderson, James C., Narus, James, A., *Business Marketing Management*, 2nd edition, © 2004, pp. 138–9. Reprinted by permission of Pearson Education, Inc., Upper Saddle River, NJ)

When making acquisitions at the rate of four per week it is vital to have a systematic approach to managing both corporate brand and its subsidiary brand portfolio. That is why GE developed its proprietary *acquired-affiliate naming scheme*, which is part of GE's Identity Program.

Because GE's overall brand strategy has historically been technically monolithic – focusing on GE as the only core identity – this process encouraged linking GE with its acquisitions, but it also considered the external variables that influenced the degree to which a particular acquisition should be associated with GE. Therefore, the objective of this five-level naming scheme was twofold: to protect the equity of the GE brand and to leverage the brand equity of the acquired company, where appropriate. The levels were as follows:

- *Naming Level 1* represented the highest level of identification and the strongest association with GE. The acquired company's name would become a combination of GE and a succinct generic name describing the business. An example of this level is Thompson CGR, which became GE Medical Systems Europe in 1987.
- *Naming Level 2* associated GE with the main name of the acquisition. This was done when the acquired name had a high degree of brand equity and when a lesser association with GE was desired. For example, because Fanuc had strong brand equity in the industrial automation market, the company was named GE Fanuc. By contrast, at GE Medical Systems, the acquired brands with equity such as OEC (surgical C-arms) and Lunar (bone densitometry) saw their names placed below the GE Medical Systems name in the GE logo format (called a *graphic signature*).
- *Naming Level 3* corresponded to a logo endorsement, where only a strong visual association was desirable. The acquired brand name was used in the GE logo format. When GE Medical Systems acquired Marquette Medical Systems

in 1998, the brand had such recognition in the cardiology market that the existing Marquette logo was transitionally incorporated into the GE logo format.

- *Naming Level 4* created only a verbal association with the acquired company. The acquired company's existing name and logo were kept (the GE logo format was not used) and were combined with a reference to GE in a tag line. An example is Transportation International Pool, *a GE Capital Company*.
- In *Naming Level 5*, GE would be invisible, because there was no benefit in associating GE with the acquired brand. An example is medial conglomerate NBC, which is a GE company but retained its own separate identity.

GE determines the appropriate naming level for an acquired business by considering three types of issues, each requiring subjective judgment. *Business issues* focus on management control (Does GE control the company?) and commitment (Does GE have a long-term commitment to this company?). *Industry issues* deal with the image value of the industry (Is the industry perceived to be dynamic and innovative?) and performance expectations (How well is GE expected to perform in this industry?). *Identity issues* are tied to the equity of the existing brand (Is it strong?) and the impact on GE (What is the impact when the new brand is associated with the parent company?). GE uses these kinds of questions as sequential steps of a decision tree to determine the best naming strategy.

The scheme described above is designed to integrate and manage *newly* acquired brands. With time, brands evolve and may move up the ladder of association with GE after a transitional period. The Marquette example mentioned earlier illustrates this point. In 2000, approximately two years after the acquisition of Marquette (when the Marquette logo was integrated into the GE logo format), the company was renamed *GE Medical Systems Information Technologies* and given a new logo. *Marquette* no longer appeared as part of the name of the company or in its logo. Instead, it was transitioned to be an umbrella product brand. Eventually, it was phased out completely.

GE's acquired-affiliate naming scheme provided branding guidance that could be applied consistently across a firm as vast and diversified as GE. The structured alternatives enabled GE to protect and build its brand equity, yet leverage the existing equity of acquired brands. Through this process, the company gained the greatest return on its brand resources.

GOING GLOBAL

The pace of cross-border merger activity is on a sharp upward swing in a fast-globalizing world. But if a local acquisition is fraught with difficulties and trip-wires, then a cross-border transaction reaches a new dimension of complexity, as the large multinational corporations know from experience. But there are many other corporations in the early stages of becoming transnational and they seek to grow globally through acquisition.

Of course, all the factors present in a merger between two national organizations will be found. To these must be added specific new considerations. The most important of these is to take time to understand the new markets and their environments. This will include a study of the culture and customs of the countries to be entered. Time must also be taken to check out the regulatory structure and the competitive landscape. According to Caroline Firstbrook of Accenture UK, any oversight of these factors can lead to overly optimistic assumptions about revenue growth or cost saving opportunities. She says:[4]

> For example, when North American buyers fail to understand Europe's different labor laws, they make overly optimistic projections from headcount reductions at the acquired company. Naïve reliance on the protection offered by contract or intellectual property law in some of the more chaotic developing markets can lead to significant write-offs or even the inadvertent creation of low-cost competitors that benefit for a company's proprietary knowledge.

THREE-STEP PROCESS

Lippincott recommend a three-step process (Figure 11.2) to ensure brand success flowing from mergers, a process in which I believe that the chief corporate communications officer should play a key integral role within the core team.

CASE The Bentley story

If ever there were any doubt about the importance of brand in M&A deals, the tale of Volkswagen's 1998 acquisition of Rolls-Royce Motors will erase it. As critics charged at the time, VW slipped up by paying £430 million for the Rolls-Royce company without acquiring the world-famous Rolls-Royce brand as part of the deal. Instead, VW's arch-rival BMW acquired the rights to the Rolls-Royce brand and its visual icons for £40 million.

Due to a history of company splits, brand cross-licensing and legal trigger clauses, Rolls-Royce effectively had to sell the brand separately from the company. Confirming the value of the brand, BMW created a new business that is already arguably the size of the original, starting from only a name and a radiator grille. It claimed for 2004 "the largest number of Rolls-Royce

ACTIVITIES AND KEY PLAYERS

1. Pre-deal Phase
The Pre-deal phase is driven by senior and strategic management for both parties and determines the brand strategy and architecture for the merged entity.

Strategy clarification	Brand audit and valuation	Intent to merge announcement

KEY PLAYERS

Core team, steering committee, senior management, brand management	Core team, steering committee, senior management, brand management	Core team, steering committee, senior management, brand management, communications

2. Brand Transition Phase
Significant brand transition planning involving most functional areas should occur prior to deal close.

Inventory/requirement audit	Transition planning and budget development	Deal close announcement

KEY PLAYERS

Core team, steering committee, brand management, communications, sales and distribution, HR, IT, legal	Core team, steering committee, senior management, brand management, communications, sales and distribution, IT, HR, finance, legal, external vendors	Core team, steering committee, senior management, brand management, communications

3. Post-deal Phase
In the Post-deal phase, a number of activities should be carefully coordinated to ensure successful implementation and brand rollout. Most functional areas of the organization need to be involved.

Redesign and implementation	New brand launch	Evaluation and monitoring

KEY PLAYERS

Core team, steering committee, brand management, communications, sales and distribution, HR, IT	Core team, steering committee, senior management, brand management, communications, HR, sales and distribution	Steering committee, brand management, senior management as required

Figure 11.2 The three-step process (Source: Lippincott)

brand vehicles to have been sold for 14 years." That is the value that VW missed out on.

But there was much more to the story than that. VW found hidden value in the business that it purchased. The Rolls-Royce Motors company included the Bentley brand – lustrous in its own right, but long overshadowed by the Rolls marque. VW set about transferring some of the Rolls-Royce brand equity to Bentley. In 1998, the year of the deal, Rolls-Royce Motors had sold 1,600 high-end cars – a mix of Rolls and Bentleys. Five years later, when BMW sold 800 Rolls-Royces, VW sold 700 Bentleys – along with more than 6,000 of its new Bentley Continental GT, a racy new model priced at $200,000, which is quite affordable for that market segment.

In short, VW has deftly used its new, higher-volume Continental GT not only to grow the Bentley business in its own right, but also to create the visibility that Bentley needs to be an aspirational luxury car brand. For proof of VW's success, just look at the crowds gathered around the GT display models at major European airports.

Both VW and BMW have achieved impressive successes with their respective acquired brands. Although commentators at the time of the deal saw BMW as the clear winner, their "rear-view mirror" perspective of historic brand asset value blinded them to the potential value of the Bentley brand, now realized by VW through its business, product and brand strategies. (Interestingly, BMW can tell a similar success story about the Mini, previously an iconic British brand.)

Source: Lippincott

The real lesson of the story is not just about the importance of brand in the deal. It is also about assessing brand value in the post-deal context.

I know this to be true. I have been involved as PR consultant in many mergers and strategic reorganizations planned by US companies to improve or rationalize their operations in the newly forming "single" market of Europe. In almost all cases the plan called for the closing (or, at least, downsizing) of production facilities located in France. I cannot think of a single instance in which the alliance of French workers, their unions, the national government and the local community did not emerge victorious and the strategic plan had to be reworked. It is interesting that the record and case studies were all there but each corporation approached the task without reference to history. Many suffered severe brand reputational damage as a result.

Caroline Firstbrook highlights another classic mistake:[5]

Assuming that customers in new markets are fundamentally the same as those at home. A key driver in the 1998 acquisition of US carmaker Chrysler by Daimler-Benz of Germany was the assumption that product development costs for the joint company could be slashed by developing common models for both markets – an assumption that failed to recognize fundamental differences in road infrastructure, driving habits and customer preferences between Europe and North America.

Notes

1 *Graziadio Business Report*, 2004, Volume 7, Issue 1.
2 *Outlook*, October 2005, Issue 1.
3 Personal communication. See www.lippincott.com for more information.
4 *Journal of Business Strategy*, 2007, Volume 28, Issue 1.
5 See www.lippincott.com.

12

Rebranding the corporation

In a dynamic and globalizing economy the one thing you can be sure of is the constancy of change – technological, societal and political. Add to this the speed of change and it is clear that only the most agile businesses will survive and prosper. Brands must use the winds of change to propel themselves into a stronger position or be blown off course and, on occasion, into oblivion.

Consider this: of the top 20 brands in the Brand Finance 500 (2008) seven did not exist 25 years ago. And of the remainder, six have changed their business model in the same period.

Moore's Law[1] of computer hardware, that the number of transistors that can be inexpensively placed on an integrated circuit doubles exponentially every two years, is a rate of change that many believe in principle applies to many other aspects of science and society.

By some calculations the sum of human knowledge that existed in the year AD 1 took 1500 years to double and another 250 years to double again. The doubling speed is now every one to two years. (Oh, if only information and knowledge was wisdom!)

Change lies at the heart of the seemingly different reasons why corporations choose to rebrand themselves; or feel compelled to do so.

IMAGE LAGS REALITY

Long-established corporations may have developed a brand that is both widely recognized and has a broadly positive image. But it is often true of such corporations that the brand image lags well behind the reality and no longer reflects the company's activities or attributes. The company's management thinks that wrong perceptions might hamper the company's ability to perform and compete in today's marketplace. The outdated image needs to be revamped.

An example is United Parcel Service, which celebrated its centennial in 2007. Over the years UPS had undergone a number of transformations but none involved changes so dramatic as those that took place between 1988 and 2002. Given that the last brand review that had taken place was 46 years earlier when the logo was redesigned, it was clearly time to undertake a branding review. Over its entire history UPS had had only three previous logo designs.

Figure 12.1 UPS logo designs from 1919, 1937, 1961 and 2003

The team assigned had to consider not only the point of development the company had reached; if its proposed branding was to last even half the 46 years between the last reviews, it had to provide a solution that would describe the company in the future.

Since 1988 UPS had changed in a number of ways. It moved from being a US domestic service provider to a global corporation offering service in 200 countries; it made a massive investment to leap from being a technology laggard to leader in its industry; it added supply chain expertise and services, logistics, freight forwarding and multimodal (train, truck, ship and plane) movement of packages to its list of services; it built the world's 9th largest airline with a state-of-the art fleet of jets; customers could access a whole new array of services from finance to smart systems for advance customs clearance for international shipments; they could also tap UPS insourcing services in which UPS would take over complete responsibility for running the customer's shipping department.

And it was precisely because United Parcel Service had such a strong brand image as a specialist company (the premier and totally reliable package delivery company) that it was so difficult to gain recognition for the new multiservice, multimodal and multinational organization. So it was that in 2002 United Parcel Service began a brand review, working with Futurebrand, with the intention of completing the process in time for a launch in the spring of 2003.

As challenging as the theoretical process of identifying the correct brand image for UPS might be (and, yes, a fundamental early decision was to change the master brand name from United Parcel Service to simply UPS with an updated logo) it did not compare with the demands that would be made to execute the change of visual identity in an organization the size of UPS. It was essential that the creative wing of the team should understand the complexity of the task facing those responsible for implementation.

Just consider:

■ the insignia on the uniforms of more than 400,000 employees world-wide had to be changed
■ 120,000 vehicles would have to be repainted, as would 250 aircraft
■ about 60,000 UPS facility or storefront signs would have to be produced and erected
■ the documents relating to 4 billion packages would have to be printed in the new livery.

The massive task and cost of changing the face of UPS meant that it could not be done at a stroke overnight. There had to be a phased plan in which the new UPS logo and design would be introduced. For example, to avoid any hitch in customer service, too many vehicles could not be taken off the road at one time for repainting.

UPS, in keeping with its reserved corporate culture, decided that the primary target for its rebranding announcement would be the company's 400,000 employees. If they were to be the ambassadors of the "new" UPS they would need to be fully informed and convinced of the relevance of the repositioning. Beyond that, UPS adopted a PR-led communications strategy ahead of any significant TV and press advertising.

Before any formal announcement, UPS's PR agency, Edelman, conducted a teaser campaign in which coupons for a box of specially minted coins featuring the four UPS lifetime logos were sent to media in all key UPS markets and they were invited as special guests to a series of 30 unveiling ceremonies for staff at facilities in 26 countries. The new logo in gold and brown had a "slash" conveying smooth speed, replacing the original parcel tied with string. No longer was the near-centurial corporation engaged only in package delivery, now it was helping its customers by "synchronizing global commerce".

UPS One, the first jet of UPS's newly branded fleet, went on an around the world flight, landing in several important key markets for ceremonies, while senior UPS executives undertook a world speaking tour in the launch week.

Only when the novelty of the UPS transformation began to fade (key message: it is UPS that has changed, not just the logo) did paid advertising appear to drive home the story.

But UPS knew that a true transformation could only take place by a consistent corporate brand communication long after the immediate launch. Employee and external communications, executive speeches and advertising were all aligned to underscore UPS's ability to synchronize the three flows of commerce – goods, information and funds.

This theme was also the central focus of a series of high-level 'by invitation only' symposia titled "Longitudes", eight of which were held in New York, Chicago (twice), Paris, Frankfurt, Barcelona, Shanghai and Toronto in the period 2004–2008. At these events, leading academics and business leaders debated the strategic importance of the supply chain to the success of global corporations.

In this way UPS elevated its brand to number 38 in the Brand Finance 500 (2008), with a brand value of $14,840 million. No longer was theirs a service simply for the mailroom. They had earned recognition by the members of the executive suite.

The success of the rebranding of UPS has been measured and monitored in many ways, but one outcome encapsulates the achievement. The "new" UPS described in the company's rebranding caught the attention of Thomas Friedman as he was researching and writing his best selling book *The World is Flat* and he visited the UPS headquarters in Atlanta, Georgia to find out more. Friedman's theory is that digital technology has leveled the global economic playing field, allowing new corporations and nations of different sizes to compete effectively in the marketplace. He devoted one whole section to describing how UPS was an important "equalizer", especially through "insourcing" – the arrangement in which UPS subcontracts to take over various supply chain functions by putting its own people into the company and managing the process – the reverse of outsourcing. No longer was UPS a company with an illustrious history, it had become a technological leader and a shaper of the future of global business.

REASONS FOR REBRANDING

Buggy whip factor

The buggy whip factor is important in driving many rebranding decisions. When a company's management determines that its brand seems to be irrevocably linked to an industry that is in decline (or disrepute) but is in reality succeeding in new sectors, it is time to make an intense effort to communicate its new vision and mission to its stakeholders. In such cases management has to make a choice: to take the equity in an existing well-known name and give it new meaning, transferring the goodwill and linking it to the growing new markets in which it plans to succeed; when this is seen to be too difficult or costly a task the decision is usually made to change the name. IBM is an example of the first approach, the mutation of Philip Morris into Altria of the second.

Mergers and demergers

Mergers or break-ups or demergers are all reasons that make rebranding necessary rather than an option. In these circumstances the real character and mission of one or perhaps more of the other parts of the corporation must be rebranded to reflect the reality. Examples of brands that have been created as a result of mergers and acquisitions are discussed in Chapter 11 but here we will look at an example of a global mega brand that emerged following a change of domicile, a corporate restructuring and a series of acquisitions around the world.

CASE The World's Local Bank

It has been a long journey for HSBC to its position as the world's most valuable banking brand in rankings published by *The Banker* on March 2, 2008[2] from its foundation in Hong Kong and Shanghai in 1865 by Scotsman Thomas Sutherland and other British and American traders. The bank has retained its position as the most valuable banking brand in the publication's survey published in February 2009, although turmoil in the financial markets caused many changes in the rankings and the exit of some illustrious names. The Shanghai Banking Corporation was established to finance the growing trade between China and Europe and it was domiciled in Hong Kong until 1991 when HSBC Holdings was set up in London as a result of a series of acquisitions of banks and financial institutions around the world, including the Midland Bank in Britain. It is now, by many measures, the largest bank in the world.

In 1998 HSBC embarked on the first step of a rebranding or positioning process with the execution of a new visual corporate identity. This had to be a design that could be applied to all the banks that HSBC acquired and where names would be changed.

The ID that emerged from the process was the hexagon symbol originally adopted by the Hong Kong and Shanghai Banking Corporation as its logo in 1983. It was developed from the bank's house flag, a white rectangle divided diagonally to produce a red hourglass shape. It was based on a Scottish flag, the country the founder of the company was born in. Like many other Hong Kong company flags that originated in the 19th century, the design was based on the cross of Saint Andrew, the patron saint of Scotland. The logo was designed by graphics artist Henry Steiner.

With the acquisition and renaming of a host of well-known local banking icons – Midland Bank in the UK, Marine Midland and Household International in the USA, the British Bank of the Middle East in the UAE are some examples – HSBC was anxious to defuse any notion that it was an impersonal "foreign" global giant. The first preparatory step towards the goal of a single brand was taken n the mid-1990s when HSBC started using the hyphenated form for some of its capital markets businesses, to start projecting "HSBC" beyond the holding company and the Hong Kong and Shanghai Banking Corporation.

The Group understood that it would meet internal resistance to the eventual rebranding because the staff felt loyal to their heritage banks rather than to the Group. Says Mary Jo Jacobi,[3] architect of HSBC's rebranding:

> With this in mind, to give staff something they could relate to, and to help project "HSBC" globally, we decided to sponsor Stewart Grand Prix. Formula 1 has the largest annual television audience in the world in non-World Cup years, and we knew that having the brand and logo on the car would attract a lot of attention.

> When we finally launched the global rebranding publicly in 1999, the brand was known and, importantly, had been demystified for the staff.

> The final big branding effort before the major advertising campaign that became "The World's Local Bank" was the

sponsorship of the jetways at Heathrow, Gatwick and Stansted Airports in the UK. This was the first time this medium was used for branding. It was so successful and caused so much comment that it has been replicated at airports all over the world.

In 2002 the advertising campaign created by Lowe & Partners Worldwide was unveiled, proclaiming HSBC "the world's local bank".

HSBC says that although consumers appreciate the value of international organizations, they want to be treated as individuals, and to feel that companies care about them, recognize their needs and understand what makes their community unique. This is particularly true for customers who don't travel internationally.

An example of this was told me by Mary Jo Jacobi:

In Kuwait all members of the population are paid a monthly stipend by the government and these are deposited in our bank. However, many desert tribesmen are suspicious of paper statements. They often ride into town and call at the bank and ask to "see my money". The manager always has to be ready to produce the hard cash to prove it is safe and available, even though the customer often does not make a withdrawal.

HSBC's global brand advertising, sponsorship, PR and communications outreach is widely recognized as a brilliant concept of twinning the attributes of individual service with those of a full range of financial services offered globally. It is also an example of inside-out branding. Chris Clark, head of marketing at HSBC Group, told *The Banker*:

We are thrilled to be number one in your top brands list. It's reflective of an organization that now believes branding is the job of the 310,000 people who work for this company, rather than primarily a function of the marketing department. We believe customer recommendation and brand health are probably the only two leading indicators of future business performance. If you have a healthy brand and high levels of customer advocacy, it is probable that if you price, promote and distribute your financial services and products properly – you should do well.

And, of course, customer recommendation is a direct result of excellent customer service, which according to Mary Jo Jacobi is "the essence of a good brand. When we launched the HSBC brand it was based on the fact that in retail banking, the brand is only as strong as the service provided by the worst cashier/teller on his or her worst day."

Brand fatigue

Revival of a brand may be provoked by a very basic motivation. If a brand is tired, old, losing its place in the market or in the rankings of reputation, it is not surprising that the management will consider a rebranding exercise. This makes sense but only if accompanied by a full top to bottom strategic review of the corporation's operations. Brand fatigue is seldom something that will be solved by a design makeover alone. Nevertheless, the very process involved in rebranding will bring to the surface other necessary changes in the structure, marketing, operations and management of employee relations if the corporation is to get back on the path to success. In this regard the process can act as an important catalyst and should not be too easily dismissed as cosmetic. It will uncover much about the brand, but among the findings are likely to be:

- the brand has lost its moorings and drifted too far from the values that helped it succeed in the first place
- the brand has become sclerotic and no longer serves a needed purpose or has been overtaken by rivals
- the brand merely needs updating in minor ways and more targeted and energetic promotion
- the brand team is tired and needs to be rested and a fresh team brought in.

Make news

Rebranding is an opportunity to make news and put the spotlight on the corporation to all its stakeholders. If it is creative and well planned, it enables the corporation to use the platform to tell its story and describe how it is relevant in the current marketplace. This can be especially important with employees whose "living the brand" and advocacy can benefit from the excitement involved in a brand revival project.

It might not seem necessary for the world's largest industrial company, as well as one that is in the top ten of every brand ranking table to make news but for GE it was important to communicate substantive changes that were taking place at the corporation. Following the retirement of CEO Jack Welch, arguably the best-known business leader of his generation, his successor, Jeffery Immelt, needed to stamp his own "brand" on the organization. In the USA itself it had become imperative to shake off the bad reputation effects of a controversy over GE's disposal of PCBs in the Hudson River. The topic kept returning to the news to haunt GE as litigation and government enquiries generated decisions or reports.

Here was an opportunity for Immelt to mark out the theme of his stewardship of GE and at the same time rebrand the corporation as a committed member of a sustainable society. The overall theme selected for the new era was GE: Imagination at work.

Under this umbrella, proof-point initiatives were undertaken, none more dramatic than "ecomagination". This proclaimed a new thinking at GE – that an aggressive clean tech initiative would benefit the bottom line of GE and its customers. According to research undertaken by PR agency Edelman, environmentalists and the business community would be most likely to view ecomagination credibly if it was seen as a natural extension of GE's business and technological strengths.

Ecomagination certainly made news for GE. As a central focus of speeches given by Jeffrey Immelt, GE was able to put its polluting past behind it and become the champion of a much more vigorous private sector role in meeting global environmental challenges.

Need for new brand architecture

Those corporations that have been assembled through a process of mergers, perhaps without a dominant brand and brand naming process like GE, can find themselves in a muddle, both organizationally and from the point of view of brand clarity. So there comes a time when the decision is made to pause and address the issue through a strategy review and rebranding process. It becomes necessary to assess the potency and relevancy of a group which might have several well-known brands, all with different meanings and qualities and adherents. A new brand hierarchy and architecture needs to be created. In this process either one name will be chosen from among the existing brands or a completely new one created to act as the master corporate brand. Whichever alternative is selected, it will create the need for a major internal and external communications program.

MAKING CHOICES

Once a decision in principle has been made a corporation is then faced with a choice, whether to view the rebranding effort as evolutionary or revolutionary. The answer to this question will be predetermined as shown in Table 12.1.

Table 12.1 Reasons for rebranding

Problem or opportunity	Style of implementation
Update image to match reality	Evolutionary, but expedited if major change involved and publicity impact is sought
Merger/acquisition/demerger/spin-off involving change of name or brand architecture	Revolutionary, synchronized and well-publicized overnight switch-over
Buggy whip factor	Evolutionary, heavy reliance on intensive, creative and sustained communication
Brand fatigue or to make news	Dramatize evolution or revolution to achieve impact at switch
Crisis recovery/damaged brand reputation	Can be evolutionary or revolutionary, as discussed in Chapter 14

Two global brands in very different sectors – consumer products and banking – are cited by Muzellec and Lambkin[4] as examples of revolutionary rebranding according to the reasons given by the companies. The first is Danone, which described its strategy thus:[5]

> In June 1994, it decided to drop BSN, which seemed to reflect the company's past rather than looking ahead to the future, and adopt the name of The Groupe Danone, symbolized by a little boy gazing up at a star. The Group thus took advantage of the resonance of its leading brand, which was famous the world over, produced in 30 countries, and accounted for about a quarter of its turnover. Danone is the Group's standard bearer and has become the link between the various families of brands: biscuits, mineral waters and baby foods were soon being sold under the new name.

After a series of acquisitions, UBS decided to do away with certain venerable brands in the interests of promoting the UBS name alone. Its announcement[6] said that the firm was undertaking:

a further evolution of its brand strategy and portfolio. From the second half of 2003, its businesses will be represented by the single UBS brand. The firm will no longer market services using the UBS Warburg or UBS PaineWebber brands. The move to a simpler branding accurately reflects UBS's integrated business model and the "one firm" approach UBS delivers to its clients.

But circumstances change and UBS has recently suffered reverses of fortune that might force it to sell off certain of its divisions or lines of business. It could well be that following the completion of the disposals, UBS will once again have to rebrand itself to reflect the reality of its operations. There has even been media speculation that the discarded brand names (for example Warburg and PaineWebber) might be revived.

BRAND BLUNDERS

Any corporation intent on rebranding itself should do so with extreme care according to Muzellec and Lambkin.[7] They point to the project to rebrand the UK's Royal Mail as Consignia as a case in point. In addition to provoking a public outcry, it cost £2.5 million to become Consignia plus an additional £1 million to change the name back to Royal Mail – the brand that was cherished by the British public.[8] It seems imperative, therefore, that such decisions be informed by strong theory and research.

Another example from Britain is the misstep taken by British Airways (BA), one of the best in class organizations as regards branding. After a very successful advertising and communication strategy of positioning themselves as "The World's Favourite Airline" with more destinations covered than any other, BA made the fateful decision to unhitch itself from its British base and link more strongly with the many markets it served. The visible expression of this was the removal of the British flag from the tailplanes of the BA fleet of aircraft and its replacement with images created by artists from many international countries. The redesign was announced with great fanfare and in the expectation of a favorable reaction everywhere. The opposite turned out to be the case. There was a public outcry in Britain where many people saw the move as unpatriotic. Overseas, especially in the all-important North American market, there was disappointment; it turned out that "Britishness" was seen as a key marketing advantage by travelers, especially those loyal to BA. The rebranding move also allowed an opening to Richard Branson's feisty rival airline, Virgin Atlantic, to exploit the error and position itself as the more patriotic of the two carriers. It was not long before British Airways aircraft were returned to the paint shop and the tails were once again flying the union flag, albeit in a more surrealist design.

ALPHABET BRAND SOUP

You must have noticed the proliferation of acronymic brands in recent years – brands whose familiar names have been replaced by a set of anonymous initials.

Of course the use of initials has been with us for a long time, mostly as a convenient abbreviation which then, in many cases, grew into a corporate identity or logo, symbolizing the corporation. Examples are IBM, GE and HSBC.

But there are many other newer reasons for making a conscious transfer to an acronym in today's global economy. Here are some of them:

- Many names do not travel well and would hamper the ability of corporation or product to find new markets around the world. You might tingle with anticipation at buying a new BMW and feel confident in the performance and quality of a product from Germany. But would you be quite as excited at the prospect of taking delivery of a product from the Bayerische Motoren Werke? Perhaps not, and nor would many BMW fans living outside German-speaking countries.

- In addition to being unwieldy and difficult for non-German-speaking people to pronounce, Badische Anilin Soda Fabrik no longer describes the full range of chemical products made by BASF. The same is true of the American Telegraph and Telephone company whose activities are no longer restricted to the USA or to the traditional services of telegraphy and telephony. Another company is United Parcel Service, which now offers an array of global supply chain management services well beyond package delivery and has transitioned to UPS, a name by which it was known colloquially anyway. The recent rebranding of UPS is described earlier in this chapter.

- For companies such as UPS, IBM (International Business

Machines) and GE (General Electric) the change to an acronymic description has other attractions. A transition can be made smoothly without too much disturbance to the longer-serving employees as can happen when the decision is made to coin a completely new name.

■ The change of name to an acronym often applies primarily to a holding company. This allows the corporation to acquire other businesses while the heritage name can remain active as a division or subsidiary operating company. Earlier in this chapter you read about HSBC, which still operates under its heritage name, the Hong Kong and Shanghai Bank, in markets in East Asia.

■ Another reason for the switch to an acronym can be particularly relevant to professional service and consulting companies. While Barton, Batten, Durstine and Osborne has a lovely ring to it, the name is something of a mouthful and became moot as a descriptor when the named founding partners had left the company or passed on. The same is true of Doyle, Dane Bernbach. Today these two giant global advertising agencies are known as BBDO and DDB and all but those with the most interest can be forgiven for not knowing the original names. Both these advertising agencies are now owned by Omnicom.

There can be mundane reasons to support the idea of a change to an acronym, which is invariably shorter than the original name. Cheerleaders are graphic artists and typographers who can not only be creative with logo design but simply find that they can fit a compact name onto a page, ad or package more easily.

Notes

1 Gordon Moore was one of the founders of Intel Corporation.
2 *The Banker*'s Top 500 Financial Brands (March 2008) is based on data provided by Brand Finance plc. In addition to leading the list of financial institutions, HSBC is ranked 7th among all brands behind Coca-Cola, Microsoft, Wal-Mart, IBM and GE. Its brand value is noted as $35,456 million.
3 Personal communication.
4 Muzellec, L. and Lambkin, M. (2006) "Corporate rebranding: Destroying, transferring or creating brand equity?", *European Journal of Marketing*, **40**(7/8): 803–24.
5 Danone Group, n.d., cited in Muzellec and Lambkin.
6 UBS (2002), cited in Muzellec and Lambkin.
7 Op. cit.
8 Haig, M (2003) *Brand Failures,* Kogan Page; and "Brand new name game", *Europe Intelligence Wire*, 2004.

13

Crisis – the defining moment

Every corporation is likely to face one or more major crises during its lifetime. A crisis or catastrophe is the crucible in which the resilience of the brand is tested, sometimes to destruction because not all survive the test. Among those that did not survive the test of a severe crisis is Arthur Andersen, the accounting firm that was destroyed by the Enron scandal. Enron itself came out of the affair as a mere shell of its former self. Two of the USA's most famous airlines – PanAm and TWA – had prolonged declines and deaths that many experts trace back to the terrorist crises that each suffered and from which they were unable to recover.

But in order to understand the full cycle of events it is necessary to start long before a crisis occurs because almost every crisis is not a matter of bad luck; most are the result of poor risk or issue management. If as much effort and attention were to be given to risk and issue management as to preparation for crises as if they were inevitable, then not only would many be avoided but reputations would be held intact.

Figure 13.1 is a simple depiction of the circular nature of risk, issues and crisis management. It is a sad fact of business life that it seems necessary for most managements to give their full attention and funding to the topic only when they are located in the reactive zone. It seems to take the experience of a full-blown crisis for the purse strings to be opened and management resources to be devoted to proactive measures that will build reputation and brand equity. But why should this surprise us? Even in the field of personal healthcare it is customary to give short shrift to sensible prevention measures and early diagnosis, leading to much greater costs and anguish when symptoms present themselves.

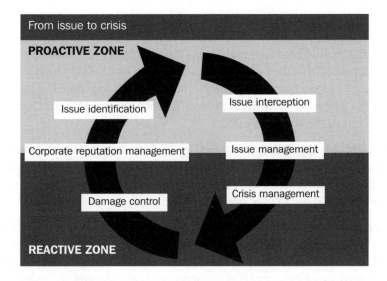

Figure 13.1 From issue to crisis (Source: *How to Manage Your Global Reputation*, Palgrave Macmillan © 2002 Michael Morley)

No business sector has a greater vested interest in crisis management than the insurance industry. It is where the buck stops – or rather it is where the bucks are kept that get paid out to crisis victims. The motivation to ensure crises are avoided or mitigated when they occur is a powerful one for all those underwriting risk.

Aon, a leading global insurance specialist,[1] is at the forefront of the industry in studying the dynamics of the various kinds of crises and evangelizes greater effort in crisis prevention and management. What Aon has learned through its investigations is important for anyone involved in brand management on a global basis – that the most serious risk facing corporations is "damage to reputation." This is the finding of the *Aon Global Risk Management Survey 2007*, which gathered responses from 320 organizations in 29 countries. Participating organizations had annual revenues equivalent to US$1 billion or greater and represent a broad range of industry sectors in the Americas, Europe and Asia/Pacific. The majority of organizations are publicly owned (70 percent), a further 25 percent privately owned and a majority of the balance government-owned or not-for-profit organizations. According to Randy Nornes, Executive Vice President of Aon:

The findings of our survey demonstrate the dynamic nature of risk as management priorities shift over time. Whereas senior management and risk managers have traditionally been concerned with operational and financial risk they now have to deal with issues as diverse, complex and esoteric as reputation crises, sustainability, labor unrest, pandemics and the impact of new regulation all around the world. This thinking is reflected in the top risks cited.

Damage to reputation emerged as the most frequently noted risk concern. While intangible, reputation is one of the most important corporate assets and also one of the most difficult to protect; it takes years to build but can be destroyed overnight.

While some consider damage to reputation a risk in its own right, others may consider it as a consequence of other risks; either way, it is clear that all risks may impact or be impacted by it. Damage to reputation is an enterprise-wide event that can lead to negative publicity, reduction in earnings, costly litigation, credit downgrades, a decline in market share and the inability to recruit and retain top talent. The process of globalization, linked with the acceleration and flow of information further accentuates vulnerabilities.

POTENTIAL FOR RISK

It is one thing to recognize the potential for risk, and another to take preventive action. Figure 13.2 shows several risks in order of importance to the survey's respondents, along with their level of preparation.
Says Randy Nornes:

It is quite surprising to find this lack of preparedness for the key risks identified. Risk concerns for which respondents overall reported the lowest state of preparedness are typically more complex, difficult to control, carry a degree of unpredictability and are enterprise-wide. These risks, while difficult to manage and in some cases not insurable, must still be addressed and require innovative forward-looking solutions. Historical priorities and treatment may not prove adequate for dealing with future risk trends.

There are ten kinds of crises which have the potential to cause reputational damage if ineptly handled. Five of them are slow-burning issues,

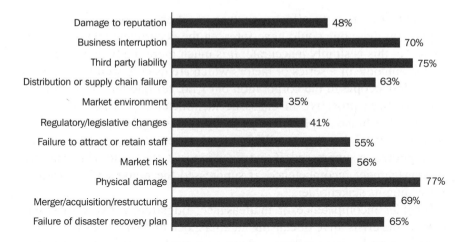

Figure 13.2 Key risks and level of preparedness (Source: 2007 Aon Risk Survey)

which can be detected and managed by using identification and intervention techniques:

- Litigation
- Product liability
- Action by pressure groups
- Labor disputes
- Financial irregularities.

The other kinds of crises usually come as surprises, even though most of them are potential hazards for all businesses and, with some exceptions, should have been foreseen. In all cases, advance preparation can limit the reputational damage from such crises and ensure a prompt and effective response when they occur:

- Exposé or whistleblowing
- Hostile takeover bid
- Disaster, accident, explosion, oil spills
- Production mistake, product recall
- Terrorism, tampering, extortion.

It is natural and very common for corporations that have become engulfed in a crisis to affect a posture of surprise, communicating the impression that none could have foreseen the occurrence that caused the crisis. Yet this is simply inaccurate. It is much more likely to be the unalterable outcome of a series of factors which are usually well known by at least a few people in the corporation but who, for one reason or another, have not been proactive in the issue identification process. When this happens, the brand is placed in jeopardy because subsequent investigations will reveal that the contributing factors were known in advance and were ignored or suppressed. If they were ignored, the brand will be tainted by management incompetence; if suppressed the brand will be seen as misleading its stakeholders.

Whether incompetence or malfeasance, litigation is likely to ensue, keeping the crisis alive or causing an aftershock that will place the corporation in a prolonged position of damage control and delaying a return to the proactive zone.

There are plenty of examples of recent "surprise" crises which turned out to have been quite predictable. In each case, measurable damage was sustained by the corporate brand.

BEYOND PETROLEUM?

BP, the world's third largest oil company had, starting in 2000, rebranded itself. It changed its name from British Petroleum to reflect its new status, having acquired three other major oil companies in the USA. It adopted a new slogan – Beyond Petroleum – and a new logo that proclaimed its commitment to developing renewable and environmentally acceptable forms of energy in the future. The award-winning advertising went some way to distancing BP from its rivals and its CEO, Lord Browne of Madingley, gained iconic status as perhaps the most applauded business leader in the media in the period 2000–2005.

But while BP's strategy and aspirations were no doubt truly transformational, it was not possible to change the realities of corporate activities and the company was soon to be hit with a series of hammer blows to the image of both the corporation and its CEO. Lord Browne, whose sexual orientation was an open secret among business associates and had no bearing on his successful career, became involved in a scandal which he sought to suppress. The surrounding publicity forced him to take early retirement because it increased attention and day-by-day reporting that focused on other – more serious – operational troubles facing the oil giant which put into question BP's commitment to living its proclaimed values. Important among these were an explosion in 2005 at one of BP's largest refineries in Texas, causing 15 deaths and 100 injuries. Official government and internal investigations concluded that mismanagement contributed to the disaster. The following year there was a leak in one of BP's pipelines in Alaska and this caused an oil spill into the tundra. Later in 2006 BP announced the closure of its last oil wells in Alaska, which had been leaking crude oil and diesel. In both cases environmentalists claim that the spills and leaks were the result of corrosion that had occurred because of corporate decisions to cut maintenance.

While many of these "crises" came as a surprise to those who had their brand image shaped by the powerful green "Beyond Petroleum" campaign, subsequent investigation and analysis showed that the company's description of itself had gone "Beyond Reality" and it had been unable to accelerate operational change in step with its promotional messages. There were plenty of people inside and out who were aware of the reality and who could (and maybe did) predict the course of events.

FRAUDULENT MANIPULATIONS

The Enron affair had all the telltale signs of a major crisis for several months before its "surprise" meltdown in late 2001 when it filed for bankruptcy. Here was an unusual combination of a corporation; one part was an old-fashioned utility with profitably operating physical assets such as power plants that delivered natural gas and electricity to its customers, a business easily understood by investors and analysts. The other part was considered exciting and innovative and involved online trading and the creation of a series of increasingly exotic financial instruments that captivated investors by their brilliant performance but were much less well understood. In fact, the Enron house of cards had been based on a series of fraudulent manipulations by a number of its senior executives who have since been convicted. Here was a company that promoted itself and its business model with evangelical zeal and succeeded in creating a faithful following even among normally skeptical analysts and media commentators; it seems that, once they had joined the flock, it would be hard for many of them to see any flaw in the idol that they had helped create.

Yet, even as *Fortune Magazine* named Enron "America's Most Innovative Company" for the sixth successive year in 2001 and it was included in the magazine's 2000 list of the 100 Best Companies to Work For, staff writer Bethany McLean wrote an article published in *Fortune*'s March 2001 issue with the headline "Is Enron Overpriced" pointing out many of the anomalies in Enron's financial reports that should have been amber lights to any investor or vigilant analyst. Yet the warning signs were ignored until the eventual denouement as the year drew to a close.

HIDDEN LOSSES

Enron did not sink alone. It dragged down the great accounting firm of Arthur Andersen, its auditor and financial adviser, which was implicated in the construction of the exotic financial instruments used by Enron. This included the transfer of losses to "special purpose entities" which were limited partnerships that Enron controlled. It turned out that the primary special purpose of these entities was to hide losses and bad investments so that they did not show up on Enron's financial reports to shareholders.

It is doubtful if Andersen would have weathered the storm created by the scandal alone. But it's the second shoe that dropped that ensured its downfall. This was when the accounting firm was charged and convicted of obstruction of justice in 2002. The indictment claimed the company had arranged for the systematic destruction of documents relating to the Enron audit. By the time the guilty verdict was overturned by the Supreme Court in 2005, the firm had to all intents and purposes ceased to exist and all the partners and key staff not implicated in the Enron affair had been hired by one or other of the major firms (who now were no longer referred to as "the big five" but had been renamed "the final four"). Here was a case in which the result must have been predictable to the firm's leadership. There had been – as we now know – whistleblowers within Enron whose warnings were ignored or rebutted. And surely the criminal manipulations should have been spotted by even the least experienced CPA. This was also an example of how a brand can be destroyed when it becomes uncoupled from its founder's values. According to Wikipedia:

> Arthur Andersen, who founded the firm in 1916 and headed it until his death in 1947, was a zealous supporter of high standards in the accounting industry. A stickler for honesty, he argued that accountants' responsibility was to investors, not their clients. During the early years, it is reputed that Andersen was approached by an executive from a local rail utility to sign off on accounts containing flawed accounting, or else face the loss of a major client. Andersen refused in no uncertain

terms, replying that he would not sign the accounts "for all the money in America." Leonard Spacek, who succeeded Andersen at the founder's death, continued this emphasis on honesty. For many years, Andersen's motto was "Think straight, talk straight."

REFRESHING CANDOR

Today American Express is one of the strongest global brands (15th in the Interbrand/*BusinessWeek* rankings) with stellar financial results and an equally stellar reputation, as has been true for most of its history of more than 150 years. But the company is refreshingly candid in describing a period when, following several acquisitions, it became overextended. Under the heading "Trying Times" in the company's history posted on its website (www.americanexpress.com), it records that:

In 1987, American Express Bank added $950 million to its reserves against outstanding loans in Latin America. Later the same year, the U.S. stock market experienced its largest drop since the Great Depression; and in the aftermath, Shearson was rocked by a series of serious missteps and setbacks. The situation ultimately became so dire that in 1990 American Express repurchased all of Shearson's remaining publicly traded stock for more than $1 billion and provided a critically necessary capital infusion.

Continuing problems at Shearson masked an ultimately more disturbing development. Serious problems were developing in the core American Express Card business. Despite the introduction in 1987 of a new revolving credit product in the United States, the company's share of the U.S. card market fell during the late 1980s and early 1990s. Trouble was also brewing on the merchant front. In Boston in 1991 a group of restaurateurs, upset about what they felt were American Express' unfairly high rates, staged a revolt that came to be known as the Boston Fee Party. Outside the United States, card suppression – when merchants try to dissuade customers from using the American Express Card – began to rise.

Years later, the company's chief executive, Kenneth Chenault, would say, in retrospect, "If not for the strength of our brand name, American Express would have collapsed by the late 1980s."

MANAGING A CRISIS

This volume is concerned only with corporate brand management on a global basis so it is hardly the place for a full discourse on crisis management as it needs to be practiced in the reactive zone once a crisis has been triggered. There are many excellent substantial volumes, articles and manuals offering good advice on how to respond to a wide variety of crises. In this pantheon of literature I can mention my own book, *How To Manage Your Global Reputation*, which contains a chapter on crisis management.

It is sufficient here to draw on the "Golden Rules" I concocted as simple basic guidelines that any company can follow. Here they are in shortened form:

1. The CEO takes charge
The chief executive officer must be informed of any *major* crisis *immediately*, wherever he is and whatever the time. The ultimate impact of the crisis on the company's reputation and bottom line is shaped in the first few hours after a "surprise" crisis occurs. His first duty is to apologize to those affected even if the company is not to blame. At the same time, he must reassure and commit to doing everything possible to minimize any negative impact. He must take control and get to the site of the crisis immediately.

2. Issue holding statement within two hours
Two hours is the maximum length of time that should pass before you issue a statement summarizing the facts of the matter as far as they are known. Stick to the facts and do not elaborate or try to interpret them. Every minute you delay with your statement means reporters must find alternative "experts" to explain the cause. Corporate and industry enemies will be eager to step in and give their views.

3. Create a crisis task force
The CEO should nominate a special task force early. The task force leader should be a senior executive of the company, who will be able to take on some of the time-consuming communication duties that will emerge as the crisis evolves. The task force should consist of a legal representative, a communications officer and the technical specialists appropriate to the incident.

Members of the task force should be assigned full time in the heat of the crisis, with counsel and support from a specialist PR agency team. The secondary effects of a crisis can be extremely damaging and the huge time demands it creates distract the company and its executives from their true purpose. The company must field two teams, defense and offense, at the same time.

4. Set up and announce an internal investigation

Set up your own internal investigation to be ahead of the official investigation that follows most crises. Select a chairman who is independent and respected. The purpose is not to whitewash but to get to the truth first so you can plan remedial action and control your messages internally and externally before the official enquiry.

5. Arrange brief media training refresher course

Although the CEO and other senior executives have probably undertaken media training previously, it is a "must" to arrange a short refresher course – even if only for an hour or two – to remind your spokespersons of the tenets of a successful interview and to rehearse them on the key messages to be communicated, along with answers to likely questions.

6. Call on civic and other government leaders for help

In cases of loss of life, property and similar dangerous situations, do not try to fight the crisis alone. Call on civic, police and other appropriate leaders for help. Not only will this help to mitigate the disaster more quickly, it will make the impact of the crisis a shared problem.

7. Announce establishment of a disaster fund within 24 hours

The victims of some disasters are faced with immediate, unusual expenses for medical treatment, travel and shelter, and often have no money to cover these costs.

8. Institute news conferences up to four times daily

Establish a routine in the immediate aftermath of a crisis that reflects the 24/7 news gathering needs of the media but also allows the press center to operate efficiently. By scheduling a news conference to provide progress reports at a time that fits in with deadlines, press officers can respond publicly to a variety of media inquiries and extend an invitation to participate in the next press briefing when there will be a Q&A session. This system ensures that *all* media are equally well served and no favorites are given exclusive treatment, something that would be guaranteed to alienate the majority of reporters.

9. Communicate proactively

In the pressure of a crisis situation, it is easy to become reactive under the onslaught of media attention and questioning. Yet it is vital for successful crisis management that you take control and communicate proactively. Do not wait for questions to be asked. In addition to the daily news conference, make sure you release regular news bulletins – by fax, video news release, web page and all the other means at your disposal. Report what you have found out about the cause of the crisis, what the company is doing to put things right, how it is helping those affected, and steps being taken to prevent future occurrences. This is the first step in damage control.

10. Survey public opinion

Do not fly blind in a crisis. Opinions may vary among senior management as to the extent of public awareness of the crisis and its effect on your company's reputation. The impact of the crisis will also vary widely in different parts of the world. You should know at intervals how your response to the crisis is being viewed by employees and audiences key to your business, for example opinion leaders and members of the public.

RECOVERY

It can take time for the wounds of a crisis to heal. Many corporations make a mistake in trying to undertake proactive programs unconnected with the crisis to deflect attention or to act as a balance. These seldom work. One reason is that it is the crisis alone that is of interest to the media and the public. Time alone (and the limits of media and public attention span) will allow the crisis story to move from the front page to the inside pages and eventually out of the news altogether unless revived by aftershocks (as described elsewhere). During this period a "recovery" team, separate from the task force handling the crisis itself, should be put to work on creating and crafting a program to rebuild the business, any damaged reputation and brand equity, to start when the crisis has receded sufficiently. In most cases, this will be focused on the existing corporate brand; in a few it might mean a complete rebranding, with new name, logo and management (for almost every significant crisis provokes a change in a corporation's CEO and top management).

Not all crises are confined to one corporation when they are caused by an external event. An entire industry can be affected. The airline industry is a case in point. It is especially susceptible to public anxieties about security and safety.

CASE British Airways and the world's biggest offer

It is not sufficient to prepare for and manage a crisis when it hits. Forward planning requires that there be a "recovery" plan in place to rebuild the business that might have been badly damaged by a catastrophe. It does not matter whether the cause was human error, engineering failure or "act of God" as the insurance companies categorize events over which you have no control.

Companies that operate globally feel the impact whenever there are tumultuous world events.

The repercussions of a long list of crises are especially dramatic for the travel and tourism industry, as British Airways and other airlines learned in 1986, immediately following the bombing of Libya and the Chernobyl reactor explosion. Four years later, the passengers, crew and ground staff of a British Airways' (BA) flight landing in Kuwait were detained as "guests" of the Iraqi government, during the Gulf War. A recession was already under way and air travel had been substantially reduced. News of the Kuwait incident appeared on television and in newspapers, precipitating further losses.

Early on in the Gulf War British Airways recognized that there was little they could do to encourage air travel while hostilities continued. However, they did create a "recovery" task force which spent three months planning a high profile campaign to "jump start" air travel once again after the war ended. There was a big gap to make up because business had dropped by 30 percent. The model for action already existed. It had been created in response to the 1986 losses. Then, the "Go for it America" campaign had sent 5,000 lucky travelers on cost-free sprees from the USA to Great Britain. This earlier success prompted BA to create "The World's Biggest Offer" in 1990, a $100 million promotion "to get the world flying again".

Every seat free

Working with Edelman Public Relations Worldwide, BA announced that on April 23, every seat in its system would be free. People holding tickets would fly free and other seats would be raffled through a coupon entry, for a total of 50,000 free seats. As in the earlier program, the new campaign would include special offers from hotels, car rental companies, restaurants, theaters and stores.

The global campaign, masterminded in London, required secrecy until launch day and was coordinated among BA's in-house PR managers and 42 consultancies. The tactics had to be replicated throughout the world and all press materials were localized and translated.

Announcement press conferences around the globe were held simultaneously. The entry and selection process was then monitored for anecdotes with publicity potential.

On April 23, dubbed "Up and Away Day", bobbies, bag pipers and other costumed characters were in 62 airports in BA gateway cities, and 435 previously pitched reporters, photographers and broadcast crews from 60 countries covered the winners' trips to London. Photo opportunities were set up with the British prime minister and transport minister.

The complete effort yielded major print and television coverage, including all national TV networks in the US. Worldwide, some 500 million people read about the campaign and 200 million saw it on television. There had been a grand total of 5.7 million entries and BA was able to add millions of qualified names with travel preferences to its database. Recovery from the travel slump was complete within 120 days. Every major travel market in the world was stimulated and BA's brand reputation as the world's favorite airline was enhanced by its display of bold imagination at this defining moment.

CORPORATE BRANDS AND NEW MEDIA

Internet-based communications are today a central component of all successful corporate brand management strategies. Only a short time ago, in the early years of this new century, the corporate website had already established its place in the communications quiver of most corporations. But blogs were little-understood new tools and social media such as Twitter, MySpace and Facebook were exotic sites in a universe inhabited only by a small group of early adopters.

All that has changed. Personal and corporate blogs are commonplace.

If you do not have a Facebook entry and are unaware of the latest hot video you will be a wallflower at your next cocktail party. You will be unable even to make sense of some network or cable TV news items which are increasingly regurgitating disclosures or rumors that first appeared in a social media site. You will be blind to the importance of this medium in shaping brand reputations or – more importantly – in damaging and even destroying them. Now there is an increasing body of evidence of the power of new media to attack a brand and to organize an online alliance of detractors; there is also evidence of their power to drive corporate brand reputation in a positive way for corporations that make the effort to understand the code words and code of conduct of the open source online universe.

And in the world of politics the potency of new media was demonstrated by the Obama presidential campaign in 2008. Much has been written since his successful election about the understanding his team had of communications in the digital age and their use of it to create what is widely called "the Obama brand".

Only one thing is certain in this fast changing world. That is that anything written here will be out of date by the time this volume is finished, edited, printed and distributed.

Note

1   Aon Corporation (www.aon.com) is a provider of risk management services, insurance and reinsurance brokerage, human capital and management consulting, and speciality insurance underwriting. There are 43,000 employees working in Aon's 500 offices in more than 120 countries.

14

The pillars – creating the brand foundation

There are many routes to the creation of a global corporate brand. Or, as is more frequent, taking an existing corporation and defining or redefining it as a brand. And there are as many different proprietary methodologies offered by branding consultants as there are routes. Often they are described as unique, as if the promoted procedure includes the secret formula of the next Coca-Cola.

When dissected, it turns out that most methodologies are somewhat similar in the basic steps that must be taken to build a secure brand platform. Their promotional materials describe a basic service based on the intellectual property and experience of each, using different jargon and explanations to convince potential clients of the superiority of their particular methodology. In fact, the first task of a branding consultancy is to achieve a powerful brand identity for the corporation itself and many have done this successfully.

For the purpose of this chapter I have chosen to illustrate the process by describing the fundamentals of the methodologies of just a few prominent consultants in some depth, rather than undertake a more superficial comparison between several competing approaches.

INITIAL RESEARCH

The first step in the process is research. This is always one of initial deconstruction in which the brand is taken apart and examined in its various pieces to sift the essential from the unimportant, the unique from the generic. This can be a complicated and arduous process with established organizations. In the first instance there may be multiple audiences of stakeholders, not all of which will be making brand evaluations in the same way. Second, the corporation itself may be multi divisional and operating as a single brand in many industry sectors (GE, Philips, Siemens) or as a house of brands (Unilever); in both cases the corporate brand strategy will have to consider the product brand strategy and work within – or perhaps reconstruct – the brand architecture. There are also likely to be many contrary views regarding the brand among the company executives themselves.

It is this degree of complexity that led Alan Siegel of brand consultancy Siegel+Gale to develop a two-step brand process of "Simplify and Amplify".[1] The first step of simplification is essential, he says, if a brand is to be easily understood and evangelized:

In the Simplify phase, we analyze the strengths and capabilities of the organization, the environment in which it operates, and its audiences to define the brand platform. The brand platform is composed of a brand promise that defines what the organization stands for, values that govern the behavior of the employees, and the voice, which provides criteria for all external communications. Together, the brand platform provides a lens through which all decisions, strategic and creative, are measured, evaluated and made.

If your goal is to simplify then it is appropriate to use a method that is itself very simple and clear, such as the DDB Worldwide brand foundations process described to me by Keith Reinhard, the agency's Chairman Emeritus. "Brand Foundations", he says, "is a simple process for examining a brand's unique history, the organization behind it, the future strategy and the stakeholder and competitor environment."

The process calls for a series of questions that you have to imagine the brand asking itself as it seeks to consider where it is now and where it would like to be in the future.

Look at the grid in Table 14.1. Although, as one of the world's iconic advertising agencies, its process might have been developed primarily with products in mind, the questions are equally relevant to every corporate brand.

Table 14.1 Brand foundations process, step 1 (Source: DDB Worldwide)

Where do I come from?	The origins, history and "anchorage" of the brand
What do I do?	The brand's field of competence – what does it make or do? What are its skills?
What makes me different?	What unique qualities differentiate the brand from all others?
Who am I for?	How can we define the target user or need stated that the brand addresses? What do we know about them?
What am I like as a person?	How does the brand behave, express itself? What personality does it have?
What do I fight for?	What is the brand's unique, driving purpose in the world?
What do I value?	In a word, what does the brand stand for?
Strategic concept	The whole brand vision in a single phrase

Origins and history

In DDB's "The Springboard Approach" brand training volume,[2] the agency asserts that:

> Every brand has a unique asset that cannot be copied—its own past. Understanding and re-interpreting what made a brand successful in the past can be a powerful source of inspiration for the future. Values remain relevant even when the world appears to have changed beyond recognition.

> Every Brand Foundations project should include researching and telling stories about the brand's past, especially its origins and foundation. And then creatively re-interpreting these stories for insights about what the brand could do now and in the future.

DDB suggests this example from long-time client McDonald's: "What would Ray Kroc do if he were starting the McDonald's business today? What were his values and goals, and what might those mean in today's world?"

For Keith Reinhard, who now spends most of his time as President of Business For Diplomatic Action, an organization dedicated to rebuilding the USA's reputation around the world, his questioning might have been directed at the founding fathers of the nation. What would have been the branding recipe offered by Washington, Franklin, Jefferson, Hamilton, Adams or Madison?

A sense of specific mission and purpose can be the single most powerful element that creates a strong brand. This does not mean a competitive goal ("be brand leader"), nor a bland general statement of excellence ("delighting customers"), but a very particular statement of how the brand wants to make a difference in the world. Reinhard says:

> The power of questions on what do I fight for or what values do I stand for is that it forces us to look beyond the simple financial goals of the brand to considering its impact on society, on the environment, on culture or on individuals' lives. This makes it a challenging but potentially liberating question.

Because the Founding Fathers were no longer available to help Roger Dow, CEO of the Travel Industry Association (TIA) (of the USA), in his quest to distill the essence of the appeal of America to tourists, he and Reinhard convened a meeting of 15 representatives of the travel and tourism industry instead. They worked through the DDB brand foundations process to create the theme of a new communications initiative. Says Dow:[3]

> We arrived at the conclusion that the essence of the American tourism brand was "discovery". We are a nation of pioneers, explorers and discoverers. We still have many frontiers for the visitor to explore – including frontiers of science and art, of nature and commerce and much else. So we changed our name to the U.S. Travel Association and we changed our call to action from See America to Discover America. Thus we hope to touch the spirit of the explorer in everyone.

Exhibit 14.1 describes how the group worked through the brand foundations process to arrive at the new branding of America as a tourist destination.

Exhibit 14.1 TIA Brand Foundations Worksheet (Source: Travel Industry Association)

Where do I come from?

"I am a nation of immigrants drawn by the possibility of life, liberty and the pursuit of happiness. I am an amalgamation of cultures from around the world. I am born of optimism and hope for a better future. I am, by inclination and necessity, a pioneer."

What do I do?

"As a vacation destination, I enrich people's lives with new experiences, new perspectives and lasting memories. I fulfill dreams and expand personal horizons. I reinvigorate."

What makes me different?

"I welcome you to explore the frontiers with me – frontiers of nature, music, science, entertainment, commerce, art, fashion, architecture, cuisine, medicine, education. I offer you unlimited access to larger than life experiences that can be found nowhere else – nature and culture at its most remarkable."

Who am I for?

"I am for the 'explorer' in everyone."

What do I fight for?

"I fight for expanding the frontiers of science, commerce and art. I fight for preserving the frontiers of nature, for defending the defenseless and for skewering the pretentious."

What do I value?

- Fairness
- Equality
- Inalienable rights
- Access to opportunity
- Freedom

Reinhard likes to distill the answers arrived at through the brand foundations process into what he defines as the essence of the brand or its guiding concept. This, he told me, "consists of the right combination of three elements: The Brand's point of view – how it views the world and its role in it – out of which springs a promise, either explicit or implicit, which is relevant to all stakeholders. Both the Point of View and the Promise are clothed in an attractive, differentiating and, one would hope, compelling personality."

In the case of the USA, these "three Ps" were determined to be:

- **Point of View:** Life is more interesting, more fun and rewarding, on the frontier – the frontiers of entertainment, music, art, science, nature, fashion and commerce.
- **Promise:** Your life will be uniquely enriched when you visit America and explore our frontiers with us.
- **Personality:** A modern-day pioneer, young and enthusiastic, adventurous, plain-spoken and eager to help.

Having distilled the essence of the corporate brand into the brand platform, the process moves to what Alan Siegel refers to as the "Amplify" phase, which he describes in Exhibit 14.2.

Exhibit 14.2 Siegel+Gales' brand development strategy

In the Amplify phase, we bring the brand alive in everything the organization says and does. We start by developing strategies for naming, brand architecture, and messaging. We then develop the **identity elements**, including logo, colors, and imagery style, and the **identity system** for interactive, print, vehicles, uniforms, and environments, which are the foundation for creating a consistently branded **experience** at every touch point.

Our process is illustrated by a confidential project we have recently undertaken on behalf of a client.

The premier North American insurance brokerage firm for clients in the entertainment industry engaged S+G in 2007 with a fundamental strategic challenge: its strong but narrowly defined reputation in entertainment was limiting its ability to grow beyond the entertainment niche.

Few people realized that our client was more than "just an insurance broker for Hollywood." In reality, it also provided financial planning services for customers similar to those provided by high net worth money managers, family office practices of major banks, and wealth management firms.

Our client asked us to rethink their brand strategy and tell a story that more accurately reflected the breadth of services they provided. The specific objectives of the project were to develop a strategic platform that:

- Differentiated the company from brokerages, high net worth advisory firms, and private banks
- Increased awareness of its breadth and depth of offerings
- Served as an internal guide for decision making, succession planning, and hiring and retention programs
- Unified employees across practice areas and geographic locations
- Informed internal and external communications.

Strategy development process

Our process consisted of two steps. First, we examined three core questions and developed a set of insights for each:

- What opportunity does the marketplace present?
- What do key customer groups want?
- What are the organization's core strengths?

Once we developed these individual insights, we then examined the intersection of those insights and, through a combination of art and science, identified the core idea for our brand strategy recommendations.

Individual insights

- Marketplace

The growing importance of brokers to deliver product and provide valuable market intelligence, combined with an industry that had recently been tainted by bid-rigging and kick-back scandals, created an opportunity to reposition the role of brokers from "transactional middleman" to "focused adviser."

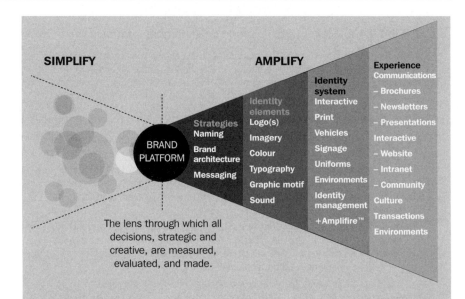

Figure 14.1 Simplify and amplify (Source: Reproduced with permission of Siegel+Gale)

■ Target
Customers were desperately looking for more than a transactional broker. They were looking for an advocate or a steward to help them navigate exposures to risk. They were seeking a trusted adviser who could provide sound counsel on risk, and a long-term relationship with someone who cared about their needs. In addition, specialty clients who exist in complex, niche marketplaces demanded specialized expertise.

■ Organization key strengths
Our client was well positioned to take advantage of the marketplace opportunity and the customer needs. From the start, the firm has exhibited an absolute commitment to client service – which is recognized and valued by clients – and has operated under principles of integrity, honesty, innovation and industry expertise. *Ultimately, we found that our client had the unique insider perspective to anticipate future uncertainty, and the reputation and client relationships to be heard.*

■ Core insight
From these three individual findings, we developed a core insight: We're much more than a brokerage firm. We're a group of highly experienced risk advisers who help clients navigate the uncertainties of business and life.

We used this core insight to serve as the foundation for the brand's strategic platform. We then developed a brand voice – rooted around the firm's values of insight, hospitality, and proactive behavior – to support this platform and ensure that all of the company's communications spoke with a consistent tone and manner.

Brand implementation

Following agreement on the Brand Platform, we brought the strategy to life in a new logo and visual system that strongly reinforced the idea of navigation. We also established a new approach to the marketing section of their website, focusing on navigation success stories across the organization – truly illustrating how the company did indeed help clients navigate the uncertainties of business and life.

Notes

1 This section is based on my personal communication with Alan Siegel and extracts from Seigel+Gale company brochures.
2 Version 2: 2003.
3 Personal communication.

15
Corporate social responsibility

"Whatever the corporate-social-responsibility gurus say, business is a force for good in itself: its most useful contribution to society is making profits and products" states *The Economist* (June 28, 2008) in a leading article about Bill Gates. The world's richest man had just announced that he was stepping back from executive duties at Microsoft to devote most of his energies to his charitable foundation.

There are two points to be made about this assertion.

The first is that *The Economist* has not taken the position of free market purists who see the quest for profit and the need to satisfy the appetites of investors as the only purpose of business. By choosing the words "most useful contribution to society" the newspaper is implicitly suggesting that business has some other, albeit subsidiary, roles to play. One does not have to be a corporate social responsibility guru to believe that in today's economic environment business should be able to manage a number of useful roles at the same time.

The second is the common mistake of equating corporate social responsibility (CSR) solely with philanthropy.

While both play an important role in shaping a corporate brand, CSR is about how an enterprise conducts its business and makes its money. Philanthropy is about how the company devotes its profits to charitable causes.

On one thing all can agree. The primary duty of any business is to succeed financially. If it does not, or cannot, then it is bound to fail in social responsibility (creation of jobs, wealth, and so on) and an empty bank balance offers little chance for philanthropy.

Corporate social responsibility might at first sight appear to be a phenomenon that first gained currency in the latter decade or two of the 20th century but has established itself firmly as part of the management agenda during the first years of the 21st. Yet it has been with us under various other names since limited liability corporations were formed.

The only elements that have changed over the years are, first, how we define "social responsibility" and second, how practices that might have been considered elementary corporate good behavior have been crystallized into a structured management function staffed by trained specialists.

Leaders in my own craft of public relations have long been evangelists for CSR. Edward L. Bernays, considered by many to be the "father" of modern public relations, wrote in his still relevant book *Crystallizing Public Opinion*, published in 1923: "The public relations counsel will find that the conditions under which his client operates, be it government, a manufacturer of food products or a railroad system, are constantly changing and that he must advise modifications in policy in accordance with such changes in the public point of view." Bernays adds: "He acts (in a capacity) as a consultant both in interpreting the public to his client and in helping him to interpret the client to the public. He helps to mould the action of his client as well as to mould public opinion." Nearly 90 years ago Bernays had equally well given a broad job description of a modern corporate responsibility officer. He knew that the job of a serious and dedicated PRO or CRO involved encouraging a change of behavior when necessary.

In the early days of my own career in public relations the most-used colloquialism was "corporate citizenship" and this is a term which I feel still conveys the essence of a socially responsible corporation, especially within a global context; for it is necessary for any socially responsible multinational company to ensure that it is a good corporate citizen in each of the countries and communities in which it operates.

The first line of my earlier book, *How to Manage Your Global Reputation*, states that Marshall McLuhan's "global village is here". I now know that while the Canadian philosopher and scholar's prediction made nearly 40 years ago has come to pass, "the global village" is open to misinterpretation. Perhaps a better description might be a "universe of interconnected villages". This is a lot less catchy but it underscores what we now know; which is that along with the seemingly relentless globalization that is connecting the world's economies and communications there is a counter trend of regionalization, localization and nationalism.

Although public relations people have been in the vanguard encouraging corporate social responsibility and some major firms have created special practice groups to counsel clients, they are no longer alone. Their right to dominate the market has been hindered by the desire of firms to avoid any suggestion that their commitment to social responsibility is driven by the wish to achieve good publicity. So specialist firms devoted exclusively to this topic have mushroomed in recent years, staffed by recruits drawn from other disciplines such as management consulting, accounting, the law, public and international affairs, science, research and development and human relations.

Most business leaders are so convinced of the benefits of globalization that they tend to think of it as an unstoppable train, conveniently forgetting economic history which shows that earlier periods of momentum towards globalization were stopped by the collapse of empires, wars and depressions that fostered periodic returns to protectionism. The logic of it all seems so clear that any suggestion that globalization might be fine for big business but not for everybody is characterized as an uninformed opinion. The view of elites in developed countries is not necessarily shared by workers whose jobs have been outsourced or "exported", or by people in smaller developing countries who feel their views and needs have been shut out by the clout of the G8 nations. The painfully slow progress of the 'Doha Round' is testament to that.

To succeed as a corporate brand in today's universe of connected villages, companies must find a way to operate as both good global and local citizens. The demands created by this need have helped create the new profession of corporate responsibility counseling.

DEFINING CSR

Every profession or management function needs a description or definition and these abound for CSR.

There is the pithy "doing well by doing good".

Or "the triple bottom line" of social, environmental and financial success.

Or the ponderous definition of the International Standards Organization (ISO 2600:13):

Social Responsibility refers to the activities of an organization aimed at contributing to a sustainable society and environment, as well as maintaining the organization's continued existence, by minimizing negative impacts and maximizing positive impacts on the society and environment through proactive stakeholder communications and engagement throughout the organization's sphere of influence. Social Responsibility is about organizational initiatives that start with, but go beyond, any legal requirements and that contribute to social acceptance. An organization obtains its social acceptance by observing national laws and applicable international agreements and by responding to an eve changing society that has constantly changing expectations.

Another approach is promulgated by Rachel Simmons (brandchannel. com) of the William J. Clinton Foundation's Healthier Generation initiative. She believes that companies can create social brand capital (SBC), which is defined as "the loyalty value that stakeholders attribute to a company's brand as a result of that company's commitment to social/ environmental causes". She points to the 2006 Cone Millennial Cause Study in which nine out of ten Millennials (born between 1979 and 2001) surveyed stated that they are likely or very likely to switch from one brand to another (price and quality being equal) if the second brand is associated with a good cause. And nearly eight out of ten want to work for a company that cares about how it contributes to society. However, there is often a big gap between research that reports intentions and an audit that monitors actions. After all, who would respond that they wanted to work for a company that did not want to contribute to society?

Ms Simmons says that companies that have a high degree of SBC meet the following four criteria, when their commitment to society and the environment is:

- the key point of competitive differentiation
- part of day-to-day operations
- inherent in the company from its foundation and not an afterthought
- relevant, authentic and sustainable.

She cites Aveda, Avon, Ben and Jerry's, Green Mountain Coffee, Newman's Own, Patagonia, Seventh Generation, Starbucks, The Body Shop and Whole Foods as examples of some companies with high SBC.

This is a topic in need of greater exploration because it is hard to resist the thought that the further a product moves away from satisfying a basic human need for survival (where its social purpose is self-evident), the greater the need for a corporation to link itself with improving activities. It is surely a win–win to salve both corporate and consumer consciences, the one troubled by marketing frivolous products and the other for desiring them in a world that treats so many of its inhabitants so very harshly.

Whatever the reasons, there is a strong body of evidence suggesting that

CSR is now a permanent feature of business management and not merely a passing fashion. Here are some of the hallmarks of a discipline that is no longer on the fringe but mainstream:

- There is now a dedicated management specialty and a large number of corporations have corporate responsibility officers, although many operate under another name and might be responsible for an additional management portfolio. All CRO's are senior managers and some report directly to the CEO.
- Most corporations produce a CSR Report. Some are supplements to the regular Annual Report to Shareholders while other companies prefer to publish them separately.
- Beyond a lively blogosphere, CSR has its own specialist journals and website/wire service, CSR*wire*.
- As you might have expected, there is an annual ranking of corporations undertaken by *CRO Magazine*. Scores are awarded in several categories: climate change, employee relations, the environment, financial performance, governance, human rights, lobbying and philanthropy. The process is still imperfect as evidenced by the passionate postings by corporations which feel their efforts have not been recognized.
- The number of ethical or "green" investment funds has blossomed in recent years.
- The field of CSR has been accorded academic recognition and respectability. Harvard University's John F. Kennedy School of Government now has a program titled the Corporate Social Responsibility Initiative, and Boston College has established a thriving Center for Corporate Citizenship. Many other universities and business schools around the world have similar bachelor's and master's degree programs or run specific shorter courses and seminars for business executives.
- CSR has now attracted its own cadre of "watchdog" organizations, usually NGOs, which monitor the performance of companies in each of the various subsets of CSR. They are always ready to publicize winners and losers, especially if they have well-known brand names. One example is the organization Climate Counts, a non-profit that publishes a scorecard ranking corporations on their efforts towards mitigating climate change. Their listing is broken down by industry category to keep comparisons fair. So, for example, in the electronics category, IBM and Canon come out as clear leaders with scores of 77 and 74 respectively but Apple is described as being "stuck" with a meager 11.

It is of course vital for corporations to observe all treaties, laws and regulations if they are to be accepted as good citizens. But in today's world, legal compliance is merely the price of an entry ticket to join in the race for honors. Corporations with a brand halo will have been pursuing policies in every aspect of their business that are several steps ahead of any legal obligation.

The defining characteristic of the best corporations is that a culture of responsibility will be embedded in its DNA, in every policy and action, from hiring to firing, from R&D to production and marketing – and beyond. This is the route to the accumulation of strong reserves of social brand capital.

STAKEHOLDER MAPPING

A valuable first step in assessing a corporation's standing as a corporate citizen is to undertake a stakeholder mapping exercise. This will enable you to identify all the elements in society that are affected by your business operations. You will research their current perceptions and initiate dialog that will lead to the formulation of policy and action in the future.

Stakeholder mapping is a tool designed to help an enterprise identify specific issues in the public domain that could impact its brand reputation. It will help to identify and then engage organizations and institutions that can serve as key influencers. Chris Deri, who leads the CRS practice at Edelman, explains his company's process:

> Through a series of internal and external interviews, we first examine those issues that matter most to an organization and its stakeholders. Then, through a systematic five-step process, we identify key opinion leaders and assess their ability to influence the external environment on these key issues. Backed by facts and figures – not speculations. This tool provides a proven approach for greater strategic integration across an entire organization based on qualitative considerations and quantitative metrics that can be effectively triangulated to shape policy and programs.

The final report includes a detailed analysis of key stakeholder groups based on the following six dimensions of activism and influence: Media Visibility; Public Policy Activism; Community Activism; Business and Corporate Influence; Organizational Resources; and Thought Leadership. Stakeholders are then plotted on a chart (see Figure 15.1) according to their ability to influence the external environment (Y-axis) and a company/organization's ability to engage the stakeholder (X-axis). The result: a targeted list of stakeholders that allows a company/organization to prioritize engagement and track shifts over time.

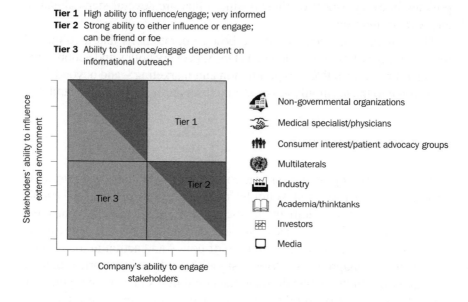

Tier 1 High ability to influence/engage; very informed
Tier 2 Strong ability to either influence or engage; can be friend or foe
Tier 3 Ability to influence/engage dependent on informational outreach

Figure 15.1 Stakeholders: influence and engagement (Source: Edelman)

ELEMENTS OF A CSR PROGRAM

A systematic Global Responsibility program will need to cover the following:

Shareholder relations

Consistent and clear communications with the owners of the corporation about its triple bottom line performance.

Employee relations

In Chapter 10 we discussed the importance of "living the brand". This begins with a well-informed and motivated group of employees at all levels and in all the locations of the corporation. Moreover, a 2007 survey[1] conducted jointly for PR agency Fleishman-Hillard and the National Consumers League found that nearly one in two US Americans believe that the most important proof of corporate responsibility is treating employees well. And only 21 percent of Americans give US corporations good marks for CSR. According to John D. Graham, Chairman of Fleishman-Hillard:

> What American consumers are telling us – perhaps influenced by ongoing coverage of corporate layoffs and employee-benefit reductions – sheds new light on how we view corporate social responsibility. If companies want to maintain and strengthen their reputations, it will be essential for them to invest actively and visibly in their employees.

> Average Americans feel strong about buying products from or working for a company whose values are aligned with their own personal values. Survey respondents say it's 'extremely' or 'very' important to work for (79 percent), buy products and services from (65 percent), and socialize with (72 percent) those who have similar values and principles.

Community relations

Good citizenship begins at the local level and every corporation needs to build strong relationships within each community (country and town) where it has operations.

NGO relations

Non-governmental organizations are the representatives of varying special public interests and need to be heard by corporations, just as they are heard by the various branches of government and the media. Some are militant and confrontational while others seek to partner with industry in the achievement of their goals. The successful corporate citizen will find a way of working with both wings. NGOs cover the full spectrum of elements that make up CSR.

Each NGO has its own mission but their combined goals are succinctly described in the statement of ten principles established by the United Nations Global Compact. Any company committing to membership of the compact must agree to subscribe to these principles (see Exhibit 15.1).

The UN Global Compact describes itself as: "A framework for businesses that are committed to aligning their operations and strategies with ten universally accepted principles in the areas of human rights, labour, the environment and anti-corruption. As the world's largest global corporate citizenship initiative, the Global Compact is first and foremost concerned with exhibiting and building the social legitimacy of business and markets."

Exhibit 15.1 The Ten Principles (Source: The United Nations Global Compact)

Human Rights

- **Principle 1:** Businesses should support and respect the protection of internationally proclaimed human rights; and
- **Principle 2:** make sure that they are not complicit in human rights abuses.

Labour Standards

- **Principle 3:** Businesses should uphold the freedom of association and the effective recognition of the right to collective bargaining;
- **Principle 4:** the elimination of all forms of forced and compulsory labour;
- **Principle 5:** the effective abolition of child labour; and
- **Principle 6:** the elimination of discrimination in respect of employment and occupation.

Environment

- **Principle 7:** Businesses should support a precautionary approach to environmental challenges;
- **Principle 8:** undertake initiatives to promote greater environmental responsibility; and
- **Principle 9:** encourage the development and diffusion of environmentally friendly technologies.

Anti-Corruption

- **Principle 10:** Businesses should work against corruption in all its forms, including extortion and bribery.

Participating companies are required to communicate annually with their shareholders on progress made in implementing the ten principles. In June 2008 the UN Global Compact announced that 630 companies were being removed from the list of participants for failing to do so. However, the number of participating corporations continues to increase. The total of business participants is now 4,619; if non-business stakeholders are added the total is 5,982.

TIMELESS

While these principles are timeless and most certainly worthy for the world, it is important to remember that how corporate responsibility is defined depends upon both the time in history and geography. In both cases priorities might well be different to those you might expect from your own vantage point today.

Consider this story told me by Dr Hans Fehr, spokesman for the Swiss chemical/pharmaceutical concern Hoffman-La Roche. Always in the avant garde of design, Roche had in the 1930s built a state of the art facility at its location on the banks of the Rhine in Basel. The Chairman commissioned a well-known European artist to paint the land and townscape in which the new building had been set, blending beautifully with its natural surroundings. The completed painting was proudly placed in a prominent position in the building for all to see. Critics applauded but instead of drawing admiring comments from employees there was silent consternation. On deeper investigation Roche discovered the reason. In his eagerness to achieve an idyllic image the artist had painted unsullied sunny skies unaware that smokeless chimneys were directly linked in employees' minds with idle factories and unemployment. The painting was returned to his studio and there the smoky emissions that we find so offensive today were painted in (at least on the canvas). The painting reappeared to universal relief and approval.

Similarly, what is considered socially responsible might be different in different parts of the world or in different cultures.

According to Kosta Petrov, who was manager of the 4th CSR Conference,[2] which took place in Dubai in 2007:

> CSR cannot be bought off the shelf; different regions have different priorities and tenets which should shape the way business entities function.
>
> Typically corporate organisations in the United States place an emphasis on a tax-deductible philanthropic model, something which has been copied by many businesses in the Middle East, even though the tax element doesn't enter the equation. In Europe the accent is more on operating in a socially responsible manner, which includes investing and dealing with other like-minded organisations and justifying support for their local communities with a solid business case.
>
> The business case for CSR in the Middle East region is gaining momentum. Islamic finance is setting a good example and in many ways runs in parallel with socially responsible investing.

SOCIAL-CAUSE AND AFFINITY MARKETING

One way companies seek to brighten their brand halo is through undertaking social-cause-related marketing initiatives. When relevant and well executed, it is thought that these can win a marketing advantage while giving visibility to an organization's commitment to society.

In such efforts a company seeks to take a step beyond its basic mission, which is to live up to the promise it has made to satisfy its customer in terms of quality, safety and value for money. It adds a commitment to support a cause or organization which it has established is important to its customers and potential customers and may not be directly related to the performance of the product.

Mitch Markson, President of Edelman's Global Consumer Brands practice, told me:

> We see a new phenomenon emerging called "Mutual Social Responsibility", where consumers and the brands they interact with every day take a mutual interest in and a mutual responsibility for being good citizens. It's a natural fusion of corporate social responsibility and traditional cause-related marketing.

> Consumers are seeking a more personal, co-creative role in everything from product development to brand marketing. A survey of 5,600 consumers in nine countries (the United States, China, the United Kingdom, Germany, Brazil, Italy, Japan, India, and Canada), conducted by StrategyOne, revealed that consumers are more involved than ever in social action, with 88 percent saying they feel it is their duty to contribute to a better society and environment. Among all respondents, "helping others and contributing to the community" was cited as the second most important source of personal contentment, after "spending time with family and friends".

> Seventy percent of consumers say they would be prepared to pay more for a brand that supports a good cause they believe in. More than seven in 10 (73 percent) would be prepared to pay more for environmentally friendly products.

> Markson adds, "The success of popular brands like Dove, Rama, The Body Shop, Virgin, and Coca-Cola, which are connected to social purposes in the minds of millions of consumers, are a testament to the active role that brands can play in advancing good causes."

The problem with such programs can be competing claims of the two different goals – linking the brand with a social cause or winning market share.

If the second of these is the more important to the corporation's management, it raises the question as to whether a cause-related initiative is the most effective route to success. As an article[3] in *MIT Sloan Management Review* in 2006 points out:

> What has been lacking from case histories and previous academic research has been a comparison of the beneficial effects of a social-cause affiliation with the effects of other types of affiliations. Most companies are faced with a choice of spending some of their marketing budget on either a social cause or a more commercial promotional venture. Comparing the performance of a societal marketing initiative to that of no initiative at all, which has been done in most of the previous experimental studies, does not provide very compelling evidence to managers about the value of societal marketing.

The authors recommend a thorough research process at the center of which is a technique known as conjoint analysis:

> This technique asks consumers to review a set of profiles, each consisting of a combination of various hypothetical attributes of a particular product or service; each consumer ranks the different profiles according to his or her preferences. The profiles are varied systematically so that a range of attribute combinations are considered, with some profiles containing high levels of certain attributes, and some containing low levels of those attributes. Based on how a consumer shows preference for the profiles, statistical techniques can be used to determine which attributes the consumer weights most strongly positively, most strongly negatively and in between.

PHILANTHROPY

There are different kinds of philanthropy spanning the full spectrum from wholly altruistic to self-serving. They are:

- **Pure philanthropy**. This is the anonymous donation of money to charities, specifically nominated or via a distribution committee to worthy causes. The donor does not wish to have his name disclosed or to have any credit. According to an article in the *New York Times* of January 26, 1997, this kind of donation is declining and now represents a mere 3 percent of charitable giving in the USA. Interestingly, the writer points out that the pressure to publicize the names of donors is not coming from donors themselves, many of whom are publicity shy, but from the recipients, such as hospitals and universities. They have discovered that the way to attract contributions is to publicize major gifts received from prominent people; this sets up a "top that" kind of competition among the rich, which swells the coffers of the luckier institutions. "To those that have, shall be given."

- **Posthumous philanthropy**. Beware of the creation of a major trust fund by individuals who have accumulated exceptional wealth during their lifetime by methods that some might consider to have been excessively harsh and callous and, on occasion, unethical. Cynics dub this "conscience money". The trusts may be set up late in life or willed upon death. Some prominent trusts that have attracted notice because their independent boards have sometimes given money to causes and institutions that would have been anathema to the donor are the Ford Foundation, the Carnegie Foundation and the Rockefeller Foundation. There is, of course, truly altruistic posthumous philanthropy, too.

- **Smart philanthropy**. This is a term used by organizations that want to build a bridge between charitable giving and self-interest. In essence, this means they want to donate money (or services, or something else of value) to charitable causes that are strongly related, if possible, to their business and its goals. It is perhaps a new variant on the saying "charity begins at home". It can mean that there is some direct payback, not always in monetary terms; or it can mean that the organization is in a special position because of its own know-how or resources to offer help unavailable from any other sources.

Notes

1   The full survey results can be found at www.fleishman.com.
2   See http://www.albawaba.com/en/countries/UAE/214303.
3   "How social-cause marketing affects consumer perceptions", by Paul N. Bloom, Steve Hoeffler, Kevin Lane Keller and Carlos E. Basurto Meza, *MIT Sloan Management Review,* January 1, 2006.

16
What's it worth?

Brand is an intangible and that is enough to make some people doubt its reality and importance in the business context.

But just because something is intangible does not mean it cannot be defined, measured and valued. Today there are a large number of organizations that have developed formulae and methodologies to calculate the value of individual and corporate brands.

Some of the firms are branding consultants, or agencies, whose primary income is derived from fees paid by clients who engage the firm to undertake a brand analysis and new brand strategy, or architecture, or even a complete rebranding. Some have grown out of advertising agencies or corporate identity consultancies. Examples of such firms abound and references to them will be found elsewhere in this volume.

Perhaps the most widely known name is Interbrand, a member of the Omnicom Group, by virtue of its collaboration with *BusinessWeek* magazine in the publication of an annual league table of global brand rankings.

The methodology by which Interbrand calculates the value it attributes to the brands in its rankings is disclosed briefly in Chapter 1. For the purpose of this chapter, however, I have chosen to describe the methodology developed by another firm, Brand Finance plc, to illustrate that brand valuation can be reliable, real and an indispensable tool for running a successful business.

One reason for this selection is the heritage of those who run the firm and maintain its impartiality: the leadership of the firm has a training and background in accounting rather than marketing. Another is the credibility of the Brand Finance valuation method with important third parties such as the major auditing firms, national tax authorities and the International Accounting Standards (IAS) Board. The firm's approach has also been accepted by the UK Takeover Panel.

Of course the ultimate determinant of brand value is established by the market itself, and because of IAS rules the sale of a brand may be the only time an accurate valuation takes place. Under present rules, the value of a brand can be recognized on the balance sheet of the acquiring corporation. But it cannot be recognized on the balance sheet of a company if the brand value has been internally generated.

By deconstructing the purchase price when one corporation buys another into that which is paid for tangible assets, on the one hand, and for the intangible assets on the other, it is possible to arrive at the value of the brand or brands being bought.

Jaguar is one of the most illustrious of automobile brand names. Twice within recent years the company has found itself unable to operate profitably and has had negative equity. But twice it has been purchased for a significant sum, first by Ford in 1990, which owned Jaguar for 18 years without making a profit, and then by Tata Motors of India who purchased the loss-making duo of Jaguar and Land Rover in 2008 for $2.3 billion, signaling the value placed in the name.

Brand value is also clearly established when one corporation purchases the rights to a brand name from another corporation without purchasing any tangible assets in the form of real estate, manufacturing equipment, employee contracts and so on involved in its production. Such transactions are similar to arrangements under which corporations license the use of a brand name owned by another entity and pay a license or franchise fee or royalty.

For this reason, Brand Finance thinks there is a strong case for the inclusion of internally generated brands on the balance sheet. It is also why its methodology is based on the "royalty relief" approach which CEO David Haigh says is:

recognized by technical authorities worldwide that ties back to the commercial reality of brands: their ability to command a premium in an arm's length transaction ... Brands fulfill the definition of intangible assets ... in that they are controlled by management, provide future economic benefits and are identifiable and therefore can be sold, transferred or licensed as appropriate. We are increasingly seeing companies taking advantage of this transferability by moving brands (including trademarks and other associated intellectual property, such as design rights and other marketing collateral) to special purpose vehicles, such as brand holding companies, for the purpose of raising finance and tax planning.[1]

In Exhibit 16.1 Haigh describes the process used by his firm to compile its Brand Finance 500.

Exhibit 16.1 The Brand Finance 500 process (Source: Brand Finance plc, 2008)

Brand valuation approaches. There are three widely recognized approaches to valuing all assets, including brands: cost, market and income.

Income approach. An example of why the cost and market approaches are often inappropriate can be found in the art world. Vincent Van Gogh's portrait of Dr. Gachet was painted in 1890 at a cost of less than 100 francs. Reproductions from China can be bought today for less than US$100. Yet a century after it was painted, this work of art sold at Christies [*sic*] for US$82 million. Its market value today is estimated at close to US$130 million. This estimate may be true and if it could be achieved, then this would be today's FMV [fair market value].

However, markets fluctuate for many reasons and even in the art market there is a lack of liquidity and transparency to determine values reliably at a given point in time. As a result, most valuers use the income approach for estimating the FMV of assets, particularly commercial assets such as brands.

The income approach is used to estimate the value of a brand by considering the net present value of the stream of future benefits accruing to the brand owner. This is done by taking future brand earnings and discounting them back to a net present value (NPV) in a discounted cash flow (DCF) valuation model using the hypothetical buyer's weighted average cost of capital (WACC).

Approach used to determine the 500 Most Valuable Global Brands. There are different ways of calculating brand value under the income approach. All involve the creation of a forecast financial model. However, there are five alternative ways of identifying brand earnings for inclusion in the model. These are: price premium, excess margin, economic substitution, earnings split, and royalty relief. We rejected the first four methods and decided to go with the royalty relief method.

Royalty relief. The royalty relief method is based on the notion that a brand holding company owns the brand and licenses it to an operating company. The notional price paid by the operating company to the brand company is expressed as a royalty rate. The NPV of all forecast royalties represents the value of the brand to the business. The attraction of this method is that it is based on commercial practice in the real world. It involves estimating likely future sales, applying an appropriate royalty rate to them and then discounting estimated future, post-tax royalties, to arrive at an NPV.

We use the royalty relief method for two reasons: it is favoured by tax authorities and the courts because it calculates brand values by reference to documented, third-party transactions; and because it can be done based on publicly available financial information.

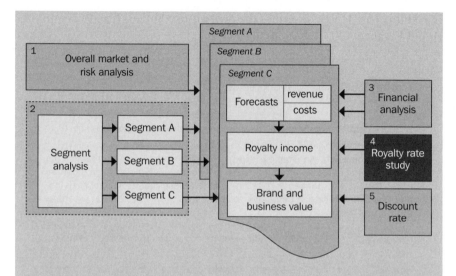

Figure 16.1 Brand Finance valuation process (Source: © Brand Finance plc, 2008)

Steps in the valuation process. There are a number of steps in the royalty relief brand valuation process. These are detailed below.

1. Obtain brand-specific financial and revenue data.
   This quantitative data is obtained from Bloomberg, company data sources such as websites and annual reports, investment analyst and industry expert reports, and other publicly available data sources.

2. Model the market to identify market demand and the position of individual brands in the context of market competitors.
   Three forecast periods were created for each brand:
   - Estimated financial results for 2007 using Institutional Brokers Estimate System (IBES) consensus forecasts.
   - Estimated four-year financial forecast (2008–2011), based on historic growth trends for the brand, IBES consensus forecasts and OECD GDP growth forecasts.
   - Perpetuity growth, based on a combination of growth expectations (IBES and OECD forecasts).

   Where appropriate, data sources varied by industrial sector.

3. Establish the notional royalty rate for each brand.
   There are a series of steps to take when determining the notional royalty rate. The first of these is to establish a royalty rate range for each industrial sector. Royalty rate ranges were set for each industry by reference to a review of comparable licensing agreements and industry norms. A review of publicly available licensing agreement indicates the royalty rates set between third parties in arm's-length commercial transactions.

   Having done this, it is time to compare royalty rates with operating margins in the industrial sector. Fundamental profitability in each industrial sector influences the determination of royalty rate ranges. This must be taken into account when determining the royalty rate ranges. A rule of thumb exists within the licensing industry (rule of 25), which states that, on average, a licensee should expect to pay between 25% and 40% of its expected profits for access to the licensed intellectual property.

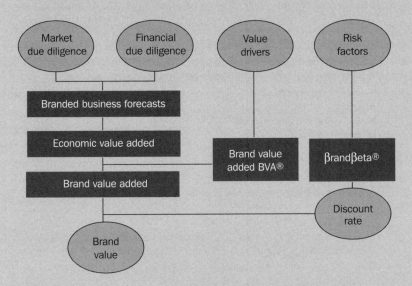

Figure 16.2 Brand evaluation model (Source © Brand Finance plc, 2008)

For example, if profit margin is 20%, an appropriate royalty rate should fall between 25% of 20% for a royalty rate of 5% and 40% of 20% for one of 8%. The rule is based on heuristic evidence of a relationship between market royalty rates and margins earned in licensee businesses. Royalty rates may be higher or lower than 25% of profits, depending upon a variety of quantitative and qualitative factors that can and do affect commercial negotiations. When determining royalty rate ranges, the 25% rule is a useful indicator of what an appropriate royalty rate range might be in each industrial sector.

Having found a general royalty rate range, the next thing to do is to conduct a brand value added (BVA®) analysis. This is a research-driven process, which estimates the proportion of income attributable to each category of intangible asset, including brand, to determine the proportion of margins which should be attributed to the brand. This process uses a brand power matrix to map the relative importance of different tangible and intangible assets in the value creation process. The results of this BVA® analysis refine the margin analysis in determining royalty rate ranges.

With this done, you can establish the appropriate royalty rate within the range for each global brand.

Having established the royalty rate range, it is necessary to pinpoint where in the range is appropriate for each brand under review. This is calculated by conducting a BrandBeta® analysis, which is a benchmarking study of the strength, risk and future potential of a brand relative to its competitor set. It is conceptually similar to a credit rating. Brands are awarded brand ratings based on their strength, risk and future earnings potential. A brand rating quantifies the strength and performance of the brand being valued; and provides an indication of the risk attached to future earnings of the brand.

To find the world's most valuable brands, the Brand Finance Brand Ratings panel considered a variety of factors in this BrandBeta® analysis process. Factors included both hard and soft brand performance measures.

- Market concentration.
- Distribution penetration.
- Marketing investment levels.
- Sales growth.
- Market share growth.
- Margin levels.
- Consumer awareness.
- Functional quality perceptions.
- Image or emotional perceptions.
- Brand preference and brand loyalty.

Brand ratings incorporate both quantitative and qualitative data. *Qualitative data is compiled by Brand Finance from secondary research.*

The final brand ratings are expressed as an index score from 0–100. They are also expressed alphabetically from AAA to D:

- AAA – extremely strong.
- AA – very strong.
- A – strong.
- BBB – average.
- BB – under-performing.
- B – weak.
- CCC – very weak.
- CC – extremely weak.
- C – failing.
- D – moribund.

The ratings can be altered by including a plus (+) or minus (–) sign to show their more detailed positioning.

4. Calculate the notional future royalty income stream for each brand.
   This is done by applying the royalty rate, determined in step 3, to sales in the explicit forecast and perpetuity periods.

5. Calculate discount rate specific to each brand, taking account of its size, international presence, reputation and Brand Rating.
   Brand ratings are used to determine a weighted average cost of capital (WACC). Debt costs, equity costs and the debt-to-equity ratio are all given a discount or premium based on the strength of the brand; the principle being that a strong brand should command a lower discount rate in the valuation calculation than a weak one.

6. Discount future royalty stream to a net present value (NPV).
   The result is the brand value for inclusion in our table. Where enterprise values can be calculated by reference to public market information, the brand value is expressed as a percentage of enterprise value (EV).

According to Brand Finance, the total value of the 500 most valuable global brands is close to US$3 trillion. Contrary to conventional wisdom, much of this value is not located in the consumer goods sector but is spread across the full range of industries. In fact, in spite of the decreases in brand value caused mainly by the sub-prime mortgage crisis, the total value of brands in this sector remains the highest in the league table.

Over half of the top 100 brands are domiciled in the USA. And in the top ten, only HSBC (UK) and Nokia (Finland) are located outside America.

Table 16.1 The Top Ten (Source: Brand Finance plc, 2008)

1	Coca-Cola	US$45.4 billion
2	Microsoft	US$44.5 billion
3	Google	US$43.1 billion
4	Wal-Mart	US$39 billion
5	IBM	US$37.9 billion
6	GE	US$36.1 billion
7	HSBC	US$35.5 billion
8	Hewlett-Packard	US$34.1 billion
9	Nokia	US$33.1 billion
10	Citi	US$27.8 billion

The biggest global brands are not, however, necessarily those with the highest brand rating. Those honors go to those brands which have the highest brand value relative to the value of the enterprise as shown in Table 16.2. From this it will be noted that only Coca-Coca and Hewlett-Packard make it into both tables.

Table 16.2 The highest brand values to overall enterprise value (Source: Brand Finance plc, 2008)

Nike	72%
Dell	45%
Budweiser	36%
McDonald's	32%
American Express	31%
Coca-Cola	31%
L'Oreal	30%
Tesco	27%
Disney	26%
Hewlett-Packard	26%

Note

1   See www.brandfinance.com.

17
The role of public relations in brand building

Many hold the view that the term brand is firmly fixed in the sphere of marketing and sales, applies to products and is misplaced in the context of corporate communications. In the public relations community the preferred term is reputation. Brand is considered to be too ephemeral and somehow linked to the superficial rather than to substance. Brand managers and CEOs who have risen through the marketing ranks invariably differ. They recognize brand equity, but struggle to define the real value of reputation.

The fact that we are playing with words and feel "we all know exactly what we mean, but we cannot explain it precisely" is why definition does matter. And public relations is not a profession for people who do not want to clarify the meaning of words.

Let us consider the following three words: Brand, Reputation and Relationship.

In my experience, public relations people in general – there are of course exceptions – are much more comfortable with prose rather than pictures, with facts and rational argument rather than oratory or emotional connection. They tend to equate brand with products and reputation with corporations and other institutions. Branding is for selling. Reputation is associated with values. Advertising builds brands, public relations builds reputation. These are outdated concepts.

If proof were needed of the thinking of the PR establishment it can be found in the "Authentic Enterprise", a white paper prepared by a team of leading public relations professionals who are members of the elite "Arthur W. Page Society"[1] In the 56-page report, the team sets out its view of the evolving role of the chief communications officer (CCO) in the 21st century.

(The first step was to change the name of public relations to communications, a rebranding that in my view was quite unnecessary and relegates the role into a function rather than one serving a strategic purpose. Communication is a tool with which you achieve good relations with your publics.)

In a section that charts the mission and role of the public relations professional yesterday (1945–1995), today (1995–2007) and in the future, the report uses the word "brand" just once. The same role specification they assign to the chief marketing officer uses the word brand yesterday, today and tomorrow no less than eight times.

The report states in its summary that there are four new priorities and skills for which the CCO must now assume a leadership role:

1. Leadership in defining and instilling company values;

2. Leadership in building and managing multi-stakeholder relationships;

3. Leadership in enabling the enterprise with "new media" skills and tools; and

4. Leadership in building and managing trust, in all its dimensions.

While the word trust is used, brand is nowhere to be seen. "Trust mark" is a commonly used synonym for brand identity or logo.

It seems clear to me that this excellent four-point mandate exactly outlines the key elements of global corporate brand management.

Clearly important for all corporations that have the same corporate and product brand names (for example Microsoft, IBM, Kodak, Disney), it is also increasingly important for multi-brand corporations in a world in which, research shows, consumers want to know about the company behind the products they are buying. Thus, Kraft, Procter & Gamble and Unilever have embarked on corporate PR programs in recent years. These are companies that have accumulated a deep understanding of the anatomy of global and local brands, and have the skills and heritage to apply disciplined brand management techniques to their corporate communications.

Successful and long-established transnational corporations also understand the paradox that all successful global brands are local. That is, the brand – whether it is a product or a corporation – must be so deeply embedded in each individual community that it is seen as being intrinsically local.

In Britain, there are many people who believe that the Ford Motor

Company is British owned. Lever Hindustan is seen in India as a national company. And Michelin was not targeted by those who held anti-French sentiments leading up to, and during, the war in Iraq because most US Americans think of it as a company with US roots.

Increasingly, the age-old arguments over the relative merits and value of paid advertising, public relations (earned media), direct marketing, Web and viral marketing, and all the other tools of communication, will be seen in relation to what each contributes to product or corporate brand equity.

BRAND

The corporate brand is the definition of a company. The brand equity of the company represents the entire monetary value of the enterprise over and above its net book value. (And, yes, if the corporate brand is subpar, this value might be negative.) A fundamental feature of a successful corporate brand is stamina, meaning it has strength and flexibility and is not derailed by changes in fashion. The recent crop of boom-and-bust brands from the dot-com era briefly had billion-dollar names that have now been forgotten.

More important, the successful corporate brand will transcend almost any CEO's ability to depreciate its underlying equity, though brand equity will always be increased under strong leadership. In fact, the corporate brand is the legacy a retiring CEO hands on to his or her successor.

Coca-Cola, Daimler-Benz, Nike, Perrier, Nestlé, Ford and Sotheby's are examples of brands with sufficient stamina and equity to allow them to recover from temporarily damaged reputations.

Arthur Andersen, WorldCom and PanAm are companies that lost their reputations. All their accumulated brand equity was not enough to carry them through a fatal loss of public trust.

And in the financial crisis of 2008 (which in fact had been brewing for the previous two years) even storied Wall Street giants were brought down or absorbed by others. To those who argue about how and why this happened and focus only on financial metrics, I say it was basically a failure of the firms to live up to the promise of their brands. In reaching out to achieve ever greater returns they assumed levels of risk that led to their downfall. These risks were neither recognized nor understood by many investors who trusted that their money would be safe in the hands of prudent professionals.

Among those that have disappeared or been absorbed are Lehman Bros., Bear Stearns, Merrill Lynch and Countrywide.

REPUTATION

Reputation is a snapshot of an organization's brand equity at a single point in time. As such, it is of vital importance to PR practitioners. While they cannot change the course of a corporate brand's past history, they can and must work on achieving the best possible reputation in the present, the only period in which they can exert direct influence. This will help to secure the brand's future by building a reserve of goodwill.

RELATIONSHIPS

The last corner of the triangle, relationships are by far the most important. The very term public relations underscores the understanding our profession's founders had when they chose those words to define our work.

Our achievements manifest themselves and can be measured in the quality of the relationships our organizations establish with their stakeholders and the public at large. It does not matter if they are corporations, non-profits, NGOs or government branches.

Relationships provide the basis of an organization's present reputation; they are the bonds that create a lasting brand.

When PR practitioners remind themselves that they are in the business of helping to establish and maintain relationships, and apply themselves to that task, reputation will be enhanced and corporate brand equity strengthened over the long term.

After all, considering all their responsibilities and expertise, public relations directors and their staffs are in the role of crossing guards at the intersection where many of the elements that shape the destiny of the corporate brand meet. The PR director either directly controls or influences how the corporation manages its:

- **Employee relations**: Many corporations divide responsibility for internal and external relations to different executives, with the director of internal relations reporting directly to the VP of Human Relations. In other cases, the VP of PR might oversee both functions, reporting to the CEO. In either case, he will exercise influence on those responsible for "living the brand" (see Chapter 10).

- **Media relations**: This is the central duty of the PR director. With the fragmentation of traditional media and the advent of digitized media in all its forms, he is responsible for managing relations that can build or destroy brand equity.
- **Financial relations**: The PR director must work with the director of investor relations to enhance reputation with financial media and analysts.
- **Corporate social responsibility**: This was part of the job description of the PR director until recently when it has been split off into a separate function. Nonetheless, the PR head of the enterprise will have a great influence in CSR strategy and its communication internally and externally (see Chapter 15).
- **Sponsorship and event management**: The PR director has input to the selection of sponsorships and will play a leading role in their exploitation to ensure benefit to the brand.
- **Government relations**: PR embraces public affairs and relations with local, national and supranational governments – lawmakers and regulators.
- **Corporate advertising**: Corporate image issue and advocacy advertising is an instrument of corporate communications and falls under the PR director. His job is to manage paid and free media.
- **Issues and crisis management**: The corporate brand is always enhanced or damaged by perceptions of how it deals with issues and acts at times of crisis. Issue and crisis communications are the direct responsibility of the PR director (see Chapter 13).

In short, there is no other officer within a corporation, other than the CEO, who has a 360° mandate of responsibility for managing the corporate brand.

The leading global public relations agencies have for decades understood the importance of their skills to promoting product brands. Only recently have they begun to apply the same process, creativity and execution to corporate brands.

Ketchum, for example, has a proprietary research-based methodology called Corporate Brandbuilder™ to link a company's reputation characteristics to profit or loss or other business results. Brandbuilder also serves as an indispensable tool for PR professionals in crafting a reputation management strategy.

David Rockland, Ketchum's Managing Director of Global Research and Interactive Communications, describes the process in Exhibit 17.1.

Exhibit 17.1 Ketchum's Brandbuilder methodology (Source: David Rockland, Ketchum)

First, a survey is fielded among target audiences, which are defined as narrowly and specifically as possible. The questionnaire usually covers:

a. Awareness, aided and unaided
b. Overall reputation
c. Stated importance and relevance of certain reputation attributes to the company's business
d. Company and competitor rankings vis-à-vis these attributes
e. Desired or actual behaviors, including such factors as stock purchase or recommendation, defense of the company's reputation, purchase and recommended purchase, and others
f. Exposure to various marketing communications about the company, including advertising (aided and unaided) and traditional and on-line media channels
g. Recall of specific events or activities – either positive (e.g. merger or acquisition, new product launch) or negative (e.g. lawsuit, boycott).

Second, In addition to reporting the results and net scores from the survey, the researchers conduct statistical analyses that answer the following questions:

a. How much does reputation drive the desired or actual behaviors?
b. What values and attributes are the real drivers of corporate reputation?
c. What lift does the company's reputation derive from general awareness?
d. How much does each marketing channel contribute to movement in the reputation metrics?
e. How do specific events or activities affect the company's reputation and the drivers most important to its reputation?

What emerges from this analysis is a very clear picture of the company's reputation and a guide for developing reputation management strategies: what attributes to focus on, what to ignore and whether certain events or activities will help or hurt a company's reputation. Most critical are the causal linkages between reputation attributes and desired and actual business behaviors.

Ketchum has conducted approximately 150 Brandbuilder studies in the last few years among a wide range of audiences, including influential consumers in Kuwait, students in China and employees in South Africa. Here are some examples of how companies have worked or are now working with Ketchum Brandbuilder:

■ A major chemical company uses Brandbuilder to design advertising and public relations programs in 17 countries, as well as to test the reputational effects of management changes, acquisitions and joint ventures.
■ A restaurant company assessed the impact on its reputation of a lawsuit regarding discrimination in hiring practices.
■ A grocery retailer determined an optimal positioning in the health and wellness space.
■ A tire manufacturer determined whether to continue its sponsorship of a racing program.
■ An oil company used findings from a Brandbuilder survey to help establish its strategic philanthropy program.

The most important aspect of Brandbuilder is that it not only provides a brand reputation ranking versus competitors and other industry leaders. It also provides an essential tool to help a company chart and manage its brand reputation more effectively over the long term.

CASE From Ma Bell to Baby Bell to the new AT&T[2]

At Fleishman-Hillard, corporate branding is seen as a natural fit with what the agency sees as its overall mission, which it describes as: "to use communications to deliver a meaningful, positive, and measurable impact on the performance of a client's organization." Says the firm's chairman, John Graham, "One of the things that's differentiated our approach is an ability to align an organization behind a common goal and get everyone marching in step toward that goal. An important way we do that is by making employees a key part of any corporate branding program."

Perhaps the most ambitious example of Fleishman-Hillard's corporate branding approach at work is the agency's role in evolving Southwestern Bell's brand to the new AT&T. It's a process that began several years after the old AT&T was split into the seven regional Bell operating companies, or "Baby Bells" as they were commonly known in the USA. Southwestern Bell Corporation was left with some of the least populated states in the country, and was ranked in terms of market value near the bottom of the pack. Although the company quickly rose to distinguish itself by delivering the best shareholder return since divestiture of any Bell company, research revealed that the company still was not perceived as a major player, and that a large share of this problem could be attributed to the "Southwest" in the company's name.

Fleishman-Hillard worked with Southwestern Bell Corporation to develop a new corporate name and logo that would reflect the company's growth into a multifaceted, global communications business. After extensive research with key stakeholder audiences, several new names and company logos were developed and tested. The final candidate was SBC.

The next step was the development of a communications plan designed not only to announce the change, but also to serve as a springboard for discussion of SBC's unique standing among the Bell companies and its rightful place among the world's leading telecommunications companies. The strategy included:

- Broad media outreach
- Advertising in key publications

- A comprehensive program of employee communications
- A strategic analyst relations program.

The effort resulted in major coverage of the 1995 brand change in leading national business and regional publications, accompanied by fast assimilation of the change by key national business media (for example, in the first issue following the announcement, *Forbes* began indexing SBC rather than Southwestern Bell). Just as important, the change drew a positive response from analysts. Of course, many factors influence a company's stock price. But in the month after the name change, SBC stock gained ground – this during a time when the stock price of most other major telecommunications companies lost value.

Fast forward to 2005. After executing a series of strategic mergers, SBC had grown in stature as a national brand. Now it was poised to make telecommunications history by acquiring its former parent, AT&T Corp., to create the nation's largest communications company. But, unlike its previous mergers, SBC wasn't simply bolting on a new wireline company from a different region. Rather, it was becoming a new kind of company and – on top of it all – rebranding the entire enterprise with the name of the acquired company. While the AT&T brand had a historic legacy, the 130-year-old moniker also was seen as an older brand tagged with a few negative attributes, including poor financial performance.

In addition to managing the overall communications of the merger, the company and the agency needed to reintroduce an American icon: "the new AT&T". This involved making the AT&T brand relevant again, especially to a younger generation that did not grow up with the famous icon. The overall effort was a highly integrated and extremely sensitive communications operation, aimed at positioning AT&T as the company that would set the industry standard in communications, entertainment, and service for the 21st century.

As with the SBC rebranding effort, rigorous research was conducted with key audiences – both internal and external – including employees, customers, shareholders, marketing partners, suppliers, community stakeholders, media, and analysts. The challenge was to ensure that all were reached with timely and relevant information on the decision to carry forward the new AT&T brand, and that the strengths and attributes of both the SBC and the former AT&T brands would translate to the new AT&T. Explaining the decision to brand the company AT&T to the nearly 160,000 employees of SBC, the acquiring company, was also mission-critical and would receive reinforcement from top management.

Based on this research, a three-pronged strategy was developed:

- Recruit third-party brand influencers to carry the message and validate the brand decision.
- Reinforce the larger brand attributes in all external and internal communications.
- Formally launch the brand through a sequenced approach: announce the brand decision; unveil a new AT&T logo; and announce a massive brand advertising campaign.

After briefing a select group of third-party branding thought-leaders to reinforce and validate the strategic significance of selecting this brand, the three phases of the announcement were rolled out in late 2005, culminating in a heavy publicity push for a New Year's Eve launch of the new AT&T's "Your World. Delivered." brand advertising campaign.

The transition was reinforced by a redesign of the company's corporate website to reflect the look, feel, and positioning of the new AT&T brand. In keeping with the emphasis on employee communications that characterized the earlier SBC rebranding, the company's intranet site was also redesigned and all 160,000 employees received a commemorative book that stirred excitement about the future of the new AT&T, while also celebrating the company's rich history.

The launch, combined with an ongoing campaign of sustaining communications, quickly and significantly changed how key audiences perceived the new AT&T. For example:

- During the first quarter of 2006, AT&T *won more than 36,000 contracts with companies across the world* and nearly 75 percent of all deals that the company competed for globally.

- In 2005 and early 2006 the new AT&T was *upgraded by 15 sell-side analysts*, which represented 40 percent of the analysts who cover the company.
- During the first half of 2006, *unaided brand awareness* of the new AT&T more than tripled ... *unaided advertising awareness* of the new AT&T more than quadrupled ... and, nationally, 68 percent of consumers believed AT&T delivers technology that is relevant to their needs.
- During the same period, aggressive media outreach generated extensive positive coverage and brand validation of the new AT&T with nearly 700 stories worldwide, reaching more than 13 million people.
- AT&T moved into 19th position in the 2008 Brand Finance league table that assigns a value to the world's top 500 brands, moving up from 67th position the year before.

As further evidence of the success of this long-term corporate branding campaign, since 1996 AT&T has garnered the No. 1 spot 10 times on *Fortune*'s list of America's Most Admired Telecommunications companies – more than any other telecom company.

Notes

1 See www.awpagesociety.com.
2 This case study was developed from personal interviews with John Graham and his assistant.

18
Researching brand reputation

The largest and most sophisticated corporations know the value of research in all phases of their business. But many do not know the right research methods and instruments or appropriate level of spending to use to gain insights of true value for the management of the corporate brand reputation.

Research is especially important at key moments in the life cycle of a corporation when changing circumstances create the need for a redefinition of the brand. Examples of moments when corporate brand managers stand at a crossroads are:

- With a new CEO or leadership change. Researching the health of the brand internally and externally becomes vitally important to help steer new strategies and directions.
- Following a merger or acquisition. At such times the brand profile can become blurred with competing claims of the new partners. Research can help clarify and create a new brand for the new joint enterprise.
- Following a major crisis which may have damaged the corporation's reputation. Research should be used to calibrate the extent of damage, identify areas for reputation repair and the actions needed to regain brand stature.
- When it is decided that it is time to undertake an evolutionary or revolutionary rebranding of the corporation.

These and other lifecycle change moments of corporations are discussed in other chapters of the book in more detail.

PERIODIC CHECKS

Even in normal times research is important. Just as the captain of an aircraft that has achieved cruising altitude must keep alert and check his instruments regularly, so the corporate brand reputation manager needs to have a number of metric controls in place to ensure continued brand relevance and success.

The first step should be to decide what you want to find out. Some of the key questions in your mind are likely to be:

- What are the drivers of my corporate brand and others in my industry sector?
- How is my brand perceived by its stakeholders? What are its strengths and weaknesses?
- How well does my brand compare and compete with its peers/rivals? What differentiates us?
- Is my brand poised to comport with changing attitudes and trends among stakeholders?
- What promotional tools should I use to build and protect the brand? And, can I rank these to discover which offers the best ROI?
- What are the best practices?
- How big is the gap between the desired brand image and the current reputation? That is, where are we starting from and how far do we need to get people to?
- How can I monitor progress to make sure we are on track?

These questions beg answers in every location in which the corporation operates around the globe. It is not unusual for the senior public relations/reputation manager to be personally knowledgeable about his home market but he will also be required to make judgments about markets with which he is unfamiliar and may never have visited. This is where a professionally research-based foundation is essential before decisions are taken.

This chapter does not attempt to be a primer on research. There are many books and courses available for anyone wanting to study the subject at length. I hope to provide a helpful guide for the person who wants to embark on this process and would like to know of money-saving shortcuts where they exist.

CHECK EXISTING SOURCES

It is quite likely that some of the data you need already exists in some form or another. It is just a matter of finding out where, and if it is available to you in order to make what you may already have work harder for you.

THE FIRST PLACE TO LOOK IS INTERNALLY

Large companies are the repositories of huge amounts of data. Most of it has been acquired over the years by various departments and seldom is it concentrated in one place. It is not uncommon for different divisions to be questioning the same people – even for different departments in a division to do so – without being aware of what each other is doing. Data is accumulated by one brand that is not necessarily shared with other brands. At the time of writing, many companies are appointing chief knowledge officers, one of whose responsibilities will be the assembly and arrangement of this information in easily accessible form to approved users. Meantime, your first step must be to question the person responsible in the central research department archive (if such exists) and/or existing research suppliers. Step two is to contact other company PR, advertising and marketing people to establish what recent studies they have undertaken. They will likely have an Aladdin's cave of information about the market trends, your company's or brand's position in the market, its qualities and comparisons with competitors.

What you find may enable you to piggy-back on these studies. And even if you decide you need additional data, the available information will help you to focus your new studies more accurately and thus save time and money.

Among the most important calls to make is to the human resources department, which will likely have stored a wealth of data garnered from employee satisfaction surveys. (If they do not, that will be your cue to institute a study straight away.) Employees are arguably the most important group of stakeholders that influence corporate brand perception (as discussed in Chapter 10, Living the brand) and it is certain that their attitudes will be reflected in those of external audiences.

Make sure you contact the chief financial officer. You will find he also has a storehouse of information, starting with reports of analysts from financial institutions. It is their job to know more about your company than you know yourself and to rate it against its competitors, and they have the resources to find out. In their periodic reports, you get superb appraisals of your industry and insights into your own company. And it all comes FREE.

BRAND AND OTHER "BEST OF" RANKINGS

There is a treasure trove of information about brands residing in the public domain and this should be studied before commissioning any *de novo* research. Many annual league tables are published in the media. Examples are the Interbrand/*BusinessWeek* Top Brands report, and a similar collaboration between the *Financial Times* and research company Millward Brown. The *BrandFinance 500* is a study published by that firm and there are others from a variety of branding consultants. Even if your company does not qualify for inclusion for technical reasons (for example it is privately held or is a "house of brands") these lists can be useful in providing interesting data about peers and competitors.

The many and varied "Most Admired" lists published in the business and trade media can be an equally useful hunting ground for the corporate brand manager, especially when the rankings from publications circulating in different regions and countries are compared. It will become immediately apparent in most cases that there are geographic areas of weakness and strength and this will help shape policy and communication to bring laggards in line.

Another viewpoint is provided by specialist media "Best of" rankings which grade corporations on their corporate social responsibility, work environment, diversity, treatment of special groups and so on.

By triangulating the data that can be found in these reports and producing a SWOT analysis it will be possible to undertake the first steps in planning measures to build and protect the brand. And it will greatly reduce the need for newly commissioned and costly research.

HISTORICAL DATA FROM CONTINUOUS STUDIES

Check out the major research companies for the historical data that is available from the studies that they may have been conducting continuously over several years.

You may be surprised to find that your company or brand has been included for comparison purposes in the regular panel audits that ACNielsen conducts in shops and the home, or in a variety of research projects routinely undertaken by Gallup, ORC, IpsosMORI, Harris and others. This will give you a head start in establishing your current position. All you need to do is to join the study – and pay up – to establish how your efforts are changing the company brand perception.

An annual study that has become required reading for all those involved in global brand reputation management is the Edelman Trust Barometer which surveys OFEs (opinion forming elites) in a number of countries. It sheds particular light on which sources respondents rely upon for credible information as the basis of their decision making.

SOCIETIES, RULING BODIES AND OTHER ORGANIZATIONS

You may be called upon to become an instant expert in some special population sector. For example, someone might propose that a PR program be undertaken that involves anglers or hobby fishermen, or perhaps Boy or Girl Scouts.

The best sources – and the least costly – are always the ruling bodies or societies that serve these interest groups. The society or association will usually send you, at no charge beyond postage, a wealth of material containing demographic and psychographic information about its members. This will quickly help you to establish just how useful a group it will be to your company. More often than not, nowadays, information from these societies is also available from the websites they maintain.

In the major field of healthcare, a prime source of data can be the patient support groups and networks that exist in most countries and are very well organized. Examples are patient associations for people suffering from kidney ailments, heart conditions, cancer, MS, diabetes, AIDS and other illnesses. In addition to being a source of information, these groups can be excellent partners in communications initiatives, offering a direct and highly targeted channel to a group of people of specific interest to you; or they can be formidable adversaries.

COUNTRY INFORMATION

Those practicing PR on an international scale will often want to gain objective information about a specific country to match with the information being presented by the company representatives there.

The first port of call should be to the local embassy or consulate general of that country, which will usually provide you with a great deal of useful information about the country. From this you can build up your own picture, perhaps in advance of a visit. The second should be the Foreign Office or Department of Trade (Export) of your own country's government. You will find that they usually have a wealth of knowledge about overseas markets and will also give you their opinion on such important matters as the political stability of the country and even some dos and don'ts of doing business there. Remember, you have paid for this through your taxes, so you have a right to the help from your own public servants. Mostly, they are glad to oblige.

You should complement this by requesting the most recent study undertaken of that country by the Economist Intelligence Unit, which will be available at a cost of around $200. Or collect the most recent advertising-supported "special report" or supplement on that country published by *The Economist*, the *Wall Street Journal*, the *Financial Times* or another reputable and serious journal.

CARAVANS AND OMNIBUS STUDIES

Caravans and omnibus studies are regular researches undertaken weekly or monthly by many specialist research organizations under contract to major corporations. They offer a very cost-effective way to track product purchases, opinions and voting intentions.

As a rule of thumb, you can ask questions on an omnibus for roughly $1,000 per question, so a mere $5,000 can sometimes provide you with insights of exceptional value.

FOCUS GROUPS

Focus-group testing provides information that is highly qualitative and detailed. Beyond learning how people feel about a certain product, person or concept, the skilled researcher can establish the strength of feeling, and the ease with which that opinion might be altered and how that might be done. Focus groups, because they involve people for several hours – for which they get paid a fee – are also able to establish the acceptability of alternative product offerings and ideas. This method is routinely used by politicians and political parties to check how the public might react to various initiatives.

Focus groups are the testing ground for ideas and messages, the grist to the mill of all who practice brand communication.

New technologies are available to conduct virtual focus groups, whereby a geographically scattered sample of, say, medical specialists, of whom there may be only one per city, can come together in an online focus group and share views in response to picture stimuli across the internet.

SURVEYS AND POLLS

Surveys are the single most important research instrument for the corporate brand manager. But there is often confusion over the terms "survey" and "poll", according to Don W. Stacks, Director of the University of Miami School of Communication Program in Advertising and Public Relations and author of the *Primer of Public Relations Research*. Stacks writes:

> A survey is a method of gathering relatively in-depth information about respondent attitudes and beliefs ... Surveys are fairly long and compli-cated attempts to gauge how the public perceives an issue or event or person, and they allow the researcher to probe in a controlled and prescribed way why respondents feel as they do. The survey is a care-fully constructed measuring instrument. A poll, on the other hand, is more "shallow". Polls seek to very quickly and efficiently gauge simple opinion or certify what behaviors are or are likely to be.
>
> When you need in-depth analysis, such as whether a client's product is being perceived positively, whether a company's corporate culture has been accepted by employees, or whether a candidate's position on the issues is getting through to potential voters, you turn to the survey.

REPUTATION DRIVERS IN STAKEHOLDER RESEARCH AND CONTENT ANALYSIS

In every corporate brand management program a first step is to establish what drives the corporation's reputation and then devise a method of measuring performance. This means that the components have to be broken down into the key individual attributes that go to make up the overall perception.

These components will vary in their relative importance from company to company depending on its own goals and its industry sector. It has also become clear that most clients would like to have some form of measure-ment against their peer group, rather than being viewed in isolation, although many are unable to bear the incremental costs of moving to a full benchmark study. At the same time, the absolute requirement to preserve client confidentiality has meant that hitherto it was not possible to share data between clients. According to Echo Research, a company that specializes in global research to protect brands and reputation, its industry award-winning Reputation Drivers measurement model provides clients with a sense of their position in relation to competitors within their sector or best in breed, overall, as Sandra Macleod, Group CEO of Echo, explains in Table 18.1.

Table 18.1 Echo's Reputation Drivers measurement model

Capgemini www.capgemini.com	FORTUNE www.fortune.com	management today www.clickmt.com	Echo – Corporate Sector	Echo – Government/ Not-for-profit Sector	Echo – Professional and Financial Services Sector
Leadership	Quality of management	Management Quality	Quality of management	Accountability	Financial performance
Products and services	Product/services quality	Quality of goods and services	Leadership	Competence and professionalism	Quality of management
Innovation	Innovation	Capacity to innovate	Products and services	Internal and external relations	Leadership
Workplace	People management	Ability to Attract, Develop & Retain Top Talent	Innovation	Transparency and accessibility	High-caliber personnel
Performance	Long-term investment	Value as long-term investment	Workplace and employment	Social engagement	Client focus
Citizenship	Financial soundness	Financial soundness	Financial performance	Trustworthiness	CSR/Ethics/Governance
Governance	Social responsibility	Corporate and environmental responsibility	CSR/Ethics/Governance		Trust
	Use of corporate assets	Use of corporate assets	Trust		Innovative solutions
		Quality of marketing			

GLOBAL RESEARCH PROTECTING BRANDS AND REPUTATION www.echoresearch.com

The key to tracking reputation is to understand the concept of reputation for what, among whom. This will vary from group to group according to their own needs (for example employees vs. customers vs. financial analysts), and be impacted both by experience and by external influencers such as the media.

Echo's Reputation Drivers are designed as a standardized set of topics that are known to shape perceptions and expectations within that sector. Each "driver" is recorded in relation to its importance and relevance to the stakeholder groups analyzed (the Image), along with endorsement or criticism of the brand (and its competitors) found within press cuttings, broadcast or internet items subjected to media evaluation (the Influence).

Echo's Reputation Drivers have been corroborated by other established monitors of corporate reputation such as the *Fortune* list of "Most Admired Corporations", *Management Today*'s "Most Admired Companies in Britain", and Cap Gemini Ernst & Young's global "Invisible Advantage" as being the key attributes that contribute to an organization's reputation (see Table 18.1).

Echo believes that by introducing a global system of measurement for the key elements of reputation of its clients and their competitors, it is able to provide a significant advance in the assessment of current image and expectations among key stakeholders and sources of influence such as the media to measure organizational reputation. While varied according to sector, in the Echo model, the main drivers of reputation measured in the corporate world include: Financial Performance, Quality of Management, Leadership/Strategy, Products and Services, Corporate Responsibility/Ethics/Governance, Workplace and Employment and Trust.

Since 2004, all Echo client research programs include the option of the appropriate Reputation Drivers, allowing for significant normative data to be examined by industry, by region, and, increasingly, by stakeholder profile.

Reputation Drivers can also be used to track a specific area of concern over time, among a "basket" of similar companies or companies within a geographic region; and the model can be customized to meet specific and differing client needs.

Reputation driver analysis shows how one company is faring in a particular sector, and how another is performing against an all-industry average (black lines on the "spidergrams", see Figures 18.1 and 18.2) in the view of their stakeholder groups.

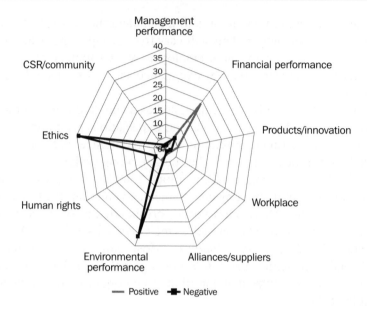

Figure 18.1 Reputation Drivers spidergram 1 (Source: ©Echo Research)

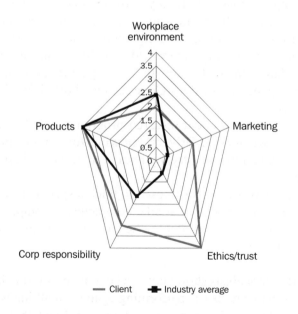

Figure 18.2 Reputation Drivers spidergram 2 (Source: ©Echo Research)

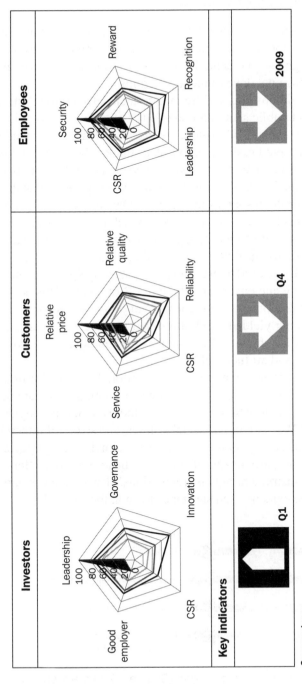

Investors	Customers	Employees

Investors

Leadership
100
80
60
40
20
0
Good employer
CSR
Governance
Innovation

Customers

Relative price
100
80
60
40
20
0
Service
CSR
Relative quality
Reliability

Employees

Security
100
80
60
40
20
0
CSR
Leadership
Reward
Recognition

Key indicators		
Q1	Q4	2009

Commentary

The latest data on perceptions gives cause for concern – while we have made progress against both target and exemplar targets in Investor Perceptions, the Customer Perspective shows a continuing decline most worryingly in perceptions of relative price and quality. Also disappointingly, the latest "people pulse" survey indicates that overall perceptions are down on the latest annual figures. Perceptions of job security have improved but the "dip" in perceptions of recognition requires further investigation.

Figure 18.3 Illustration of Echo's Integrated Reputation Measurement Scorecard (Source: ©Echo Research)

OTHER APPLICATIONS FOR RESEARCH

As the PR person's often unsung friend, research has many other functions in the toolkit of the corporate communications team, which is why it is increasingly been taught as an essential and core component of university PR degrees and professional development programs.

Not least, as organizations aim to differentiate themselves through their thought-leadership and public stand on issues, PR-based research provides useful ammunition to explain or explore trends and changes for media consumption. What the public, or a section of it, thinks about an issue or product may be surprising enough to make a news story, and if it is both topical and sound, the media are often interested in revealing angles that they themselves do not have the resources to examine. Devising questionnaires to yield newsworthy results is a specialized skill which research companies can help with, as well as with technical aspects such as sample size, which the media often insist on to make the story "stand up" and be credible.

Research may equally be used to pre- and post-test campaigns to support messaging and targeting and ensure an effective PR outreach. This is also useful to confirm and demonstrate that a low level of awareness or favorability before a campaign yielded much improved levels afterwards. This technique is important for showing ROI, such as the relationship between campaign expenditure and attitude uplift.

Finally, Issue management, a major brand protection discipline for organizations, is dependent on investigative research to highlight reputational threats and opportunities before they arrive. Today there are multiple signals in the news media and Web 2.0 (blogs, social utilities, and so on) of impending change that may affect reputation. When these signals are aggregated with what observers and participants suspect lies ahead, research offers a formidable defensive instrument against reputational damage, and clearly arms the CCO with the evidence and substance to sit at the top table.

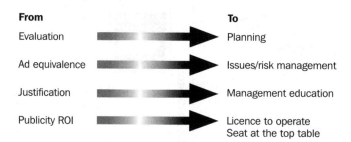

Figure 18.4 Focus on research is changing (Source: ©Echo Research)

According to Echo, there are Five Top Tips for success in researching brand reputation:

1. Understand stakeholders, issues, expectations, priorities and conflicts
2. Consider a reputation research audit, making what you may already have work harder and more effectively
3. Develop spider diagrams and gap analysis
4. Consider using holistic reputational drivers as bonusable key performance indicators
5. Be proactive: develop scorecards and warning systems as the route map for your journey. (HINT: "No-one will do this for you," says Macleod.)

Index